ACTIVITY-BASED MANAGEMENT

ACTIVITY-BASED MANAGEMENT

FOR SERVICE INDUSTRIES, GOVERNMENT ENTITIES, AND NONPROFIT ORGANIZATIONS

JAMES A. BRIMSON

JOHN ANTOS

JOHN WILEY & SONS, INC.

New York · Chichester · Brisbane · Toronto · Singapore

Library of Congress Cataloging in Publication Data:

Brimson, James A., 1947–
   Activity-based management for service organizations, government entities, and nonprofits / James Brimson, John Antos.
      p.   cm.
   Include index.
   ISBN 0-471-01351-X (cloth : acid-free paper)
   1. Industrial management.   2. Organizational behavior.   3. Service industries—Management.   4. Nonprofit organizations—Management.
   5. Administrative agencies—Management.   I. Antos, John.
   II. Title.
   HD31.B7415 1994
   658—dc20   93-36445

Printed in the United States of America

10 9 8 7 6 5 4 3 2 1

CONTENTS

HD31
B7415
1994

ACKNOWLEDGMENTS

No book is solely the effort of its authors. This book is certainly no exception, and credit must be given to all those who have commented, reviewed, and provided technical assistance during the various stages of its development.

Jim Brimson is grateful for the support he received from Robin Fraser and the consultants and support staff in the Coopers & Lybrand office in London, and Steward Lamond in Australia, whose experience and knowledge of activity-based management have helped bring this book to its overall shape.

The Wiley editorial and production team plus copy editor Susan Lauzau must be acknowledged for their professionalism and patience in bringing this book to press.

Jim must thank those special people, Maxime Flax, and his family, Jimmy and Katy, for all the support and inspiration they have provided.

John Antos would like to thank Tom Monaghan, Chairman of Domino's Pizza, Phil Rooney, President of WMX Technologies and Gerard Nierenberg of The Negotiation Institute who inspired him. He would also like to thank the American Management Association, Ron Rasopep of Boeing, Larry Huber of Centel, Wayne Simpson of the City of Indianapolis, Jim Bramonte and Mal Schwartz of Coopers & Lybrand, Jack Semler of Delta Dental Plans, John Bateman of EPRI, John Lang of Epson, Peter Wilke of Hammond Lead, Gloria Derstein of LeMANS Group, Al Discapolo of Liberty Mutual, Christine Karslake of Nutra Sweet, Dan O'Brien of Rank Video, Jim Woodward of the U.S. Postal Service, Norb Lieblang of the Board of Pensioners, Kate Morrison, CFO of the March of Dimes and Major Kruse Smith of the U.S. Air Force. John thanks those special people, his wife, Lana, and his children, Emily and Austin, for their support and inspiration.

Jim and John are indebted to their colleague Tom Pryor, who has been very influential in shaping the current state of activity management thinking.

PREFACE

This book was written for people interested in applying activity-based management (ABM) to the service, government, and nonprofit sectors of the economy and to all types of support functions. Although activity-based management may have started in manufacturing, it has practical application in the service, government, and nonprofit areas as well as support functions.

In this book, a variety of examples are given throughout. Most people learn better through examples. The challenge in writing any book on services is choosing services for examples. There is far more commonality in making cars, computers, and cosmetics than there is in insurance, banking, transportation, home building, hospitals, utilities, or telecommunications. And if nonprofits like voluntary health and welfare organizations and universities are added, there is even less apparent commonality. Add to this government agencies such as the Department of Transportation, the Legislature, the Department of Human Services, the Internal Revenue Service, Department of Defense, and appraisal and licensing boards, there isn't much apparent commonality even in just the government sector of our economy.

However, one thing these organizations have in common is activities/business processes. So in this book, we have provided a wide variety of examples to illustrate how activity-based management really applies to all types of organizations and to any department in an organization. As you read through each section, ask yourself how this applies to your organization. Most of the concepts and ideas will apply to every type of organization; however, some ideas and concepts will only partially apply. Some activities have one name or title in one organization, but a different name or title in another organization.

For example, every organization has a design activity. A hospital designs a medical procedure; an auto repair shop designs a procedure for changing engine oil; a bank designs a process for evaluating mortgages; an insurance company designs the claims handling process; a nonprofit organization designs a fund-raising event; and government designs the procedure for building roads or collecting licensing fees. So even though different departments with different titles perform this activity, every organization designs something.

If you think about activity-based management in a group, we feel that you will find it very rewarding. By understanding business processes and the activities necessary to perform those business processes, you will better understand your organization. By putting together your activities into business processes, you will learn how to minimize the cost, improve the quality, and reduce the cycle time of your services. This will allow you to become more effective in achieving organizational objectives and excellence.

We would be interested in hearing about the impact of your ABM program on your organization, and what improvements resulted from the program. In addition, we would like to hear about your activity budget. Feel free to contact us at:

John Antos	Jim Brimson
President	President
Antos Enterprises, Inc.	ABM-International
7820 Scotia Drive	2011 Ridgemont Ct.
Dallas, Texas 75248-3115	Arlington, Texas 76012
214/980-7407	817/795-1555

1

ACTIVITY-BASED MANAGEMENT AND ENTERPRISE EXCELLENCE

The purpose of this chapter is to:

- Describe the role of activity-based management in achieving enterprise excellence in all types of service organizations and support functions.
- Describe the conventional approach to cost accounting in these types of organizations
- Provide an overview of activity management
- Contrast conventional **cost accounting systems** with activity-based management systems
- Describe the role of activity management in the management process
- Describe the benefits of activity management in the service sector of our society
- Describe the benefits of activity management in support functions

EXCELLENCE CANNOT BE BUILT ON A WEAK FOUNDATION

The service world has undergone a major transformation in recent years. Today **customers** expect services with high quality, quick delivery, and low prices. Customers expect bank statements to be correct, pizza delivered in thirty minutes, garbage to be picked up on time and properly, airplane flights to arrive on time, insurance claims to be handled quickly and correctly, oil to be changed in ten minutes, and phone systems always to work. Taxpayers expect governments to run effectively, and not just raise taxes every time there is a shortfall. Society expects donations to nonprofits to be used for the mission of the organization and only the very minimum spent on operating costs. These changes are the result of unprecedented scientific and technological progress coupled with fierce global competition. Organizations in a given industry must adopt a strategy of enterprise excellence or be forced out of business. Encroaching competition can quickly turn market supremacy into oblivion. Changing tax rates and tax bases can quickly throw government units into turmoil. Changing economic conditions can send nonprofits scrambling for funds. Every organization, whether service, government, or nonprofit has limited resources. Effective and efficient use of limited resources will greatly determine which organizations survive the 1990s and thrive into the twenty-first century.

To remain competitive, it is crucial for service organizations not to become complacent. Too often organizations consider themselves to be invulnerable. Consequently, they implement a strategy of exploiting their current market position. However, proprietary advantage never lasts (e.g., Eastern Airlines, Republic Bank, Pan Am). For governments, the ever-increasing cash flow can quickly disappear, as Texas found out in the 1980s after the oil boom and Massachusetts after the high-tech boom. An attempt to keep profit margins stable by increasing price inevitably results in an erosion of market position. Low-cost, not high-price, services and products have the competitive advantage. In government organizations, the equivalent of increasing prices is to increase taxes, which eventually forces people and industry to leave or cheat the system. Raising prices or taxes doesn't work because such a strategy does not address the fundamental factors driving cost and performance.

The problem of complacency is particularly apparent in government entities. These organizations often do not have direct competitors to force a sense of urgency in improving operations. They are a monopoly and do not fear loss of market share, which is a great motivator for a private organization. Too often, government organizations turn to the taxpayer as an easy solution rather than addressing the difficult issues that have caused the need for more resources.

Government agencies, especially the Department of Defense also have the problem of establishing a fair price for their purchases. What is a fair price for programming the computers that defend our nation? This is not a commodity that can be purchased at the local computer store.

As services mature, competition increases (e.g., insurance, banking, mutual funds, hospitals, charities). Prices and margins inevitably decline as they succumb to competitive pressures. The introduction of innovative services by competitors lessens the initial advantage of the earliest organizations, and prices become increasingly important in buying decisions. When only one stock market index fund existed, then upfront commissions and operating expenses were less important. Now that there are a variety of stock market index funds, these expenses are more important to the consumer, especially when there may be very little difference in performance of the various types of funds.

As a consequence, service organizations must constantly enhance the functionality of their services, improve productivity, and reduce costs. Nonprofits must find innovative ways to increase contributions and accomplish more of their mission for less cost. Governments must meet the demands of their customers for less cost and with less revenue. However, most organizations use current period performance as a barometer of success. They don't make fundamental changes until competition, economic pressures, or an unbalanced budget force the change. With the squeeze in profit margins, donations, and tax revenues comes the inevitable short-term approaches to cost reduction:

- Freeze hiring
- Freeze overtime and salary increases
- Freeze nonessential travel
- Offer early retirement
- Cut back on services (e.g., museum and library open fewer hours)
- Reduce expansion plans (e.g., road expansion stalls)
- Layoff workers; downsize organization

These approaches may ease short-term cash flow problems. However, in the long run, these approaches hurt the organization's performance and alienate customers/citizens. These typical short-term "fixes" eliminate the worker and not the work. Too often, organizations drive some of their best employees to competitors or out of the industry. Those that remain are overburdened and unhappy. This fosters an organization whose members are so anxious about protecting their jobs that they become uncreative and averse to risk.

Rather than implement short-term fixes, organizations must:

1. Understand and address the fundamental problems and eliminate nonproductive structured cost.

2. Design cost out of services, activities, and business processes
3. Greatly improve effectiveness

The key is:

1. To manage and reduce the workload—not just the work force
2. To streamline the activities/business processes and the way the remaining workload is performed

In other words, it is essential that an enterprise continually improve the way it provides, offers, and manages its activities (work). The principles of enterprise excellence include:

- Asking the customer's advice
- Improving every process continually
- Eliminating wasteful activities
- Reducing workload
- Classifying processes properly; utilized and unutilized classifications are more helpful than variable and fixed ones
- Synchronizing activities
- Including external suppliers and customers
- Controlling the process rather than the result
- Dealing with the causes, not the effects
- Focusing on outputs and outcomes, not inputs
- Involving the expert, the one who performs the activity
- Avoiding repetition of mistakes
- Using a common language
- Maintaining consistency of purpose
- Setting targets as a minimum required level of performance
- Understanding that people will not work themselves out of a job

Enterprise excellence also requires the ability to maintain leadership in introducing profitable new services and service variations. The most visible manifestations of successful organizations in this new environment are increased automation and computerization; reduced layers of management; increased attention to service quality, service operations, service planning; development of team concepts; and shorter service delivery cycles. The revolution is based on new philosophies such as total quality management (TQM), customer satisfaction (CS); business process re-engineering (BPR); employee involvement/empowerment (EI/EE), time-based management (TBM); activity-based costing (ABC); benchmarking; target costing; and organization redesign.

Many managers have confused these tools and techniques with the actual achievement of excellence. It is easy to blame failing competitiveness on a lack of technology or capital, or on competition or the economy, rather than on a management void. New technologies and tools, wondrous or not, do not produce desired results until they are effectively employed by people. A significant challenge for service managers in the 1990s will be assisting in the discovery, choice, and application of the technologies that are best for their employees and customers. Total quality management and employee empowerment are not the sole requirement for competitiveness; they are merely prerequisites.

The second Gallup Poll for the American Society of Quality Control in 1990 illustrates this point. The Gallup Poll showed that a number of organizations expressed a commitment to quality, but the message has not really filtered down to the first-line supervisors and the hourly workers. They were still operating under the same methods, policies, and procedures, even though senior management was talking about a new way of doing things.

This is not to suggest that total quality management and employee empowerment are not important. To the contrary, they are inextricably intertwined with an organization's quest for greater competitiveness. The challenge is to perform all activities correctly the first time. This requires getting people directly involved in fixing the causes of the problems through programs such as cross-functional teams as well as total quality management. Faulty processes account for far more mistakes than human error ever has. Process thinking changes the way an organization views a problem. Today when a person makes an error, an organization tries to remedy the problem through increased supervision, training, inspecting of their work or, in the most extreme case, dismissal. Process thinking recasts the problem as a process problem. The error is the consequence of a process that relied on the experience, the knowledge and motivation of that individual. Under this way of thinking, the process can be redesigned through automation, simplification, or computerization to minimize the adverse impact of variations caused by people.

However, competitive advantage accrues to those organizations that use enterprise excellence as a proactive, rather than a reactive, strategy.

Long-term success in service organizations, balanced budgets in the government, and positive retained revenue in nonprofits is determined by the advantages or disadvantages relative to competitors, whether they be companies, nonprofits, other states, or other countries. Organizations that eliminate waste and strive for absolute quality in all aspects of management can use the increased revenue to invest in new service research, expand services, reinvest in improving organization activities/business processes, lower cost, or build a strong cash liquidity position. The organizations that achieve these results will be in a position to dictate the basis of competition in their industry whether it be for-profit, governmental, or nonprofit.

To stay ahead of the competition, organizations must have a good understanding of the factors they can influence. Management must place unrelenting pressure on the entire organization for measurable continuous process improvement, cost reduction, and productivity gains. Ongoing vigilance is critical because it is difficult to regain competitive advantage once it is lost. An organization that cuts costs using layoffs or salary freezes will only see those costs return unless they change their fundamental processes. Costs must not be allowed to get out of line in the first place.

It is interesting to note that the United States surpassed the United Kingdom this century by having productivity improvement that was .51 percent, approximately one half percent, greater than that of the United Kingdom. Meanwhile, the economic miracle of Japan occurred with the Japanese having only .79 percent greater productivity improvements than the United States. The Japanese are firm believers in dedication to continuous improvement. This continuous improvement is not large, as shown by the numbers above. Small improvements in the performance of activities add up and can make a great deal of difference. A comparative study of suggestion programs in the United States and Japan shows that the average Japanese worker provides five suggestions annually. The average U.S. worker provides only two tenths of a suggestion per year.

An important reason an organization's costs become noncompetitive is that conventional accounting systems distort service costs, hide waste and do not highlight productivity improvement opportunities. This leads to poor decisions. Most managers routinely make critical decisions without the facts. In other words, organizations that have relevant and timely information have a much greater chance of making successful decisions.

Competitive advantage demands that organizations provide accurate answers to the following questions:

1. What are the influenceable (and directly traceable) **costs** for each major service, customer, citizen, business process, and activity?
2. What are the cost behavior patterns of each activity and business process, including its **capacity?** How much can volume be increased or decreased before costs change?
3. What is the **waste** (non–value-added) component of cost, and what are the best practices for an activity/business process/service?
4. What are the **costs and profits** for each major service, customer, and channel of distribution?
5. How do the **current cost** structure, capacity utilization, and nonfinancial performance trends compare with those of other similar organizations?
6. How can low cost, high quality, flexibility, short delivery times, and **best practices** be designed into new and existing activities/business processes/services?

Cost management based on this sort of activity information is the heart of the new management information systems that help managers answer critical questions. Activity-based management profiles an organization in terms of the cost and performance of its specific activities.

ENTERPRISE EXCELLENCE

Enterprise excellence is the cost-effective integration of activities within all units of an organization to continuously improve the delivery of services that satisfy the customer/citizen. Service enterprises structured to exploit market and technical opportunities will achieve a competitive advantage. The ability to achieve and sustain enterprise excellence requires the deliberate and continuous improvement of all activities and business processes—not just the tangible service being offered. This includes market and service research, service design, human resources, information systems, marketing/sales, finance/accounting, service operations, logistic support, customer service, accounting, legal, public relations, and administration. The key elements to enterprise excellence include:

- Cost-effectiveness
- Integration of activities and business processes
- Coherence with all units of an organization

- Continual improvement
- Delivery of services
- Customer satisfaction
- Accurate assignment of costs

Cost-Effectiveness

Value-added activities should be accomplished as cost-effectively as possible. This means that an organization must be a low-cost producer, but not necessarily the lowest-cost producer. Being low-cost means one's total costs are below the average of all organizations offering equivalent services to the same customer/citizen segments. The position of lowest-cost producer is, however, sometimes achieved to the detriment of quality, service, customer/employee satisfaction, and investment in the future. For example, an airline may be able to fly older planes, which keeps its cost lower, but reduces quality of service by having more maintenance delays.

Often organizations compete on bases other than cost—such as customer service, dependability, short cycle time, rapid new service introduction, quality, and field service. However, once a competitive strategy has been defined, the business processes and activities should be structured to be as cost-effective as possible. Anything else results in waste.

Integration of Activities and Business Processes

Understanding of organizational and departmental objectives must be spread throughout the organization. Enterprises are often organized and managed with rigid specializations. Management reporting emphasizes individual organizational units almost as if they were independent, self-contained disciplines, often referred to as departmental "silos." Costs incurred in one department are affected by decisions and outputs from other departments. Under the traditional structure of responsibility accounting, the interrelationship of activities/business processes among departments is ignored. This practice is in conflict with the concept of the unified enterprise.

This separation of organizational responsibility is dysfunctional because it encourages competition among departments and provides limited incentives to take action that hinders a department's performance but is in the best interest of the organization. As a consequence, in many organizations operations view marketing as "the enemy." The financial people often take the attitude that they are the "watchdogs" trying to catch other members of management when they are wrong instead of helping solve operational problems. Attention must be directed to the real competition so that the organization can concentrate its energies on other organizations and on its mission rather than competing against one another for budget dollars.

The importance of understanding interdependencies of activities is compounded in an advanced multi-service environment. Today, organizations are implementing integrated systems and other advanced technologies in order to achieve a harmonious flow throughout the organization. Integrated systems tear down the barriers between departments and involve getting information and ideas from everyone in the organization and putting them to work.

Coherence Within All Units of an Organization

Coherence must be based on action (activities/business processes), not hierarchies. Enterprise excellence requires involvement of all units, not just those producing the service. A role of the accounting department is, for example, to provide meaningful data in a format conducive to decision making. This role is just as critical to achieving enterprise excellence as are the various service-producing functions. Similarly, the streamlining of the customer order process is as critical as is quickly producing the service.

Continual Improvement

Enterprise excellence requires continual improvement in all enterprise activities—there is no room for complacency. This requires managing business processes and activities so as to minimize waste and non–value-added activities and constantly striving for perfection in all areas of the organization.

Delivery of Services

Services are where the enterprise and the marketplace meet. Service design must exploit market opportunities within the strategic framework. Service design must balance the exploitation of market opportunities with the facilitation of low-cost production of services. Equally important are many internal activities/business processes vital to the way an organization is perceived by its customers/citizens. Even governmental organizations, such as the Internal Revenue Service (IRS), have customers; its external customers are the citizens and the congress. The IRS's mission, in part, is to "continually improve the quality of our products and services" for its customers.

Customer Satisfaction

Ultimately, the success of an enterprise is measured by customer satisfaction in terms of revenue, market share, profit, growth, and balanced budgets. Only if an organization determines what the customer wants, and provides services that satisfy those wants, will the organization be successful. Enterprise excellence requires the systematic analysis of alternate opportunities for providing services based on an understanding of the relative cost, effectiveness, and quality of those services.

Accurate Assignment of Costs

To understand cost structures and how to manage them well, a manager must understand and control business processes and activities. Many service organization have little idea of what it costs to provide a service or to service a particular channel of distribution or a customer/citizen. Each service requires that a series of repeatable business processes and activities be performed. To know the cost of the services requires knowing the cost of each activity/business process. It is not important to know the cost of the service *after* it is performed. What is important is to know what it *should* cost to perform a service given the planned way of doing each business process and each activity. Any deviation between the planned and actual cost is the result of improper execution of the activities rather than a service cost problem. It is impossible to effectively manage an enterprise by looking backward. **Focus on activities and busi-**

ness processes before or while they are being performed. Managers and associates can't remember what happened last month, however, they can improve or catch problems while they are occurring if they are given the proper tools. ABM provides those tools.

Enterprise excellence demands information that assists managers in making decisions that result in improved service design, better service quality, and the removal of waste from operating activities. New cost management systems must support enterprise excellence by providing information on how the work is currently being performed, whether it contributes to organizational objectives, what factors **drive cost**, and how the system uses behavioral incentives to improve effectiveness. The new cost management systems must identify how each activity in the enterprise contributes to the organization's success, and must encourage a commitment to total quality and continual improvement. The foundation of these new cost management systems is activity management.

TRADITIONAL COST SYSTEMS

In light of the revolution taking place in the business world, one would expect to see significant changes in accounting. After all, the conventional service cost accounting systems were designed for an era when people worked without computers. The predominant resources to do work were people, technology was stable and inexpensive, and there was a limited range of services.

Traditional cost accounting systems typically attached service overhead costs to services or departments primarily to distribute the overhead for creating financial statements. In numerous service organizations, distribution of overhead was even felt to be unimportant and a waste of time. Since the objective was to maximize labor usage, cost control was focused at the point of cost occurrence by **cost element**. For example, teller wages in a bank were tracked in the department where the tellers worked, yet teller wages might be affected by improper hiring and training by Human Resources as well as wage rates set by senior management. Waste—hidden in the traditional service accounting reports—was generated by inefficient use of the prime factors of service operations, usually labor.

Cost accounting techniques based on such early conditions still prevail despite dramatic changes in service organizations. Organizations now want to know which services are profitable and which are not. They want to know which activities/business processes of an organization have the greatest cost–benefit ratios. Organizations are deciding whether to perform services themselves or buy these services from outside (outsourcing). For example, some government entities are now buying garbage collection and prison administration services rather than performing those services themselves.

Traditional cost accounting systems provide little information to managers on the critical success factors or the sources of competitive advantage. Some organizations don't allocate administrative and marketing overhead. Others just allocate it based on sales revenue. Therefore, in some cases, true service costs don't exist. In others, they are often so inaccurate that they encourage management to adopt strategies that inhibit improvement. Managers are sometimes encouraged to manage the allocation of overhead rather than strive to eliminate waste and improve operational performance.

Conventional cost accounting systems assume that services and their corresponding sales volume cause cost. They therefore make individual budget-line items the focus of the cost system. Costs are classified as either direct/indirect to services or variable/fixed. Traditional systems often use measures such as sales revenue, total direct costs, or direct labor costs as **allocation bases** to distribute service overhead costs to services.

Traditional service costing systems report a reasonably accurate service cost where overhead activity is consumed in direct relation to service volume. For example, benefits for direct employees are related to direct labor costs.

However, service costs become inaccurate when general and administrative overhead activities related to service revenue volume increase in magnitude. Enterprise activities related to senior management time, legal services, information systems, human resources, and accounting are, at best, loosely related to current service volume. Still other activities, such as purchasing and order processing, are related to the number of different services provided rather than service volume. When a service organization allocates non–volume-related activities on volume-related bases, traditional cost accounting systems provide littler insight into the relationship between the operating activities that generate the overhead cost. A distorted service cost results.

Traditional cost systems often encourage decisions that conflict with enterprise excellence. A service overhead rate based on salaries and wages, for example, causes an inordinate focus on the salaries and wages component of cost. When hard times are encountered, organizations revert to cutting people through downsizing. Thus it masks other opportunities such as more efficient use of equipment, supplies, and information technology and other non-people related expenses. This happens because the costing system proclaims that people are very expensive.

Where the **administrative overhead rate** is 30 percent of direct salaries and wages, for example, a service automation improvement that removes $1 of salaries and wages from a service results in an apparent saving of $.30 of administrative overhead. For example, if total budgeted overhead is $30,000 and budgeted direct salaries are $100,000, then the budgeted overhead rate is 30 percent of salaries. If a new computer increases the overhead budget by $10,000 (from $30,000 to $40,000) and reduces budgeted salaries by $20,000 (from $100,000 to $80,000), then the new overhead rate will be $40,000 divided by $80,000 or 50 percent. The salaries and wages component is reduced by introducing automation. Overhead is increased by the cost of the advanced computer technology. Thus, the salary and wage reduction through automation, in reality, increases overhead through higher depreciation, training, and supplies. The new overhead rate increased from 30 to 50 percent ($40,000/$80,000). This might increase the focus on controlling direct labor. Yet our total operating cost decreased from $130,000 to $120,000. This non-overhead rate focus should yield insights into further improvements through automation. Meanwhile, the overhead rate orientation could focus management in the wrong direction, toward managing labor instead of managing total cost.

Another danger of direct-labor-based overhead allocation is that it encourages the attitude that people must remain fully occupied. Soon management and employees learn the game. They just slow down their speed in order to accommodate the work at hand. This further distorts the allocation of service overhead.

The traditional approach to cost accounting is to break down the management of an enterprise into specialized units with rigid division of responsibility. Managers of each functional area estimate the resources, by cost category (including labor, travel, supplies, facilities, and so on), necessary to accomplish their work tasks. Managers are accountable for accomplishing their tasks with the resources assigned. An accounting system monitors, by cost element, performance for an organizational unit by comparing the cost incurred with the **budgeted** costs.

For example, a purchasing department is responsible for procuring supplies needed in the service organization. To accomplish this function, the organization hires managers, buyers, and secretaries. The department manager estimates the amount of travel, office supplies, office space, and other resources required to execute the department's objectives. Costs are budgeted. Actual costs are tracked against budget by type of resource as illustrated in the following table:

Cost Center: Procurement Department

Account	Description	Actual $	Budget $	Variance $
0009	Wages & salaries, salaried	80,150	83,000	2,850
0010	Wages & salaries, hourly	124,360	110,000	(14,360)
0201	Benefits, salaried	21,812	22,600	788
0202	Benefits, hourly	37,688	32,600	(5,088)
0352	Travel	62,515	70,500	7,985
0366	Facilities	32,000	32,000	0
0380	Supplies	1,394	1,500	106
0463	Training	20,240	30,000	9,760
	Total	380,159	382,200	2,041

The assumption is that the service organization will be profitable and well run if the budgeted revenue is achieved and the actual cost of all departments does not exceed budgeted cost. The role of the purchasing department, in a financial sense, is to remain within budget. The practice of collecting actual cost by cost elements (wages, facilities, supplies, travel, and so on) facilitates comparison with budget.

Traditional cost accounting systems do not, however, provide adequate information to identify the causes of cost. In situations where costs are deemed by management to be too high, managers tend to rely on across-the-board overhead cuts to control spending in the absence of proper information. Thus, when revenue declines, service organizations usually respond by "tightening the belt" in the wrong way at the wrong point in the enterprise. Common approaches are: universal reductions in the budgets of all departments; early retirement; and freezes on training, nonessential travel, hiring; wage increase, and overhead activities; and cuts in capital purchases.

Such well-intentioned efforts are doomed to failure; they generate a self-feeding cycle of competitive decay. They do not address the demand for overhead resources—the activities that keep people busy. There is a natural tendency for managers to cut expenditure on activities critical to the future—such as marketing, new service research/development, and computer systems—or to forgo training and improvements to make short-term profits seem better or to meet budget.

A viciously deteriorating cycle gains momentum. When short-term cutbacks are removed, spending returns at least to its previous level and often to a higher level because many important activities were delayed. Deterioration in the quality of service and pressures on an overburdened staff prompt renewed spending, and overhead creeps up. The problem is that the fundamental causes of cost were not corrected. The business process used to provide services before the "freezes" remains frozen in place.

The most common and least understood factor that touches off such a cycle is management operating with the wrong type of data—data geared to accounting rather than management. The conventional cost accounting systems present distorted, aggregated numbers based on erroneous cost behavior patterns. The information comes too late to affect decisions and does not encourage making the changes necessary to compete in the dynamic service world.

The financial information generated in traditional accounting systems further hinders excellence because it presents service or operating margins. It doesn't present the true picture after all influenceable information systems, marketing, sales, human resource, legal, accounting, and other administration costs are taken into account. Finally, traditional accounting systems do not provide a clear picture of how costs and profits change as support activity volume moves up or down. Thus they are not particularly helpful to managers who must evaluate marketing, administrative, human resource, accounting, or computer alternatives that involve different levels of activity.

ACTIVITY MANAGEMENT

The activity management approach to cost management breaks down an organization into **activities**. An activity describes *what* an enterprise does—the way time is spent. An activity has inputs and outputs. The principal function of an activity is to convert inputs, using resources (supplies, people, and technology), into outputs. Activity management identifies activities performed in an organization and determines their cost and performance (time and quality).

A simple and effective activity management systems uses the following approach:

1. **Determine** enterprise **activities.**
2. Determine **activity cost and activity performance.** Performance is measured as the cost per output, time to perform the activity, and the quality of the output.
3. Determine the **output and output measure** of the activity. An activity measure (output measure) is the factor by which the cost of an activity varies most directly. The output is simply what is produced by the activity.
4. **Trace** activity **cost** to cost objectives. Activity costs are traced to cost objectives such as services, business processes, customers, channels of distribution, and orders based on the usage of the activity.
5. Determine organization short- and long-range goals (**critical success factors**). This requires an understanding of the current cost structure, business processes, and operating activities and how effectively they deliver value to the customer.
6. Evaluate activity/business process **effectiveness** and **efficiency.** Knowing the critical success factors (step 5) enables an organization to examine what it is now doing (step 4) and the relationship of that activity to achieving organization goals through long-term customer satisfaction at the lowest possible cost. Everything an organization does—or avoids doing—is measured against the short- and long-term goals. This provides a useful formula on which to base a decision of whether to continue performing or to restructure an activity/business process. Also, cost control is improved by ascertaining whether there are superior methods of performing an activity/business process, identifying wasteful activities, and determining the cause of the cost.

Determining Enterprise Activities

Activity analysis identifies the significant activities of an enterprise in order to establish a basis for accurately describing **business processes** and determining their cost and performance. Activity analysis decomposes a large, complex organization into its elemental activities. The decomposition is accomplished by examining each organizational unit to identify its business objective and the resources allocated to achieve this objective. Activity analysis, therefore, identifies the way an organization uses its resources to accomplish its business objectives. There are numerous techniques to perform activity analysis. Techniques will be explained in Chapter 5.

Determining Activity Cost and Performance

The cost of an activity includes all the resources employed to perform that activity. Resources consist of people, machines, travel, supplies, computer systems, and other expenses and capital that are customarily expressed as cost elements within a **chart of accounts**. Each significant traceable factor of service operations is included in an activity cost.

When a cause-and-effect relationship can be established between a resource and a specific activity, the cost is said to be *traceable*. In many cases, tracing cost to an activity is reasonably simple because the resource is dedicated to a single activity. A purchasing clerk dedicated to the purchase order activity is an example. When a resource supports several activities, the resource usage must be split between activities.

A purchasing department, for example, is responsible for planning procurement, selecting/evaluating vendors, negotiating contracts, issuing purchase orders, and coordinating vendors. To accomplish each of these activities, the department manager will hire people, plan travel, and procure office space and other resources.

The costs are planned and tracked by activity:

Purchasing Department

Activity Description	Actual $	Budget $	Variance $
Plan procurement	29,150	30,000	850
Select & evaluate vendors	43,360	45,200	1,840
Negotiate contracts	45,632	50,000	4,368
Issue purchase orders	121,492	120,000	(1,492)
Coordinate vendors	140,525	137,000	(3,525)
Total	380,159	382,200	2,041

How an activity manager chooses to perform an activity and the number of activity occurrences determine the resources required. For example, the activity "issue purchase orders" requires a person to make the purchase order decision and a computer system to perform the necessary calculations and data manipulation. Other resources, such as office supplies, are also required. The execution of these activities triggers the consumption of resources that are recorded as costs in the general ledger. The number of purchase order clerks, information systems resources, and office supplies depends on the number of purchase orders to be processed, not necessarily the volume to be purchased. The cost of the activity (issue purchase orders) is determined by tracing the salaries and wages, facilities cost, technology, and office supplies to the "issue purchase order" activity. A causal relationship is established between the resources and the scheduling activity. Scheduling may determine the number of purchase orders that are required.

Determining Output of the Activity

Activity cost is expressed in terms of a measure of activity volume by which the costs of a given activity vary most directly (e.g., number of purchase orders or number of purchase order lines). This is known as the *activity measure (output measure)*.

The activity measure is most often the output of the activity. For example, the input to the purchasing activity is a purchase requisition, and the output is a purchase order. The cost of the purchasing activity can be expressed as a cost per purchase order or cost per purchase order line. The selection of the activity measure is critical because it makes visible the factors that drive activity volume and, subsequently, cost.

Tracing Activity Cost to Services, Customers, or Other Cost Objectives

Activity management is based on two simple principles. First, **activities consume resources**, and second, **services**, customers, or other cost objectives **consume activities**. Costing is enhanced by more discrete tracing of the cost of providing a service, supporting a customer, or other cost objective. This is done by identifying all traceable activities and determining how much of each activity's/business process's output is consumed by the cost objective. This cost structure, referred to as the bill of activities (BOA), describes each service's pattern of activity consumption.

The discrete tracing of expenses to cost objectives, facilitated by the activity management system, allows an organization to assess the long-term cost effectiveness of the current and future mix of services. Forecasting the service mix allows the organization to assess whether the current activity/business process structure is best suited to the service mix.

The tracing of activities/business processes to services based on usage, unlike cross-subsidized allocations of revenue or salaries/wages based overhead rates, distinguishes between intensive users and infrequent users of an activity. Under traditional accounting, the cost associated with issuing a purchase order is allocated to services by using a basis such as salaries/wages or sales revenue. To properly trace costs to services requires determination of how much of each activity is consumed by a service. Consider a complex service that requires an average of twenty purchase orders while a simple service requires one purchase order. Accurate service costing requires that the complex service absorb a greater proportion of the purchase order activity than the simple service.

To continue the illustration, consider a purchasing department that spends $120,000 processing 6,000 purchase orders. The average cost per purchase order is $20. The complex service should be charged $400 (twenty purchase orders @ $20) of the purchase order activity, whereas the simple service should be charged $20 (one purchase order @ $20)—a dramatic difference. Yet if the organization used revenue to distribute the cost of running the purchasing department to their services and if the two services had equal sales, they would each receive the same amount of purchasing department overhead.

As a result of this improved tracing process, reported service costs could vary dramatically from the traditional model. One large organization found that their cost distortion was very high and caused them to be involved in activities that really weren't worth their time and cost.

Determining Critical Success Factors

An important activity of top management is to develop strategic plans based on the external environment in which the organization operates. Critical success factors could include timely performance and safety for a transportation company; low rates and/or outstanding service for a bank, hospital, or insurance company; convenient location for a store or hospital; technology for a computer software firm; or flexibility for an engineering firm, law office, or city zoning board. It could likewise be customer service for a hotel, software firm, mutual fund, contractor, or restaurant. It could be marketing for security alarm firm, direct mail firm, charity, or broker.

Enterprise activities should be structured in line with the stated strategic plans and critical success factors. Line management, however, is concerned with daily operations and meeting short-term requirements. A key objective of activity management is to match these two perspectives.

In looking at critical success factors, an organization should look at the core competencies for the industry.

Evaluating Activity Effectiveness and Efficiency

Activity-based management (ABM) encourages the continual improvement of activity performance. In structuring the way an activity is performed, an organization has a range of choices to make between different business processes and resources. Each alternative method of accomplishing an activity/business process brings with it certain implications for the organization in terms of response to markets, service operations capabilities, the level of investment required, the unit cost, and type of control and management structure. The fundamental rationale for choosing a specific method of performing an activity/business process is that it be best able to support the organization's objectives.

Activity cost is important in cost control. An *activity cost* is the ratio of resources assigned to an activity to the amount of output of the activity. An activity cost, therefore, is input divided by output—a productivity measure.

To judge the effectiveness of the purchase order activity, for example, requires knowing both the cost of the resource assigned and the number of purchase orders processed. Productivity measures show improvement by: (1) increasing output without additional costs, (2) maintaining output while decreasing costs, or (3) a combination of (1) and (2). If today's cost to process 6,000 purchase orders is $120,000, the cost per purchase order is $20. If, as a result of improvements in the purchasing department, the organization is able to process 10,000 purchase orders for the same cost, the new cost per purchase order would be reduced to $12. Productivity will have been greatly improved. Or the organizations could continue to handle 6,000 purchase orders at a cost of only $90,000 instead of $120,000. Finally, the organization could handle more purchase orders at a lower cost per purchase order.

ACTIVITY AND TRADITIONAL COST ACCOUNTING CONTRASTED

Activity management lessens the misuse of resources that is usually associated with cross-subsidized allocation. This gives activity managers an incentive to keep their operations competitive by continually identifying and cost-effectively eliminating generators of waste.

As an illustration of the differences between traditional cost accounting and activity management, assume an organization receives a request to expedite a customer order. Expediting an order may result in rescheduling (and delaying) other orders. The costs of the rescheduled orders are increased because they involve additional handling, increased computer storage, and/or complex systems to track their progress.

Under traditional accounting practices, these costs would be charged as incurred to all service orders and reported as an unfavorable variance by a standard cost system. Similarly, an actual cost system would report higher actual costs for the services that were rescheduled. There is no direct way of seeing that these costs were caused by the rescheduled activity.

In contrast, under an activity management system, all events caused by the rescheduled activity are linked and reported as separate costs. The additional expediting and related activities are traceable to the rescheduling. This results in the elimination of the unfavorable variance for orders affected by expediting.

To illustrate this point, a large organization in the United Kingdom found that an accounts payable invoice that was processed without any problems cost two pounds sterling. However, when a problem occurred, the processing cost jumped to over twenty pounds sterling per invoice. This is because of the delay and the numerous people who had to be involved. At best, a traditional system would show the total costs of accounts payable. The activity management system showed the extreme differences in cost between an error-free and invalid accounts payable invoice. This information provided management with valuable insight which resulted in an improvement program and its consequential dramatic improvement.

Activity information provides valuable input to marketing, sales, and the schedulers who caused the higher cost by making the decision to reschedule. In many cases, the order might not have been rescheduled if the true costs had been known. If a future decision to reschedule is made, then the expedited order should receive the total cost and report an unfavorable variance and lower profit margins (or loss). Or the system should be improved to better handle expedited orders if the environment doesn't allow for the elimination of these types of orders.

It should be noted that the total department cost is the same under both the traditional (cost element) and activity management approaches. The difference is that under traditional cost accounting, costs are accumulated and controlled in total by cost category for each organizational unit, whereas under activity management, costs are accumulated and controlled through activities.

COMMON REASONS THAT ORGANIZATIONS IMPLEMENT ACTIVITY MANAGEMENT

Activity management has been implemented by various organizations in a variety of ways to solve significantly different problems. Activity management can be used to support several management needs and decisions. These needs include:

- New service costing
- Managing cash and liquidity
- Cost control
- Decision support

Service Cost

Service costs are used by managers to assist with estimating and design-to-cost decisions. They can also help managers decide whether the services are more efficiently performed in-house or purchased from outside the organization. A service cost is considered accurate when it mirrors the collection of activities/business processes that creates that service.

The greater accuracy of service costs in an activity management system lessens the problem of inappropriate messages that are conveyed by traditional systems. An inaccurate service cost increases the chances of incorrect decisions.

Accurate service cost is critical in selecting services, markets, projects, and customers to be emphasized. Profit potential is the most important factor when assessing and selecting service and market segments. Too many organizations focus on expanded sales volume with the assumption that profits will follow. However, when the fight for market share in a stable or declining market intensifies, managers must specialize in the most profitable services rather than simply try to increase service sales volume. Or, managers must learn how to become more effective in providing services that customers and citizens want.

Managing Cash and Liquidity

Cash and liquidity are as essential as reported profits. Cash leads to liquidity, and liquidity is critical in a business environment of high risk and great uncertainty. Cash and liquidity help withstand surprises, facilitate adaptation to sudden changes, and enable an organization to capitalize on the narrow windows of opportunity that are common in a turbulent environment. A business can go bankrupt while reporting profits, but it will never go bankrupt as long as its cash and liquidity positions are strong. The lack of concentration on cash and liquidity are apparent in many organizations. Expansion plans and capital expenditures are justified on projected service sales volume gains or cost savings without adequate regard to the availability of funds or the cash carrying costs. Working capital is allowed to build without considering its carrying cost. Improper capital management disguises sloppy business practices. Consider work-in-progress (WIP). Examples of this in service companies would be mortgages, insurance policies, and advertising programs partially processed or completed. WIP hides quality and processing problems by buffering their effects. In service organizations, WIP is usually not posted to a balance sheet account as is required in manufacturing. Yet in reality, service WIP is similar to manufacturing WIP. It needs to be minimized. Failure to minimize WIP results in services and projects that cannot be billed. This ties up money in working capital, which results in opportunity costs and lower profits.

Cost Control

Cost information should encourage enterprise excellence. Waste cannot be tolerated. Services should be designed to optimize performance. Activities should support corporate objectives. The emphasis should be on addressing the cause of excess costs and not just the symptoms. Activities allow an organization to analyze processes that cross several departments. This analysis is done by reviewing the various activities that make up those processes. Non–value-added activities should be eliminated so as to reduce and control costs. Activity costs for value added activities should be reduced.

Decision Support

Cost information is used to facilitate decisions such as do it yourself or buy from outside, new service costing, and design-to-cost. Too often managers responsible for these decisions use cost information from outside the cost management system.

Today cost information provided by the cost accounting system is not timely and is inappropriate for decision making. It is inappropriate because it is compiled on the assumption that all support activities are related to service operations volume and it aggregates organizational units into common cost categories, like departments. Cost data is not timely because it is generated from the monthly accounting close. Cost data should be updated and made available to managers on a basis of the timing of the decision and not to accounting conventions.

USING ACTIVITY MANAGEMENT
FOR BEHAVIORAL CHANGE

Some organizations use activity management as a behavioral tool to focus attention on one or two critical aspects of enterprise excellence. One organization used activity management to focus attention on the number of different people needed to process an insurance claim. Previously, one employee took information regarding the claim over the phone, another entered the information into the computer, and a third employee set up the reserve for the loss. The insurance company cross-trained their employees so that a single employee could handle an entire claim.

This organization uses the number of claims as an activity output measure. Each claim receives the same amount of claims handling expense regardless of the total amount of the claim. Previously, claim-handling expenses were allocated based on the claim size. The theory behind allocating based on claim size was that larger claims require more time and skill to handle. Activity analysis discovered that the dollar value of the claim did not really affect the amount of time to process the claim, so the company selected number of claims as the basis for distributing claims handling expense. As a consequence of ABM, they changed to a cost-per-claim system. The new cost per claim was much less for high-value claims and much higher for low-value claims. This change enlightened management to understand that low value claims were expensive to handle. Therefore, the company could change its focus to increase high value claims while reducing low value claim business, reduce claims handling expense, or do both.

Insurance product managers each wanted their own unique forms. This made it more expensive for the organization which had to use low-volume, unique forms rather than fewer high-volume generic claims forms. The ABM analysis captured the cost of form design, regulatory approval and maintenance, and other costs regardless of policy/form volume. By spreading the costs for each policy/form based on the volume of that policy/form, the organization achieved its strategy to reduce unique policies and forms.

Product managers used substantially fewer unique policy clauses in their insurance contracts. This reduced the number of unique contracts and reduced training time, processing time, and form costs. Procurement overhead for forms fell, claims quality improved, and several policies that had previously been processed in separate departments were processed in a single department.

Traditional accounting practice distorts service cost. For example, many costs do not vary based on the size of the claim. The resulting cost distortions decrease the relevance of service cost in decisions that depend on an accurate service cost. However, using the number of claims as an activity output measure considers the following cause-and-effect chain:

- Part of the cost of the claims activity is related to the number of claims and not necessarily the type of claim.
- The activity measure is the number of claims, because the resources needed to process a claim vary by this factor.

- The cost drivers are the primary factors driving the need for the claims activity, and cost avoidance is achieved by managing these drivers. The key cost drivers include: completeness, accuracy, and legibility on the claims form; using part-time or full time employees; number of different policies; policy complexity; types of policies underwritten; and automation. However, to use these as activity output measures leads to inaccurate tracing of cost to services.

The selection of an inappropriate activity/business process measure might result in changes in organizational behavior that does not match strategic goals. For instance, employees may modify their performance in a way that lowers their cost per activity but may increase cycle time for that activity. Thus additional activity/business process performance measures relating to time and quality need to be added.

HOW ACTIVITY MANAGEMENT HELPS ACHIEVE ENTERPRISE EXCELLENCE

Activity-based management provides a foundation for achieving enterprise excellence by eliminating distortions and cross-subsidization caused by traditional **cost allocations.** It provides a base line for improving cost and performance. Activity cost information provides a clear view of how the mix of an organization's diverse services and activities contributes in the long run to organization's goals. Cost reduction potential is made visible through non–value-added analysis and analysis of best practices.

Nonfinancial performance measures (time, quality), real time control of operating activities, and activity cost information, when combined, provide the management information that organizations need in today's competitive environment. Activity information is the key to continual improvement of and achievement of organizational goals.

Activity management helps an organization achieve enterprise excellence by:

- Focusing on the process (how activities are done)
- Improving in-house versus buy-from-outside decisions, and providing estimates that are based on a service cost that mirrors the way work is done

- Facilitating elimination of waste by providing visibility of non–value-added activities
- Identifying activity/business process workload
- Identifying the source of cost by identifying the cost drivers
- Linking organizational strategy to operational decision making, thus enabling management to capitalize on activities/business processes that are an organizational strength, while restructuring activities/business processes that do not contribute to achieving organizational goals
- Providing **feedback** on whether the anticipated results of the strategies are obtained so that corrective action can be initiated
- Ensuring that time, quality, flexibility, and conformance to schedule goals are achieved by linking performance measures to strategy
- Encouraging continual improvement and total quality management because planning and control are directed at the process level
- Improving the effectiveness of budgeting by identifying the cost/performance relationship of different service levels
- Improving profitability by monitoring total **life-cycle cost** and performance
- Providing insight into the fastest-growing and least visible element of service cost—service overhead
- Ensuring achievement of investment plans by monitoring the investment through the activity management system so that when deviations from the plan are detected, corrective action can be initiated
- Continually evaluating the effectiveness of activities/business processes to identify potential investment opportunities
- Incorporating externally set target (e.g., the customer) performance and cost goals, and setting specific goals at the activity/business process level
- Eliminating many crises by fixing the problems rather than treating symptoms

It is also important to stress that the activity management system will do nothing but identify where potential problems are encountered. It is what managers do with the information that will determine whether activity management is a success.

GETTING STARTED

Before starting an activity analysis, it is important to consider that the effort involved in gathering, analyzing, and recording information on activities demands time, money, and people; it is not an effort that should be undertaken lightly or without considerable forethought. First ask:

- Does top management understand the value and effort of implementing an activity management system? Are top managers willing to commit the required time, money, and resources?
- Do managers and supervisors understand the changes that may be recommended as a result of the activity management system? Do they realize how such changes might affect them, their customers, and their employees?

SUMMARY

Activity management reshapes the way organizations manage costs. It attaches organization costs to activities/business processes. Service cost is the sum of the cost of all traceable activities/business processes based on the usage of each activity. Cost control is focused on the source of the cost regardless of the organizational unit in which it is incurred.

Managers need activity information to help them achieve enterprise excellence. Activity management identifies what the organization does. In order to improve profitability and performance, it is critical to understand where the enterprise's precious time goes and, in detail, what the enterprise does and how it does it. Ultimately, an organization can only improve when management understands what is done, how well it is done, and whether it contributes to organizational objectives. Activity management facilitates improved traceability and, ultimately, improved accountability.

Activity management is a powerful tool for managing complex operations of an organization through a detailed assessment of its activities. Activity management attributes cost and performance data to activities. Activity cost and performance data provide management with information needed to determine an accurate service cost, improve business processes, eliminate waste (non-value-added activities), identify cost drivers, plan operations, set organizational strategies, and delight the customer.

Activity management generates cost and operational information in a form that creates continual improvement and total quality. Continual improvement and total quality control are facilitated by analyzing each activity/business process and by identifying the *source* of cost rather than focusing on the *symptoms*. In focusing attention on the source of problems, management must assign responsibility to those departmental activities that drive cost and monitor their execution to see if planned results were achieved.

The U.S. General Accounting Office report NSIAD 91-190 shows that organizations benefit from "building in quality" through the use of total management practices instead of relying on traditional methods of "inspecting in quality." Job satisfaction and attendance improves, and turnover decreases. Customers' satisfaction and retention rates improve while complaints decrease. Profitability improves. Cost of quality, errors, and lead time decreases, while on-time delivery and reliability improve. Common to all organizations was a focus on meeting customers' requirements, training and empowering employees to improve quality and reduce costs, and fostering continuous improvement. Activity management is a tool to delight the customer, satisfy employees, and meet organizational objectives.

Activity information allows managers to identify and eliminate waste, and thus improve quality. It also confirms progress in removing waste from operating activities.

Eliminating waste and implementing a philosophy of continual improvement is not difficult if senior management has the will and if the activity management system is set up to assist. Waste elimination and continuous improvement can be extremely difficult, however, if the accounting systems are designed around functional organizations rather than around activities/business processes.

Nonprofits have a similar objective, which is to identify the markets, services, and customers that they can best serve. For example, should the March of Dimes have offices in large cities only or also in small towns? Should they educate only, do research only, or both? Should they work with everyone or should they take a more focused approach? Government entities may have similar objectives. For example, the post office may find that its greatest potential is to concentrate on traditional mail delivered within two or three days as well as second- and third-class mail. On the other hand, if the U.S. Postal Service can show that they can compete successfully with the next-day carriers, they should also emphasize that service. With tremendous pressure on federal, state, and local governments to balance their budgets, activity management is an effective tool in eliminating non–value-added activities.

Remember that nonprofits, according to Peter Drucker, are also businesses and need to be run that way. Likewise, governments are businesses. They may not have a profit goal, but they have a goal to satisfy the citizens by providing services while minimizing costs.

Thus activity management applies to all types of organizations, whether for-profit, nonprofit, or government.

2

THE CHANGING SERVICE ENVIRONMENT

The purpose of this chapter is to:

- Describe the changes in the service environment that lead to the development of activity management
- Project future service trends and their impact on management reporting

The service environment is awash with change. Until recently, such staples of today's business life as the personal computer and the fax machine did not exist; some governmental agencies were not concerned about customer service and costs; some nonprofit organizations were not run like businesses; robots were found only in horror stories; and free enterprise was still a forbidden notion within the former Soviet Union and the Eastern bloc nations.

Now, quite suddenly, these changes are coming together in a cascade that is causing massive reappraisals of basic business assumptions that have long remained unquestioned. The current wave of technological and management transformation, coupled with global competition, is altering the attitudes and expectations of service organizations around the world and, in the process, creating new market needs and new service organizations.

The new organizations face the formidable task of simultaneously improving quality and customer service, and reducing cost. To remain competitive and keep budgets in balance, organizations must streamline **operations**, eliminate waste, reduce cycle time, adopt a commitment to total quality, and judiciously incorporate advanced technologies such as scanning of documents, electronic data interchange, and paperless offices.

High-quality services delivered on time and at a low cost will be a competitive weapon that enables new service capabilities and enterprise excellence. Global competition has forced organizations to adopt new technology and philosophies or risk loss of market share or even bankruptcy. Not only are service companies competing, but so are entire countries.

The dilemma facing most organizations is that their facilities, management policies and systems were developed for a different operating environment. The resulting service operations and management practices are a hodgepodge of the traditional and the progressive. The software and hardware are in place, the procedures may be understood, and the people who receive information from the system may know how to interpret it. The system is "frozen" in the sense that people are comfortable with its use, whether or not they understand how to use the information and whether or not it is helpful for decision making. The conclusion is that change is difficult and management inertia is paralyzing.

Amid such profound and rapid change, the principles by which we have been accustomed to managing organizations and the tools we have used to measure progress have become obsolete. Time-honored management accounting systems present a distorted view of the enterprise and do not provide the visibility to encourage a commitment to continuous improvement and total quality. The American Society of Quality Control Gallup survey indicates that imitating the Japanese is not the answer to improving the quality of American goods and services.

Managers seeking to succeed in this environment are turning to their **management accounting** system for new types of information. Improved **capital budgeting** techniques, more accurate service cost data, and more relevant and more timely performance evaluation information are needed. Today the crucial link between service excellence and measurement systems is being rediscovered.

THE DECLINE OF TRADITIONAL SERVICE PRODUCTION

Traditional service organizations have taken a beating during the last few years. These groups were organized along functional lines. Based on the premise that repetition, experience, and homogeneity of tasks promote efficiency, functional clusters (like similar tasks and activities at the same location within an office) developed with movement of work-in-progress between clusters as the service is produced.

In this system, low cost is achieved through economies of scale and high quality through constant inspection and detection of errors. People are the dominant factor of service operations, and the role of technology (office, equipment, and information systems) is to increase the productivity of the direct laborer. John Kenneth Galbraith proudly proclaimed that the operational problems were solved.

Organizations set up by functional services created specialized workers. It was believed that highly trained specialists, who were fully utilized, minimized cost. The result was that the boom years of earlier decades created an environment where workers demanded higher wages and lenient working conditions. Management and labor were enemies. With skilled workers in short supply and service requirements tightening, managers could never quite bring themselves to say "no."

Governments have set budgets and fees not always understanding the true cost of providing those services. Recently, the city of Dallas raised garbage fees by $4,000,000 in order to make that service pay for itself. To improve productivity, the city had the employees compete with an outside firm for the next year's contract. As a result, the number of homes per day for which garbage is collected increased from 876 to 1,063.

Nonprofits emphasized gross revenue in their fund-raising efforts without really considering the costs to raise those funds. Many nonprofits did not have a formal accounting system to determine fund-raising event success. Sometimes their emphasis was on net revenue, which is what is left over after paying direct donor events such as renting a hotel, hiring a band, food, and prizes for the event. However, they didn't consider the cost of staff time and services necessary to generate that event. For some events, the vast amount of staff time and services made the event relatively unprofitable. Time would have been better spent on other events.

Few service organizations used any type of economic order quantity (EOQ) model. If they did, the EOQ model, was unchallenged as representing the optimum (least-cost) lot-size purchases. Under EOQ, the cost of holding inventories (e.g., gasoline inventories for a trucking company, airline or hospital supplies) consists of the cost of capital, storage, insurance, and depreciation on storage facilities. This holding cost was balanced against the cost of placing orders, shipping, supply movement, and quantity discounts lost—to derive the optimum order quantity. According to the EOQ model, the ordering cost per unit and handling cost go down as the order size increases. Consequently, an organization should order items or provide the same service in larger batches in order to reduce the cost of actually purchasing the item as well as reducing cost by handling less frequently (e.g., a hospital should schedule the same type of medical operation all day rather than setting up for a variety of operations that may have different requirements and multiple set ups).

The EOQ model required exorbitant levels of inventory to buffer against uncertainty and ensure high efficiency by keeping all factors of service operations fully utilized. It was not unusual to have costly **work centers** being idle far too long.

The system that evolved became characterized by one term: redundancy. Multiple systems, requiring multiple time-consuming setups and buffered by large service inventories, were used to decouple the service production process from demand, while management sought ways to capitalize on economies of scale.

The result was an unresponsive operation characterized by long **lead times**, significant quality problems, and complex forecasting techniques. Lead times were protracted because **cycle time** was secondary to resource utilization. It was not unusual for queue times and waiting processing to account for 95 percent of the total service production cycle time. Consider the length of time it takes to process a mortgage. The loan officer takes the mortgage application in less than an hour. A credit report, survey, and appraisal are ordered—approximately another hour. These reports, surveys, and appraisals are received, reviewed, filed, and approved by the loan committee—approximately two more hours. The mortgage documents are drawn up and reviewed—possibly four hours. The whole process may only take one day, yet in most cases it takes anywhere from thirty days to sixty days to close and fund a mortgage. Therefore, processing time is only 2 percent to 3 percent of the total time.

Frequent changeovers often created quality problems or amplified existing ones. The long service production cycles resulted in an increased dependence on forecasts. The problem became circular. Basing service production on forecasts, which are uncertain by nature, caused considerable re-ordering of priorities and other disruptions to the service production process. The result, more often than not, was confusion and inefficiency on all levels; inventories of the wrong forms or people with the wrong skills grew, while the number of back orders led to service production inefficiency and infighting between marketing and service production. This, in turn, increased cycle time.

The complexity inherent in functional service organizations gave rise to the need for mathematical programming and complex service production and control systems. Think of scheduling at an airline. There are thousands of pilots and flight attendants, a variety of planes requiring different pilots and flight attendants, and differing demand for the number of flight attendants depending on load factors. Given the long lead times to schedule flights, significant training time, elaborate organizations, and economic instability, it was believed that competitive advantage could be achieved through optimal use of the resources. Thus emerged linear programming. Mathematical programming was highly touted as an important tool in dealing with long lead times both in personnel and plane scheduling. Western organizations spent millions of dollars to install mathematical programming systems, often with minimal benefit. These systems accept the problem as fact and then determine optimal solutions. Progressive organizations should never accept these problems as facts, but rather should emphasize root causes of the problems.

In this environment, computer information systems proliferated. The resources required to create and maintain the computer applications grew exponentially. Yet the credibility of the information systems department was not high. Users accepted the fact that systems development would cost more and take longer than promised. Each function demanded support from the centralized systems development processing staff that promised the changes when their schedule permitted.

Worse still, the customers weren't satisfied. The marketplace demanded a continual stream of new services. For example, in 1975, there were only 426 mutual funds and $46 billion in assets. By the 1990s, assets were more than a trillion dollars and there were over 4,000 mutual funds. Now there are sector funds for high technology, health care, food companies, and even countries. There are stock index funds to match the Standard & Poor's 500 index as well as a small cap index fund. There are individual state municipal funds. For colleges, there are not only engineering, biology, and medical majors, but now there is also bio-medical engineering.

Every new service had even greater competition and markedly higher performance demands. With each new service came increased quality and reliability demands, along with shorter delivery schedules and increasing price competition. The customer demanded that when he or she took their car in for a repair, the car was actually fixed. The customer expected that the car would be dropped off in the morning and finished by the end of the day. Think about the ten-minute oil change operations. There is no need to have a friend drop you off and pick up the car. Instead, you can just wait a very short time and have the oil change done while you wait.

Managers were fixated on salaries and wages because it represented a large proportion of total service cost. They assumed that improvements in productivity came primarily from lower total salaries and wages. As a result, organizations turned all their emphasis to working harder or moving operations to areas where labor pools were less expensive, such as Las Vegas or South Dakota for credit card processing or to Colorado Springs for telemarketing.

Conventional cost accounting systems aggravated the problems. These systems viewed responsibility reporting as synonymous with control of direct cost. Thus, cost measurement focused on labor efficiencies, purchase-price variances, service overhead allocations based on sales or direct labor, and maximization of profit through control of variable costs. Proper control of direct costs required an army of cost accountants dedicated to tracking costs incurred in the office. Other organizations exercised very little control except through the monthly financial statements. These financial statements used such aggregated numbers that they were not very useful for really understanding what was going on. There have been numerous managers attending AMA seminars on "Accounting for Nonfinancial Managers" who couldn't understand their monthly financial statement. In fact, many of these seminar attendees felt the monthly financial statements were non-value-added. The managers felt they were at the mercy of the accountants to tell them what was going on. This legion of accountants could tell management the salaries and wages and service overhead component of service cost down to the fifth decimal place. Yet that information wasn't helping run the organization more effectively.

Management information was not timely. Monthly reports would indicate that certain services gobbled inordinate amounts of resources, but these reports arrived at the office weeks after the services were complete. The department managers would then try to reconstruct the previous month's events to explain to upper management what led to the disappointing variances.

The late-arriving organization reports, exclusively containing financial and accounting data, were of little help for operational decision making. The data was simply too aggregated and too old. Meanwhile, managers maintained many private, manual records, a practice that was both expensive and time consuming. As a result, the office people relied mainly on hunches and their own numbers to make critical business decisions.

Reports for regulatory agencies, weekly service production reports for corporate headquarters, and so forth, consumed an increasing amount of information systems resources. Manual gathering of more data by department managers was prohibitively expensive.

Inflation encouraged inefficiency and complacency. As long as organizations could pass on inefficiencies to the customers/citizens in the form of higher prices or higher taxes, there was limited incentive to tighten the belt. Complacency was heightened by an attitude that the marketplace had no choice but to accept price or tax increases.

Meanwhile, during the late 1970s, Japan was changing the way it managed its organizations. This signaled the end of the era of complacency and the beginning of price erosion. As a first step, several large Japanese brokerage companies and banks combined their large scale with focused operations to achieve an economic advantage through high-volume, low-variety services. In particular, U.S. banking and stock brokerage companies faced ruthless competition from Japan and the emerging Pacific Rim nations. At one time, U.S. stock represented half the market value of stocks in the world. Now they represent only one-third.

Prices had to be reduced to maintain market share in these industries. This and the slowdown in the U.S. economy resulted in bankruptcy for some companies and a squeeze on profit margins for those that remained.

It appeared to Western managers obsessed with labor costs that the Japanese were dumping their services on the world market. In most cases companies did not understand how the Japanese could provide a higher-quality service at a lower cost.

Other significant events were transforming services. While attention in Western companies was centered on finding cheaper workers and Japanese dumping, some companies were quietly developing a new system that combined the economies of large-scale service production with the advantage of service variety. This marked the emergence of Japanese companies developing software, just like they manufacture cars. Although the Japanese are far behind the United States in software development, it is interesting to note that they are catching up fast. Based on their progress in cars, semiconductors, TVs, and VCRs, it would be unreasonable to assume that they might not be a big software player in the future.

Professor Michael A. Cusumano of Massachusetts Institute of Technology feels that Japanese companies produce a 50 to 70 percent higher output per programmer, and one-third to one-half the errors of their American counterparts. He says that the Japanese improve their efficiency first and then develop better products. For example, in his book, *Japan's Software Factories: A Challenge to U.S. Management*, he says

Toyota was 50 percent more efficient than the United States in 1965, but built terrible cars. Over the next few decades the quality of the cars improved dramatically. Japanese companies often keep detailed records of successful ways to solve problems and reuse about twice as many of their basic programs compared with their U.S. counterparts.

Many service companies will not survive this transition period. Many will see little or no profit. Several quarters in a row had produced nothing but red ink for many service organizations. Dividend was a foreign word to the stockholders. With each advertising campaign failure came a muddled promise that "we won't let it happen again." Missed contracts elicited an optimistic "we'll do it better next time." Graham Phillips, the chairman of WPP Group's Ogilvy and Mather advertising agency, says that "The business has changed forever." Ogilvy eliminated eight hundred of two thousand jobs in the past five years. Advertising executives say that many of the lost jobs will never return. It's felt to be more than just the recession of the 1990s. In the past two or three years, clients have been decreasing compensation. Many clients who paid 15 percent commissions are now paying 11 to 12 percent, or even less. Ad budgets are decreasing in favor of quick-fix promotions such as coupons and sweepstakes. Technology has made this industry more efficient. This increased efficiency makes many jobs obsolete.

Management, however, often responds with across-the-board cost reductions. Senior executives announced that many office locations were "an endangered species." Workers in the offices were asked to take the salary cuts. The workers realized that a service firm closing in a region already experiencing high unemployment would be devastating and agreed to the salary cuts. Overtime was abolished. This was followed by layoffs.

Even the administrative offices were affected. It was announced that there would be a mandatory cut in office supplies and white-collar employees would now be expected to pay for their own coffee.

For a while things looked promising. Companies exploited hidden reserves (bad debt and warranty) and manipulated accounting policies to report steady earnings. Self-satisfied top managers declared, "The program is on track!" Sears Roebuck, for instance, had reorganized many times. Yet sales and profits still limped along. The company was almost ready to reinstate its bonus plan, blindly ignoring its structural weaknesses. Sears Roebuck was like the sailor on the *Titanic* who told a newspaperman: "Mister, God Almighty couldn't sink this ship."

Then companies ran out of fat to trim. The grim reality of aging processes and obsolete office technology, a frustrated, embittered, and underproductive work force, and no vision for the future came crashing in. During the 1970s and 1980s the stockholders in many companies overwhelmingly approved takeovers that management had argued were "unfriendly." This time, the layoffs came at the top.

HARD AUTOMATION HITS THE SERVICE INDUSTRIES

The new managers seemed to know what they were doing. Rather than retrench further, the trend was toward "revitalizing" companies. Technology promised an opportunity to recapture a competitive edge. The initial focus of the capital investment strategy was on replacing obsolete processes. They would begin to use technology as a competitive weapon. The new managers had visions of a highly automated service operation that would change the basis of competition in the marketplace. Think of John Reed of Citicorp, who applied assembly-line techniques used in the auto industry to processing checks. Wicknam Skinner's message that a "... facility can be either a competitive weapon or a corporate millstone" was to become a stark reality.

Managers were caught up in the whirlwind of technology. They began to act. New methods and processes were installed. Then employee empowerment systems were implemented. In addition, electronic data interchange (EDI), bar coding, and scanning were installed. Inspection was by self-inspection.

Companies began to win service contracts, and their pilot work cells became full-scale service production work cells. Before long, several new work cells dotted the office. Companies proudly proclaimed to the business world that they were committed to multimillion-dollar capital investment programs to better serve their customers. Consider how many times Merrill Lynch and American Express have come out with some new feature to enhance their service.

The new technologies created new management challenges. The accelerating rate of technological change multiplied the number of new services. The marketing and research departments were brimming with new services and expanded features. The marketing department agreed that new services were critical to the future. As these services replaced the current line, administrative and service production capabilities had to be upgraded.

One such revolutionary technology confronted by a number of industries, including transportation, warehousing and retail, is electronic data interchange (EDI). For example, a retail department store such as Foley's has a bar coding system on its cash registers. When a customer buys a pair of socks, not only is a sale recorded for financial statement purposes, but a notice is electronically sent to the manufacturer. The manufacturer now knows what was sold and at which store. Based on some agreed-upon criteria, the store would receive replacement socks within a certain number of days. If the department store chose, replenishment could be subject to a purchasing manager's review. This process reduces store inventory while ensuring that the correct product will be in stock when the customer comes to the store to buy it. Some companies have taken this a step further: at the time the manufacturer of the product is notified, the manufacturer's chief suppliers are notified as well. In this way the manufacturer and its suppliers are getting better and quicker information concerning which items to produce.

Management intuitively believed that the complete, accessible data provided by the EDI system could provide a much better insight into the increasingly complex ordering process. However, management did not have a mechanism for evaluating the cost effects of more accurate information, data validation, or poor decisions based on incorrect data. Additionally, much of the information flows that were originally manual had to be integrated to ensure that information was timely and accurate. Much of the information that was processed in batch mode, like mortgage applications, now had to be processed in real time (e.g.; approval of mortgages must be completed within forty-eight hours in some organizations).

EDI means better and faster response time with less inventory to finance. This required an entirely different set of ordering and stocking processes that were capital-intensive (in terms of computers) in contrast to the worker-intensive processes. This technology has meant a new generation of processes and methods. It is estimated that by the mid-1990s, 70 percent of companies will be using EDI. By the year 2000, EDI will probably be a requirement in order to remain competitive.

Other portions of the retail industries face similar technology challenges. With the advent of home computers and software programs like Prodigy and Compuserve, we may find that we change the way we buy items traditionally bought at a shopping mall. In a recent survey mentioned in *The Wall Street Journal* 50 percent of 1,010 people indicated that they would give up a day's pay for an extra day off each week. As time pressures mount, many of the ways we manage ourselves will change.

The short delivery cycles along with the proliferation of services put pressure on service design personnel to bring services to the market much more quickly, to get the design right before it goes into service production, and to streamline the service abandonment process.

In the past, it often took a company one to three years to introduce a new service. Management recognized that the service introduction process had to be streamlined by more tightly coupling activities/business processes to eliminate wasted time. Gone was the old practice of redesigning the service and the service production processes after it had been released to the service production departments. There was simply not enough time to recover the waste generated by an ineffective service introduction process. The first books about the war with Iraq were in the bookstores within weeks after the war ended. The key to success in the publishing business was being out first. There was no time for streamlining the editorial or printing processes. It had to be done quickly and accurately.

By the time 5 percent of the service development budget is spent, more than 80 percent of the final service cost is locked in by decisions made by marketing, senior management, and research departments. For example, a convenience store decides to locate on a certain corner in an upscale area of town. Once the decision to locate there is made, a fair chunk of the operating costs have been determined. The rent, property taxes, property and theft insurance, lighting costs, wage rates, and advertising costs to a certain extent are already pretty much determined. All the manager can control is labor hours and sales.

This points out that the service design and business processes selected were a function of service performance requirements, customer requirements, and process capabilities and limitations of the facility. The service specifications locked in the majority of the supplies cost because the performance characteristics and service cost goals were normally delineated at this time. Consider a home builder who decides to construct a home with certain quality characteristics. The selection of materials is a primary determinant of alternative installation processes. For example, using synthetic sheets in the shower as opposed to individual ceramic tiles affects not only the cost of materials, but also the cost of installation.

The IRS, for instance, has decided to provide a certain level of quality on its telephone information line. For a higher level of service, the IRS would either need to provide more training, hire more technical people, have a referral service for each area of the tax code, improve the management information system, or provide incentives for employees to remain with the IRS. Thus, service design and process decisions were the most important determinants of the organization's cost structure.

Shorter service life cycles resulted in less latitude for management error, since they involved shorter cost recovery periods. Managers realized that they would have to spend considerably more money and time in planning activities/business processes to lower service production costs, reduce time from the design phase to service production, improve quality, increase flexibility, and lower service life-cycle costs.

As a consequence, management made a significant commitment to modernize. In some companies, a document is scanned into the computer upon receipt. For example, think of United States Automobile Association (USAA) insurance application. It is scanned into the computer and stored in a database, where its image can be accessed by underwriting, billing, claims, and actuaries. There is no longer a need to file, retrieve the file, and file again. The imaging system does increase overhead, however, it allows the insurer to handle a variety of business processes more effectively. It results in increased overhead because it requires additional training, programming, systems, and computer operating resources. However, it reduces cycle time and cost while increasing customer satisfaction.

The number of new services increased dramatically because many organizations believed that a full range of services would attract customers. While the number of new services was on the increase, however, very few services were abandoned. Marketing departments cited customer expectations as a reason for keeping outdated services. Thus, the number of services proliferated. The constant flow of new services, when coupled with decreasing service life cycles, meant that management couldn't be sure what the service mix would be in three to four years. For example, think of the computer repair department, which must service the old PCs, XTs, 286 ATs, 386s, 386SLs, the 486 chips, and the pentium and 686s, which were both simultaneously on the drawing board. In addition, think of all the word processing programs, spreadsheets, databases, communication links, utilities, scanning programs, and desktop publishing programs. The implication, therefore, is clear—flexibility at every level of operation is mandatory.

A similar phenomenon was shortening service and equipment life cycles. Much of the new equipment used computer technology, in which significant advances occur at very frequent intervals—generally every three years or less. Technological obsolescence replaces physical obsolescence as the primary determinant for equipment replacement.

Automation and flexibility were often at odds—automation led to a higher percentage of fixed cost because of its capital intensity. The old worker-intensive environment had enabled management to cut costs during a recession by laying off workers, a luxury not available when managing scanners, computers, bar coders, and construction robots.

The changes extend well beyond the office floor. Personal computers (PCs) were introduced to help streamline the workload of the office worker. Typewriters were replaced by word processors and word-processing applications on PCs. PCs running electronic spreadsheets seemed to sprout up everywhere. Secretaries are now being replaced by word-processing programs in some areas, thanks to spell-checking features and grammar programs.

The role of the worker changed dramatically. Prior to the computer, knowledge resided with humans. The objective of technology was to increase worker productivity. With automation and computer networks, the skills and composition of the office worker began to change. Organizations that introduced advanced technologies found that much of the knowledge was transferred from the operator to the programmer, who created the machine instructions. The person running a claims operation for an insurance company or performing credit approvals must now be skilled in computer operations rather than claims or credit. The technology controls the pace of processing of claims and credit approvals; the worker assists and monitors. The workers in many offices tended increasingly to become highly skilled computer technicians.

A similar change is occurring in the worker-management relationship. To compete, workers and mangers are forced to recognize that industry can no longer be an arena of class warfare if companies are to match their overseas rivals.

By the late 1980s, most of the technology acquired during the previous years was operational. The impact of automation on the worker was significant. Automation, either directly or indirectly, reduced direct worker time through the substitution of improved processes or procedures. It was not uncommon for workers involved directly in providing a service to account for a much smaller percentage of total cost. However, the reduction in service workers was not problem-free. Service overhead costs rose dramatically and even exceeded direct salaries and wages in some industries. As one example, consider the original concrete pumps in the United States. In cold weather, the concrete would harden in the pump lines and had to be manually chiseled out. Eventually, the pumps came equipped with bigger motors and saved thousands of dollars in direct labor. The problem was that now, expenses such as concrete pump insurance and property taxes did not go away in the winter nor did they go away when the economy was weak. Prior to concrete pumps, direct labor could be laid off during these slower periods.

The survivors were leaner and fitter, well placed to expand when the economy rebounded. Service output climbed, yet the services were produced by fewer workers. The advertising, architecture, and tax preparation industries are striking examples of just how much service businesses have been transformed. These industries have become automated with computers, computer-aided design, and tax software programs. Also, in many industries, including government, cooperation replaced conflict in the field, and productivity soared.

However, in many cases automation did not provide a very potent strategic weapon because organizations often automated the wrong things or cost reductions simply matched similar improvements by competitors. The service process itself was inefficient and outmoded, and the competitive position was not improved merely by automation. Managers discovered that they did not possess a monopoly on advanced technologies. Now, when a customer calls to make a hotel reservation, not only the Hyatt, but a number of hotel chains, can bring up the name, address, and credit card information. A pizza chain can access a name and address from a phone number. Those who implemented strategically important technologies gained a competitive advantage through reduced cost, improved quality, faster **throughput time**, and better response to customers. There were still slippages. Many management and support personnel spent the greater part of the working day attending meetings, discussing status, or chasing paper throughout the enterprise. Even the managers were spending more time fixing problems than actually planning new and better ways to serve the customers. As Tom Monaghan, Chairman of Domino's Pizza, has said, "the goal is to exceed customer expectations and focus beyond customer satisfaction by focusing on customer delight."

As a result, some of the market is lost to cheaper, better-quality foreign competition (e.g., Russian scientists and Hungarian programmers). In some industries, competition is significant for services with large volumes, such as advertising, hotels, corporate laundry, banking, and stock brokerage. Through a joint **strategic planning** effort involving marketing, accounting, research, administration, operations, and sales, many organizations abandoned the high-volume service market and concentrated on the customized service market niches. For example, Concord Bank in Dallas services only individuals with high net worth. It pampers them with special services and parking. It can only afford to do this because of the customers' high net worths. Another bank, one of two in the country, is a cashless bank. It makes loans and accepts loan payments in the form of checks. Even nonprofits are facing greater competition. Think of all the specialty charities that solicit donations. It is no longer just the March of Dimes, Easter Seals, and Muscular Dystrophy, but a myriad of charities that serve children with specific diseases, foreign countries, the elderly, retired nuns, and so on.

Through hard work these organizations managed to hold onto an area of the market, but with small profit margins, or by barely breaking even in the case of nonprofits. Organizations became alarmed by high administrative overhead rates. There was no argument that these organizations' indirect costs were a formidable—and expanding—component of the overall cost structure. Ironically, the same modernization efforts that resulted in large hourly worker cost reductions had contributed to indirect cost increases. The capital cost of all that new equipment hit the cost ledgers as depreciation expense. Programming costs increased, as did the technical support and maintenance costs for the new and complex personal computer networks.

However, the increasing overhead was not due exclusively to automation. The number of personnel classified as managers ballooned. And top management announced: "We're too top heavy." The reason for the expansion in white-collar jobs was nebulous. External paperwork increased, internal paperwork increased, and more people were brought in to keep up with the ever-expanding workload. In fact, some of the hourly employees whose jobs were eliminated by automation never really left the organization at all. They just transferred into the ranks of the myriad of indirect employees who supported marketing, operations, and administration.

With automation came a significant amount of debt—advanced technologies were not cheap. For example, scanning systems that we described earlier can easily run into the millions. Spending $10 to $25 million for large scanning systems in an insurance company is not uncommon. As long as the technologies contributed a positive cash flow, the resulting savings would offset the debt expense. However, inappropriate investments are catastrophic and simply mortgage the future. Not only must future services be profitable, but they must also support the cost of past investment blunders. Think of universal life insurance and how it was to transform the insurance industry in the 1980s. Although it is still around today, it isn't the highly successful insurance service it was originally conceived to be.

Many organizations relied on a service costing system that distributed indirect costs to services based on sales, direct costs, or direct salary hours/costs. For example, Schlumberger, an oil service firm, spreads its administrative overhead to the divisions based on each division's percentage of total company sales. Other firms, for example companies in the defense industry—like software organizations—apply overhead on either direct labor dollars and/or total cost input. Management knew that as overhead increased dramatically, the direct labor or direct cost allocations distorted service cost. In the early 1980s, some service costing systems were redesigned to calculate service line costs where previously no allocations of indirect costs had been made.

As quarter after quarter of financial results were reported, the promises of improved performance were not realized. Management anxiously waited for the company profits to improve dramatically, as promised by the advocates of technology. The new computer systems, scanners, and EDI glistened, and the productivity gap was narrowed dramatically. Yet profits remained marginal.

In hindsight, the reason is woefully apparent—a frightening inability of top management to recognize the emerging changes. The individual automation projects employed advanced technologies to increase the productivity of the individual processes without attacking the real "cancer"— waste. Services were in a period of transition, and solutions such as personal computers and individual automation projects were simply a continuation of traditional practices.

Automation was an illusory prelude to a new service environment, an era that would not be understood until a few years later. The continued deterioration of service organizations was a result of outdated philosophies. Management needed to look no further than its competition for the answer. The productivity improvements were necessary merely to remain in business. They came largely from workers and managers adjusting to the economic realities and reversing decades of inefficiencies.

What Western management failed to recognize was that the most effective way to increase productivity is to eliminate problems rather than treat symptoms. Rather than minimizing service diversity and long lead times, organizations spent millions of dollars and countless management hours implementing scheduling programs and automation, rather than treating the fundamental problems.

The tidal wave that had begun in Japan began to be felt in the West. Study teams made pilgrimages to Japan and returned from the promised land with panaceas such as quality circles, kanban, and total quality management (TQM). If only Western companies could swallow this medicine, they could compete on the world market. Progressive companies that implemented these concepts reported glowing results (e.g., Florida Power & Light, first U.S. winner of the coveted Japanese Deming award).

Services need to embody simplification and elimination of waste through the service production cycle by cutting cycle time and eliminating mistakes. For example, Federal Express has updated its Airbill Form; the old form required double posting of information and was more subject to error. Federal Express attacked this cause of errors and reduced workload.

The new era is characterized by organizations working in cells to produce the entire service. It is supported by vendor management and logistics improvements to minimize queue and move time and work in progress, and increase accuracy. For example, certain grocery chains and department stores require deliveries to be made on a certain day of the week and at a certain time of day, or at least within a certain time span. Convenience stores, such as 7-Eleven, are built so that there is very little inventory in the back rooms. This avoids inventory holding costs. It also avoids the cost and damage from inventory being handled twice—once from the truck to the back room and a second time in stocking the shelves. Wal-mart warehouses have supplier shipments unloaded not into their warehouse, but onto trucks departing for their stores. This "cross-docking" eliminates the double handling of unloading into a warehouse and then loading from the warehouse. These just in time (JIT) examples involve substantial reductions in handling, holding costs, and streamlining.

Grocery, convenience, department, and discount stores that installed JIT found that the new system made supplier relations extremely important. Instead of the traditional adversarial relationship between supplier and customer, companies developed hand-in-hand working relationships with their suppliers. In fact the chairman of Home Depot spends time with his major suppliers and their various divisions letting them know how important they are to the success of Home Depot.

Quality control problems, particularly between suppliers and users, became important. Customers demanded high quality, and in some cases were even willing to pay for it. Suppliers found that high quality in many cases cost less to produce, since it reduced clerical, sales, and service operation errors, which reduced costs.

Inventory and space needs were reduced, and, most importantly, delivery time was dramatically compressed. The process was faster and the cash flow quicker. As lead time and flow time were reduced, forecasting became more accurate. Lead times were reduced to several days for many items, as is the case of Levi Strauss, enabling the buyers and managers to forecast only for tomorrow rather than for the next several weeks. Over time a very effective synchronous-flow system emerged.

Having the correct inventory at the correct time improved due to the new point-of-sale (POS) equipment, the use of quality circles, statistical process control (SPC), and a new commitment to quality. Just as important was the time spent socializing after work. Social prejudices and suspicions began to fade after these more informal get-togethers. The result was expanded involvement of the suppliers' workers, who met with their customers more regularly to discover and correct problems rather than burying them. Organizations moved away from confrontation toward dialogue.

As organizations embraced the new philosophies, the rules of competition changed to include short service delivery cycles, flexibility, quality, and low cost. In many industries the changes did not increase profitability, but were a matter of survival. For example, real estate management organizations either adopted the new philosophies or went out of business.

Organizations have now begun to reconsider their roles in the international market. New technologies of worldwide communications and transportation have redrawn the economic playing field. For example, European industries no longer compete against Japanese or American industries. Rather, a broadcasting company with headquarters in Italy, production facilities throughout Europe, and a marketing force spread throughout the world competes with other similarly global organizations, such as NBC, CBS, ABC, and CNN.

With the rise of the global corporations, managers, employees, and shareholders span the world. An organization's success creates a big billboard that says, "This market exists and here is how to exploit it." The old protectionist strategy of fending off global competition gives way to a strategy of using worldwide operations to provide a buffer against currency valuation changes and to expand markets. A foreign presence increases sales and gives organizations access to new technology and marketing ideas. The experience helps them fend off competition at home from foreign rivals that have jumped into the local markets. And when the economy slows, an organization can reduce the risk of an economic downturn by looking to faster-growing overseas markets. Consider the telecommunications, legal, home building, investment banking and accounting firms who have opened offices in former Eastern Bloc countries such as Hungary and Poland. Even universities are getting into the picture as they teach Western capitalism and accounting to managers and professors in Poland and Russia.

Globalization has caused as many dramatic changes in the role of the worker as has technology. In the 1980s the real earnings of the unskilled workers declined while the real wages of the "knowledge worker" increased. "Knowledge workers" are those who deal with information as the means of accomplishing their jobs as contrasted with those workers whose jobs involve the use of physical force.

More and more, the competitiveness of a worker depends not only on the individual organization's economic health, but on the worker's function within the global economy. Simply stated, a global economy will not pay for non-value-added activities. Workers who perform unnecessary and wasteful activities will not fit into the global economy because once competition has eliminated these activities, the remaining organizations must trim them or face the loss of market share. This change has given rise to a growing number of impoverished workers and a widening gap between the rich and the poor.

State and local governments will face the same challenges. They can no longer pass along increased costs to the populace with higher taxes. They also must become more efficient or lose voters, who will vote with their feet by moving to another community. Just look at New York, city and state, and Chicago. As the tax rates increase, more and more companies are moving either to the suburbs or out of state.

Another impact of globalization is that workers who perform routine services involving tasks that are repeated over and over must settle for low wages in order to hold onto their jobs. Although these types of jobs are often associated with entry-level workers such as receptionists, bank tellers, car valets, and fast food employees, they are common among many support workers who spend their days processing data, often putting information into computers or taking it out within large centralized facilities. They are overseen by supervisors who, in turn, are monitored by more supervisors. With relative ease, organizations can relocate their facilities to take advantage of lower wages in other parts of the country or the world (e.g., Ireland). The global economy places limits on how much it will pay for these activities. Through satellite communications, even routine clerical work can be undertaken far from the central offices.

Traditional cost accounting systems became increasingly irrelevant as radical changes swept most organizations. Their continued use hindered operational excellence by encouraging inappropriate business decisions. Consider, for instance, that labor efficiency measurements motivate a supervisor to keep employees busy; or that purchase price variance motivates the purchasing agent to buy in large volume to achieve quantity discounts even though there is a significant cost to holding inventory; or that the emphasis on direct labor encourages managers to try to achieve productivity improvements primarily by using machines more efficiently while overhead costs soar.

In the late 1980s organizations, mainly manufacturing companies, heard about a new method of costing called activity accounting. The aim of the new system was complete traceability of all factors that affect cost and performance. Armed with this information, an organization could more effectively make changes. Management wanted information faster so it could respond more quickly. The difference between the product cost reported under the traditional and activity management systems was dramatic. The activity management system revealed that a high percentage of the company's products generated losses in the long run. In general, many products identified as profitable by the traditional product costing system were found to be unprofitable by the activity management system. In many cases an organization's disappointing performance was a direct consequence of distorted cost information that contributed to management decisions to fill its line with unprofitable products.

The product cost was higher than reported for some products and lower for others. The ramifications of such miscosting were tremendous because it resulted in cross-subsidization of products. Products that were overcosted attracted competition that undercut the price. Products that were undercosted faced negligible competition. As a result, market share simultaneously increased for the undercosted products and decreased for the overcosted products. Profit therefore decreased at a greater percentage since overcosted products were subsidizing undercosted ones.

Organizations were led to believe incorrectly that they possessed a strategic advantage in the niche markets and were at a competitive disadvantage in markets with repetitive services. They then began to restructure their operations and facilities based on the miscosting phenomenon. Thus, it became a self-fulfilling prophecy.

A VISION OF THE FUTURE

It is practically impossible to predict exactly what the world will be like in ten years and how it will function. One thing is sure, however; it will be radically different from the one that currently prevails. The transition from the business of today to that of the future will continue to be characterized by major discontinuities.

These discontinuities are important to managers for two fundamental reasons: (1) Operating practices to cope with changes in the market and the competitive environment will be different and surprising, and (2) there is no assurance that service organizations that have been successful in the past will continue to prosper during and after this transition. Look at Pan Am Airlines, the first national airline—now it is out of business.

Taken together, these developments constitute a wave of change that challenges the existing policy of most organizations. To successfully confront the future, organizations must reconsider the very foundations of their existing enterprise. Organizations have, however, undergone major transitions in the past, and some of history's lessons remain relevant today. Thus organizations look to the future not so much to predict it as to systematically remind themselves how different it will be from the recent past.

The potential economic impact of emerging producers, such as Malaysia, India, China, and Brazil, on today's leading producers will transform the economic landscape. The dismantling of internal common market barriers will add to the competitiveness in Europe. The introduction of improved services such as telecommunications, construction, and oil drilling to the republics of the former Soviet Union and Eastern Bloc countries together with the opening of these markets to the West will again rearrange established patterns.

Technological advancement will undoubtedly continue at an accelerating pace. It is imperative, therefore, for management to develop a vision of the future and to boldly make the changes necessary to execute the plan. A key to success is the capability of an organization to create a vision of the future and manage the achievement of the vision. Too often top managers do not take decisive action until it is too late because they believe that to identify problems would largely be to identify their own failings. As a result, caution becomes paralyzing.

Over the next years we will see the development of:

- Worldwide cellular phones
- Neural/optical computers
- Holography
- Biotechnology
- Ability to medically diagnose oneself at home using artificial intelligence
- Computer/human interfunctional enterprises
- Artificial organs that can replace most human organs
- Oil derivatives that can be grown, instead of extracted from oil found in the earth.

These technologies will reverberate throughout our global societies and profoundly affect the way services are currently conceived, designed, and produced. For example, a driver's license renewal is now sent in with a check. It would be more efficient to let the county know each driver's computer number. The driver can then just look at their electronic mail, see that the license renewal is due, and authorize a wire transfer to the county. The county receives the wire transfer, and without human intervention it sends the sticker. Or better yet, it codes the license plates, indicating that the license fee is already paid. This code on the plates can be read electronically by the police force.

The profound impacts will come when these technologies "rub up" against one another, when a breakthrough in one area will ripple through to another, adding capability. We now live in a much less linear world. So left-brain, linear-type people better start rubbing their right brain to activate it.

These changes will force organizations in advanced nations to compete using three resources: capital, technology, and knowledge. Knowledge is found in large pools of educated professionals exposed to innovative, world-class methods, tools, and systems. The central offices of the global business will be filled with knowledge workers who manipulate information and then export their knowledge around the world. A company won't export its services; instead, it will produce in offices all over the globe. Currently, Citicorp processes credit cards in Nevada, so why not China?

Headquarters will export strategic planning and related management services. Elimination of waste will be a hallmark of the successful service organization. Work in process (remember those partially processed insurance policies/mortgages or uncompleted construction sites or partially completed advertising campaigns) will not be tolerated. Organizations will be expected to detect problems before they arise. The Xerox Corporation now has a copy machine that continuously monitors itself. If it diagnoses a problem developing, the machine dials a Xerox repair office to notify it of the problem and the necessary part needed. In this way, a service technician can arrive before the machine actually breaks down and repair it so customer downtime would be minimal. For frequent flyers who are delayed by mechanical problems, just think what that would mean.

Activities originating from error corrections will be scrutinized. Unnecessary paperwork will be purged, or paperwork will be eliminated altogether. There is now an office in Dallas that has eliminated all paper. File cabinet sales people and secretaries who do just filing need not apply.

The challenge is to perform all activities correctly the first time. This requires getting everyone involved directly in fixing the cause of the problem through programs such as activity analysis, customer surveys, nonvalue analysis, elimination of cost drivers, cross-functional teams and total quality management.

The future will be characterized by a movement toward flexibility and responsiveness. The 1990s will showcase flexible work centers that allow organizations to increase responsiveness to customer demands and thereby reap the advantages of economies of scope (such as variety). As it becomes feasible to reduce the number of different grades or classes of people needed to handle a situation to one grade or class, scheduling of people with different skills practically disappears, customer wait time is dramatically reduced, and hourly office planning becomes possible. One insurance company used to have different groups of people handle different type of claims. Today, whomever answers the phone can handle most claims. This reduces the need for hiring, supervising, and scheduling various people with different skills.

Flexible systems, when coupled with the concept of JIT, eliminates inventory buffer. Reduced inventory translates to a decline in space requirements. The total picture is one of leanness. There will be one database for several services/processes/departments. There will be no wasting of resources in non-value-added activities like filing. This will yield competitive advantages through both enhanced responsiveness and reduced costs.

The market will demand customized services with short introduction cycles (e.g., a sector fund for each new hot sector). The streamlining of processes is crucial to getting services to the market in a timely fashion. Also, taxpayers want more and better services at lesser costs. So waste has to be eliminated. Donors want their money going to the causes, not to salaries and offices. So nonprofit health and welfare organizations also must streamline operations and become more efficient.

A key element of the new service environment is time compression. The service production process must get out of the way of providing the service in a dynamic market. If one state government is inefficient at providing a service, it may have to hire a more effective state or private industry to provide that service.

Time compression, JIT, and total quality management are central elements in the focused office. All functions in the organization from service development to service production to logistics support must be restructured to reduce time. The benefits of a flexible system, for example, would be offset if the firm does reduce the time it takes to process service orders. Often the key to time compression is as basic as simplifying the approval process. Think of the Federal Express employee who charged a helicopter on his credit card in order to make sure the mail would get through in a snow storm. In most organizations, he would have had to have been a senior vice president to authorize such a charge. Yet the mail does get through and Federal Express does prosper. There is one office in Plano, Texas that for six months did not make an error processing airbills. It processed over 500,000 airbills error free.

The shift in costs from labor to technology is complete in a health care environment, as many indirect labor functions such as order entry and laboratory tests are automated. In fact, some doctors are using artificial intelligence for patient diagnosis. Thus, they give the patient the human touch and still have access to the experiences of many medical specialists. The computer is providing a link among seemingly diverse functions, including patient registration, progress monitoring, patient diagnosis, and reimbursement by third parties. First there were Diagnostic Related Groups (DRGs), in which hospitals were only reimbursed up to a certain amount, regardless of what they spent to provide a certain service. Then there were medical reimbursement guidelines for ambulatory (outpatient) services as hospitals performed more outpatient work and shifted the overheads to this area. Starting in 1992, there were guidelines for medicare reimbursement for physicians. Blue Cross/Blue Shield has adopted these reimbursement guidelines in some states. And some third-party insurers have likewise adopted the guidelines, with the attitude that, if it's good enough for medicare and the "Blues," it's good enough for us. This will put increasing pressures on hospitals to provide quality health care at a reasonable cost. It will also mean that many physician's incomes will probably decrease. In Canada and some European countries, a physician earns only 25 to 50 percent what they earn in the United States.

With cross-functional teams, previously separate groups will work in unison to achieve corporate goals. For example, service introduction cycles are decreased through the use of a common database that can share information across departments, customers, and services. When a customer applies for a mortgage, the bank will input all the information into the computer. So if at a later date that same customer needs a car, college, or a home improvement loan, he or she will only need to update his file, probably from his home computer. Thus, islands of information will be in one integrated system that seeks to optimize the performance of an entire enterprise.

Accelerating technological innovation will increasingly rely on information and communication technologies. The future systems will be software dependent. The task of processing and controlling information in the office of the future will require reconceptualization of the role of data processing and the use of new techniques such as object-oriented information systems, which allow the application programming to be shifted to the users of the data.

Bill Gates, chairman of Microsoft, has a dream that everyone will have a personal computer that is user friendly. Computers are getting more user friendly, but still have a way to go. Tutorials and self-help programs, pens and mouse systems, and self-diagnosis programs will continue to improve until grade schoolers will be using word processing and spreadsheets. There may no longer be a need to learn addition and subtraction. It may become more important to know how to use a spreadsheet or a ring computer.

Information and communications requirements and capabilities will more than double in the coming years. The potential will exist by the opening of the twenty-first century to have the enterprise totally integrated from the supplier to the customer. The impact on services will be to transfer routine knowledge from humans to computer systems. Look at some European hotels that now have a vending-machine approach to checking into your room. This may not give you the warm and friendly feeling of a Hilton, Hyatt, Intercontinental, Marriott, or Sheraton, but if the room is at a lower price, it will appeal to some people.

As organizations' operations facilities evolve into offices of the future, common shared data are critical. The data used by different organizations often overlap by 80 to 90 percent. Efficiency dictates that no data should ever be entered more than once and all data should be available across all applications. Some data should be accessible to the suppliers and customers.

Although a centralized database is technologically possible, the office of the future will probably maintain a distributed database because of the capabilities of minicomputer and microprocessor technology. This technology, along with local area networking, permits efficient transfer of files between databases, and provides greater flexibility and responsiveness at the machine and process level, where the transformation process occurs.

It is important that future applications be easy to modify and reconfigure. Information systems should anticipate change. Installing an application package should not require undesired changes to the activity. At the other extreme, an application package should not automate chaos. Configurable software requires the process for which the computer system is written be evaluated to determine the best way to operate before the system is developed. It also requires the application to be flexible, in order to achieve a form and fit that can be enhanced easily over time by operational personnel.

Future capabilities will include interconnected enterprise management systems with high capacity, secure data transport, intelligent terminals and workstations, and database transfer throughout the enterprise. Organizations will integrate these features and add artificial intelligence, knowledge-based systems, object-oriented systems, and real-time update.

The services of the knowledge worker will be in high demand around the world. Knowledge workers are easy to recognize. Their work environment tends to be quiet and tastefully decorated, often within tall steel-and-glass buildings. When they are not analyzing, designing, or developing strategies, they are in meetings or on the telephone giving advice or making deals.

Routine service workers can become knowledge workers by using advanced technologies and being given the responsibility to alter how their activity is performed, to increase productivity. Service production workers who have broader responsibilities and more control over how the process is organized cease to be routine workers—becoming knowledge workers at a level very close to the process.

COST MANAGEMENT IMPLICATIONS

The late 1980s represented a watershed period for cost accounting. The recent emergence of cost management is a direct result of organizations trying to manage 1990s enterprises with 1920s accounting systems. Organizations have become increasingly aware of the shortcomings of these obsolete accounting systems. Articles on the subject have appeared in virtually every business magazine.

The dramatic changes in service organizations suggest a time of transition for cost accounting—a prelude to new cost management approaches. Accounting must become more than simply recording, summarizing, and reporting the financial aspects of operations. The cost management domain must maximize enterprise rather than functional performance. Through activity management the basic functional activities and their interrelationships are readily perceived to ensure that they accomplish the fundamental goals of the enterprise.

What is quite unusual about this moment is not its coming, but its arrival in so many parts of the organization at the same time—operations, management, administration, and accounting. Many organizations, at different levels of technology deployment and in different industries, are now simultaneously seeking to revise old concepts and question conventional practices.

These organizations are demanding that the new cost management systems determine a cost that mirrors operations, identifies waste, isolates cost drivers, and provides visibility of cost reduction/performance improvement opportunities. The profitability of a service over its life cycle (e.g., a special promotion at a hotel, restaurant, or airline) becomes an important focus, characterized by full-stream tracking of costs as incurred, from inception to retirement.

Another major type of change is the shift in emphasis from a fixed/variable expense distinction in contribution analysis to cost traceability. Direct labor will continue to decrease as a component of service cost, approaching a fixed cost nature in some cases. Hence there may be a minimum of variable costs. In the new environment, the traceability of cost becomes more critical than the traditional distinction between variable and fixed. The new decision support systems will be built on traceability. Improved traceability will result in fewer arbitrary allocations and erode the distinction between direct and indirect costs.

Today it is more important to think about used and unused capacity. By tracing **unused capacity costs**, management can decide whether to eliminate them, combine operations, or cross-train associates to balance workload.

Nonfinancial performance measures will achieve a level of importance equal to financial measures. Strategies such as time compression in service delivery systems require an ongoing monitoring of time. Process balance will be more important than direct labor efficiency. New performance measures will be developed at the activity/business process level. Measures of capacity costs become critical. Bottlenecks in the service delivery system, whether in service operations (emptying a dumpster or repossessing a car) or customer service, must be identified and evaluated as cost drivers. Organizations must be able to measure improvements in the velocity of the service process (time to clean a room, process an application, serve a meal, turn around a plane), service development, distribution, and customer service.

Life-cycle management becomes important. Cost accounting systems have focused primarily on the cost of service operations, without accumulating costs over the entire service design, service operations, marketing, and support cycle of a service. Think of an insurance company selling hurricane insurance and having few or no losses for several years. That may be too short a life cycle to determine whether the hurricane insurance business is a profitable business. Or consider a car dealer looking at the car business in 1990/91. Those obviously were not good years for the car business, but the cycle was too short to review the business.

Activities related to the development of services and the service production process represent a sizeable investment of capital. The benefits accrue over many years and, under conventional accounting, are not directly identified with the service being developed. They are treated instead as a period expense, buried in service overhead, and allocated to all services (typically direct labor, total direct costs, or sales). Many organizations use life cycle models for planning and budgeting new services as part of their discounted cash flow analysis, but they fail to integrate these models into existing cost accounting systems. It is important to provide feedback on planning effectiveness and the impact of service design decisions on operational and support costs. For example, if a service is designed to change auto oil and filters within ten minutes or deliver pizza within thirty minutes, those time constraints put a terrible burden on operations and support. The pizza makers must always have fresh dough and ingredients ready to go or partially baked. There must always be sufficient drivers so that if eighteen people at different ends of town call at the same time, the marketing program can be fulfilled by delivering to all of them within thirty minutes. If an amusement park, such as Disney World, is open from 7:30 A.M. to midnight, there is a tremendous burden to have all the rides maintained and inspected for safety every day.

Period reporting hinders management decisions. Shorter service life cycles result in less latitude for management error, since the cost recovery periods are short. Today's cost accounting systems are based on period reporting and do not provide life-cycle reporting. This hinders management's understanding of service line profitability and the potential cost impact of long-term decisions such as speculative commercial office construction loans in the Northeast, California, or Texas. If those loans officers were forced to consider the impact of their loans through a probable downturn in the economy, they might have made different decisions. Would they have been cooperative with the investment bankers who made junk bond loans to West Point Pepperell or The Southland Corporation that ended in default?

Life-cycle costing and reporting provide management with a better picture of service profitability and help managers gauge the effectiveness of their planning activities.

Finally, cost management will be closely intertwined with corporate culture. The introduction of cost management has run into severe political sensitivities. While managers concede that the information in an activity cost management system is superior to that of existing techniques, they come up with many reasons for inertia. They ask questions such as: "What other organizations have implemented the system?" or "What software is available?" The cost of mismanagement is not obvious! Otherwise, managers would react much quicker.

SUMMARY

The decline of traditional services and accounting marks a historic departure. It also provides significant opportunities for creativity and innovation in investment and corporate management.

The progressive use of advanced technology and information systems made the traditional cost system obsolete by creating a computer- and service overhead-intensive environment. However, the majority of service cost accounting systems are still driven by total direct costs, direct labor, or sales volume, and provide minimal guidance for controlling service overhead.

It was interesting that even in the movie-making industry, the executives became aware of these principles. They said that they would not invest in another large-scale production like Dick Tracy (neither Warren Beatty nor Madonna comes cheap) because of the drain on financial, technical, and creative resources as well as an inordinate amount of top-management time.

This change has raised challenges to the relevance and appropriateness of almost all the systems and procedures in place at businesses, and nonprofit and government organizations, as well as to the concepts that managers have learned during their university training.

Although recognizing the problem is a good beginning, the pressing need now is for solutions. Organizations are struggling with the question of how to align their cost management system with the operating environment while instilling a philosophy of continual improvement. The challenge is to perform all activities correctly the first time. New activity cost management systems are being proposed as a solution to this problem.

3

ACTIVITIES, ACTIVITY MANAGEMENT, AND COST MANAGEMENT

The purpose of this chapter is to:

- Define and contrast activities, activity management, business processes, and cost management
- Describe a transaction process model for defining activities
- Describe the key characteristics that provide a basis for evaluating the effectiveness of activities
- Provide an overview of the key components of an activity management system

This book is about activities; more specifically about managing activities to gain and sustain a competitive advantage. An **activity** is a combination of people, technology costs, supplies, travel, occupancy costs, methods, and environment that produce a given service. It describes **what** an enterprise does: the way time is spent and the outputs of the process. Examples of activities include:

- Answering an inquiry
- Issuing a paycheck
- Providing a service such as moving products by air, rail, or truck
- Billing the customer

Ultimately, an enterprise can manage only what it does—its activities. The starting point for managing activities is to understand the resources currently assigned to today's activities (activity cost), the volume of output (activity measure), and how well the activity/business process is performed (performance measures). This information is derived from the activity management system.

Activity management is a process of accumulating and tracing cost and performance data to an organization's activities/business process and providing feedback of actual results against the planned cost to initiate corrective action where required. It's a tool for understanding cost. An activity management system assigns costs as they actually exist at a point in time, not as they should or could be.

Cost management—the responsibility of everyone—uses activity cost and performance information to guide formulation of strategic plans and operational decisions and identify improvement opportunities. An activity cost management system uses activity cost and performance information to determine a service cost that mirrors the enterprise and to challenge what costs should be.

ACTIVITY HIERARCHY

Activities form the foundation of activity cost management systems. An activity describes the way an enterprise employs its time and resources to achieve organizational objectives. Activities are processes that consume substantial resources to produce an output. The principal function of an activity is to convert resources (supplies, labor, and technology) into outputs (services). For instance, the primary activities of a credit department in a computer leasing company are obtaining credit information, reviewing information for completion, deciding on credit, setting credit limits, monitoring payment history, performing periodic analysis, and setting general credit-limit guidelines.

A **function** is an aggregation of activities that are related by a common purpose, such as the following: identifying new vendors, certifying vendors, expediting orders, and issuing purchase orders for the purchasing function. Other functions are marketing, operations, security, quality control, accounting, legal services, human resources, customer service, and logistics. Although most organizations are organized functionally, the total spectrum of activities related to the function is much broader than the organizational unit that has primary responsibility for the function. For example, the responsibility for certain quality activities is assigned to the quality department. Yet many other quality activities, such as quality planning for service design, in-process inspection as done by managers on audits, rework of a customer's tax return, and customer service, occur in other departments. Many managers fail to grasp the interdependency of activities across departments.

A **business process** is a network of related and interdependent activities linked by the outputs they exchange. The activities are related because a specific event initiates the first activity in the business process, which in turn triggers subsequent activities. An output or information flow occurs where two activities interact. The exchange of an output or information flow draws a boundary between different activities within a process and links them in a strong cause-and-effect relationship. Activities are defined in terms of the information elements necessary to perform them and to create their output. For example, the business process of hiring a new employee might involve an operations department completing a new employee requisition; a human resources person reviewing the requisition, placing an ad, and interviewing candidates; the operations department interviewing finalists; the medical team performing a physical; and security issuing a security card.

A **task** is the combination of work elements, or operations, that make up an activity—in other words, a task is the way the activity is performed. Several different organizations might accomplish the same activities using significantly different tasks. An **operation** is the smallest unit of work used for planning or control purposes.

Activities, rather than functions or tasks, were chosen because they are at the appropriate level of detail to support an ongoing cost management system. Reporting at the function level is too global to trace costs accurately, whereas reporting at the task or operations level is too insignificant—that is, localized—for control and too costly. For example, to report the task of data entry of time cards into a payroll system separately from the processing of payroll checks would provide minimal value on an ongoing basis. For this reason, activities are used to document what an organization does.

The hierarchical relationship of functions, business processes, activities, tasks, and operations is outlined in the following list:

Function: Marketing and sales

Business process: Sell service

Activity: Present a proposal

Task: Gather proposal data

Operation: Type proposal

A function is what gets done, whereas an activity is what the enterprise does to accomplish the function. For example, a salesperson's presenting a proposal, is an activity within the sales and marketing function. The activity of presenting a proposal is distinct from the activity of pricing the service, yet both are part of the sales and marketing function, and in some cases may be done by the same person. A salesperson might perform a myriad of activities including presenting a proposal, pricing a service, and handling customer complaints.

The business process of selling a service might consist of activities such as traveling to the customer, presenting a proposal, and following up. An example of a task for the activity "present a proposal" is to gather proposal data. An operation for the task "gather proposal data" might be to review customer sales history.

ACTIVITY OVERVIEW

Activities are defined in the broadest sense to include both direct service production (those processes that transform supplies and human effort into a finished service, like pick up waste) and the myriad of actions that support the direct process (e.g., responding to customer inquiries). Activities transcend all steps within the chain of value—service design, service operations, distribution, marketing, and after-sales support.

Accounting based on activities therefore provides equal visibility for support and service operation costs. All traditional managerial accounting textbooks begin by defining product/service cost as the sum of direct labor, direct supplies, and overhead. Activity management requires no such arbitrary distinctions between direct and indirect costs. The service process is described in terms of service-related activities including those that do not physically create the service. Service operation activities can be thought of as execution of the process plan in accordance with the service operation schedule. Supplies are purchased and labor and equipment is assigned to produce the service whether it is architectural, insurance, banking, legal, electrical, water, retail, phone, transportation, fundraising, medical, zoning, real estate tax appraisal, defense police, census, educational, prison, or judicial.

Activities that occur in support departments and those that occur in the direct production of the service are highlighted equally because the major activities of all organizational units are identified. A primary criterion of activity management is the ability to trace an activity to a service, business process, channel of distribution, project, or other reporting objective for which management needs cost information.

Activities are performed by people or by automated processes. Too often managers focus on controlling people-related costs, to the detriment of automated activities. In defining activities, think of time as a series of activities or tasks to be completed. Time is an attribute of both people-related activities and automated activities.

Activity definition is independent of the specific organization. Activities represent what is done in an enterprise. Every enterprise must perform many of the same basic activities to function. Depending on the size of the organization, Alexander City, Alabama or the state of California, activities may be performed by specialized workers or by more general workers who perform multiple activities. However, the activities must be performed in small, as well as in large, organizations. What varies is the degree of specialization and responsibility for decisions.

Activity Elements

It is useful to characterize an activity by reducing it to its simplest form— the processing of a transaction. An activity (a process) is described in terms of its internal/external suppliers of input, resources, tasks, inputs, outputs, output measures, internal/external customers for the activity, and procedures, as illustrated in the following Figure:

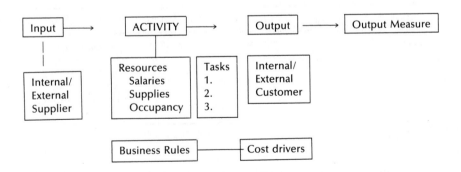

An input is the consequence or result of an action external to the activity. Inputs (events) trigger the execution of an activity. The two primary types of inputs (events) are clock inputs and external inputs. A clock input (e.g., quarterly close) occurs regularly. An external input occurs outside the activity.

Transactions are used as surrogates for inputs. A **transaction** is a physical (including electronic) document associated with the transmittal of information. The document serves as evidence of the transaction. The receipt of a customer order, for example, is an input that would trigger an order entry activity. The output of the activity would be a computerized customer order transaction. Other examples of inputs include:

- Purchase order receipt
- Labor charging record
- Supplies receipt
- Work order
- New-hire requisition
- Customer phone call

For example, a computer or switching station breakdown results in a maintenance repair order. The input was the computer or switching station breakdown, but the maintenance repair order transaction is an excellent surrogate for the input.

To illustrate the use of transactions, consider the activities associated with receiving supplies:

Input	Activity	Output	Recorded by	Resulting Activities
Shipping document	Receive supplies	Supplies receipt	Person at storeroom via CRT	Unload supplies Inspect supplies Move supplies Store supplies Pay for supplies Retrieve supplies

The supplies receipt transaction is a means of charging the cost of the supply storeroom for the specific supplies received. These costs are then traced to services and used to evaluate the efficiency and effectiveness of the purchasing department and to make decisions about whether to buy in large quantities.

An activity requires resources to accomplish its objective. **Resources** are the factors of service operations—labor, occupancy costs, technology, travel, supplies, and the like—employed to perform an activity. Examples of resources include:

Activity	Resource
Write program	Computer, desk
	Programmer
	Computer paper, disks
Service car	Skilled mechanic
	Tools
	Service manual
	Garage

Resources are purchased externally or obtained from other departments; that is, the output of one activity often becomes an input (resource) to another activity. An **activity cost** is the sum of all resources, including inputs from other internal activities. An activity's cost behavior pattern is the manner in which the resources vary in relation to changes in the number of occurrences of the activity.

An input to an activity includes the physical documents that trigger the activity or supply information. Inputs, as well as outputs, are expressed as a physical unit such as a transaction. Inputs emanate from either an internal or external supplier.

Many inputs are required to perform an activity, but usually only one event triggers its execution while other inputs supply information. The action of a trigger can be stated as, "When this event occurs, start this activity." The activity of issuing a purchase order, for example, is triggered by the receipt of a supplies request. The single triggering input (transaction) is important to manage because its occurrence triggers the execution of the activity. Additional information is supplied by the purchasing specifications and a vendor list.

Some activities can have multiple triggers. For example, the "issue purchase order" activity might also be triggered by a low inventory report.

In a management sense, the input transactions constitute the objective and verifiable evidence of consummated business transactions. Characteristically, the input is consumed by the activity process and converted to an output.

A **cost driver** is a factor that creates or influences cost. Cost driver analysis identifies the cause of cost. For example, the office layout is a key determinant of the cost of service operation movement and work-in-progress. Think of processing an insurance policy application. The closer the mailroom is to the claims department, the less distance the claims have to move.

An office organized into groups of similar activities requires a significant amount of paper movement. However, a cellular office layout concentrates all the activities necessary to complete a process in a single location to minimize paper movement and service work-in-progress. For example, IDS used to have three departments handle requests for prospectuses. One department answered the phone and recorded the information on paper. This information was then given to a second department to enter into the computer. A third department actually mailed the prospectuses. Now IDS has cellular work groups that perform all three tasks. Finger pointing between departments is eliminated, errors and cost have decreased, and productivity has improved.

A **positive** cost driver results in revenue, service operations, or support-related activities that generate profit. For example, improved procedures:

- Reduce personnel costs and time
- Help eliminate rework

A **negative** cost driver causes unnecessary work and reduced profitability. For example, improper training can result in:

- Redoing the service (e.g., reprocessing chemical waste, or fixing the same pothole a second time)
- Taking longer than necessary to perform the activity

An **output** is the culmination (the service) of the transformation of resources by an activity. It is what the user receives or what the activity produces. It is the result or objective of performing the activity. Examples of outputs include:

Activity	Output
Bill customer	Invoice
Hire employee	Hired employee
Produce service	Cargo/passengers transported

It is important to keep in mind that the output is the result of the activity, not the goal (e.g., an activity to sell a car results in a sales contract, not the profit that is the goal; food stamp requests result in food stamps being issued, not the goal, which is ultimately to eliminate the need for food stamps). The execution of an activity therefore creates certain tangible documents/results or an intangible action, idea, or concept. An **activity measure (output measure)**, is the "number of activity occurrences per period."

There is always an expected result of an activity such as a completed sales call, payroll checks, repaired equipment, educated students, delivered pizza, healed patient, real estate tax bill, apprehended criminal, satellites in the sky, or a new law passed.

Sometimes an activity might be broken into sub-activities. For example, the activity, fill job request, might be divided into the following sub-activities: fill non-exempt local, fill exempt local and fill exempt out of state. Judgement is required to decide whether to use sub-activities or just to ignore subactivities that don't take very much time or resources.

The output of an activity is intended to meet customers' demands. The customer (citizen, recipient) in this sense could be the final consumer of the service, or just the next user of the output of an activity. The customer of the activity can therefore be either internal or external to the organization.

An activity's output often becomes an input to other activities, an external customer, or a service. The completion of the purchase order, for example, is an event that triggers a subsequent activity to receive the supplies

The **process** is the manner in which the activity is performed. It encompasses all the systematic tasks and operations that contribute to the transformation of inputs into outputs. A process can be performed in numerous ways with different factors of service operations. The resources involved in scheduling nursing staff or social welfare workers manually or with the aid of a computer system are quite dissimilar, yet they are alternative methods of one scheduling process. The terms **activity** and **process** are often used interchangeably.

An enterprise establishes control procedures for activities that regulate the transformation of input into output. **Control** is the regulation of a process (activity) to ensure a predictable output of uniform quality (e.g., fires being extinguished according to the same procedures). **Control** regulates the flow of data, prescribes operating logic, and establishes parameters and tolerances.

Activities are controlled by business rules. A **business rule** defines the goals, strategies, and regulations governing the activity. For example, government employees shouldn't exceed their funding levels from congress or they are subject to prosecution. Rules take the form of policies, procedures, rules of thumb, and algorithms. Policy is essential to translate high-level enterprise objectives into detailed plans. For example, the business rules for the activity of scheduling cargo shipments might be to accumulate several orders into a batch when determining truck routing and delivery sequence. The same business rule can be used for a city needing to replace burned-out light bulbs on the city streets. These procedural rules are typically embedded in scheduling techniques.

Business rules are not changed by the activity to which they apply. For example, an activity to purchase computers depends on whether the computers are in the budget. If there is no computer budget, then the activity to purchase computers is suspended. However, the business rules that govern the purchase of computers are independent of whether it's computers, cars, or furniture being purchased.

Business rules are developed from two forms of knowledge: basic and expert. Basic knowledge is based on known relations such as time and cost. Expert knowledge is derived from experience.

Activity Classification

Activities can be classified as repetitive or nonrepetitive, primary or secondary, strategic, discretionary, or required, by degree of influenceability and by degree of leverage. The following paragraphs will explain these classifications.

Activities are repetitive or nonrepetitive. A **repetitive** activity is what the organization does on a continual basis. Repetitive activities have consistent input, output, and processing and are managed within the activity management system. For example, initially identifying a vendor is different from selecting a vendor for a particular order. Both activities involve unique repetitive processes. Because each represents a significant commitment of resources, they are separate activities. As such, they represent a defined area of accountability. A **nonrepetitive** activity is a one-time activity. Nonrepetitive activities are managed within a project management system. The latter often demands a business process analysis approach since, by their nature, nonrepetitive activities are one-time projects, and often span several departments.

Activities are either primary or secondary. A **primary** activity contributes directly to the mission of a department or organizational unit. Researching the market and modifying services are two of the primary activities of some marketing departments. They are one of the reasons the marketing department was created. A characteristic of a primary activity is that its output is used outside the organization or by another department within the division.

A **secondary** activity supports an organizational units' primary activities. Secondary activities are general activities such as administration, supervision, training, and secretarial work carried out in support of the whole or part of an organizational unit's primary activities. Often the manager of a department, for example, is not hired to carry out the activities of that department, but is trained to manage the activities in that department. Secondary activities support only a single department and should increase the efficiency and effectiveness of the primary activities in that department. Although these activities are essential to the effective execution of primary activities, they drain time and resources from the primary activities and must be carefully managed. A common characteristic of secondary activities is that they are consumed by the primary activities in an organization.

Secondary activities should be carefully scrutinized to determine whether they are necessary. The ratio of secondary activities to primary activities is an indication of an organizational unit's bureaucracy. For example, consider the activities of a loan officer:

Primary Activities	Time%	Secondary Activities	Time%
Business Development			
Sales calls—existing customer	20	Customer file maintenance	1
Sales calls—new customers	20	Cross selling	1
Commercial loan negotiation	5	Loan operations	5
Commercial loan checking	5	Community involvement	3
Customer Service		Internal reporting	1
Service commercial loans	20	Budgeting	1
Loan review	5	Training	2
Loan pricing	5	Employee relations	1
Loan review documentation	5		
Total	85	Total	15

This 85/15 ratio is considered very good. Suppose, however, that the loan officers' ratio of primary activities to secondary activities is 50/50, and that the current level of effort is 50 person-years for the primary activities and 50 person-years for the secondary activities. If half of the secondary activities shifted to (lower-paid) clerical staff, the net savings to the organization would be dramatic. The 25 person-years of loan officer secondary effort could be performed by 25 dedicated clerical staff members. This can result in considerable savings, as shown here with some representative salaries:

$$25 \text{ person-years at } \$55,000 = \$1,375,000$$
$$25 \text{ person-years at } \$30,000 = \underline{750,000}$$
$$\$625,000$$

An activity can be strategic, required or discretionary. A strategic activity is important to achieve organization goals. Money saved from eliminating waste should be funneled into strategic activities. A **discretionary** activity is optional, depending on the manager's judgement. A **required** activity must be done at the request of laws, stockholders, or customers.

It is important to determine the degree of **influenceability** of an activity. Many factors influence an activity's performance. External factors are, in general, less easily influenced than internal factors. Weather and regulatory requirements are examples of external factors. Rain on the day of the Walk-America fund-raising event or the IRS policy dealing with bingo being used by nonprofits to raise money are examples of external factors. Company policy and procedures are examples of internal factors. For example, government employees are not allowed to fly first class. They are usually restricted in the type of hotels they can stay in or at least are limited in the amount they will be reimbursed for their hotel, regardless of the room rate charged to them.

Activities also vary in their degree of **leverage** in the marketplace. For example, the activity of designing a service has a high degree of leverage: some designs clearly promote service desirability, like a newsletter promotion that guarantees your money back within three months if you are not totally satisfied. Complying with external regulations, however, has a low degree of leverage in the marketplace. Meeting external requirements at the lowest cost is an excellent goal for an activity/business process. These activities, known as compliance/oversight activities, sustain stewardship responsibility. A second category of low-leverage activities comprises transaction-related activities (e.g., paying vendors). These activities reflect the effort needed to process volumes of transactions. A prudent manager will maximize the efficiency of performing these activities. A third category comprises administrative activities. These activities support service work activities; examples include supervisory and secretarial tasks. Non–value-added activities form a fourth category. These activities correct or revise some form of deficiency. Prudent managers will seek to eliminate or minimize these activities.

Activity Considerations

In structuring an activity, an organization has a range of choices to make between different processing methods and resources. Each alternative method of accomplishing an activity will bring with it certain implications for the organization in terms of response to markets, citizens' demands, level of investment required, unit cost, and type of control and management structure. The fundamental rationale for choosing a specific method of performing an activity is that it is best able to support the organization's objectives.

It is difficult to optimize enterprise performance because many activities overlap. Too many things have to be dealt with simultaneously. As a result, the wrong activities are given priority; less important activities consume an inordinate amount of time, as actions are ruled by the daily schedule and sidetracked by responding to crises.

Because the environment is dynamic, the mix of activities/business processes must also be dynamic. When service volumes increase or decrease, for example, organizations should ideally revise their activities/business processes in keeping with the new level of volume. It is common for costs to increase easily with a higher level of volume, yet move down slowly when volume decrease. When demand for government housing permits and inspectors increases, staff may be added. However, how often is it cut when the demand for these activities decreases? Too often, organizations do not revise activities in a timely manner because the existing accounting systems do not monitor activities/business processes and their corresponding cost behavior patterns.

It is interesting to note that traditional accounting systems are indirectly based on activities. The reason is that most organizations are structured around clusters of specialists who perform related activities. Thus, the purchasing activities are performed within the purchasing department, marketing activities are performed by the marketing department, community service is done by a certain group in nonprofits, professors educate on specific topics, and so forth. However, clustering by specialty provides a homogeneous grouping of cost to only a limited degree since the cost behavior patterns of each separate departmental activity are dissimilar enough to cause service cost distortion.

BUSINESS PROCESS OVERVIEW

A business process is an orderly arrangement of activities operating under a set of procedures in order to accomplish a specific objective such as marketing services, developing new services, or processing customer/citizen orders. The activities are related because a specific event initiates the first activity in the process, which in turn triggers subsequent activities.

An important feature of business processes is that they transcend organizational boundaries. For example, the introduction of a new service would require a marketing assessment of needs, a design for the service, specifications for the service, and the development of a procedure for creating the service (e.g., how to process contaminated industrial waste). This requires effort on the part of marketing, research and development, administration, and finance.

A business process can be a part of a larger process. For example, several activities are part of the customer order business processes. The key activities include:

- Acquire supplies (obtaining proper income tax forms)
- Scheduling returns—choosing whose tax returns get done first
- Create service—completing tax returns
- Deliver service—mailing or delivering completed tax return

A business process view of cost is an essential adjunct to the traditional **organization structure**, which equates management and accountability with a vertical manager/subordinate responsibility structure. The traditional structure often leads to inappropriate competition among departments. The "creative" department thinks that account representatives are interested only in selling advertising, no matter how complex the design and how low the budget; the marketing department thinks that the people in creative are unresponsive; and the finger pointing goes on.

Anyone who has worked in a service company, a nonprofit, or a government agency can cite examples when marketing, service operations, the legislature, citizens, headquarters, and financial activities were not coordinated in the introduction of a new service, fund-raising event, or new law. For example, the process to introduce a new service would set the following activities in motion:

Activity	Responsible Department
Analyze market	Marketing
Design service	Research & development
Review design	Marketing and/or operations
Plan quality	Quality assurance
Create prototype	Operations and/or research
Test prototype	Marketing or operations
Analyze make/buy	Finance
Plan process	Operations
Analyze financials	Finance

In a typical scenario, the financial people are surprised by the additional costs of the service; marketing insists on releasing the service or new concept before it was fully tested; operations has to spend excessive amounts of money in overtime to get the service out and make up for inadequate consideration of operational issues. The productivity of the entire organization is affected when the new service is introduced but is not well tested and, as a result, gets a poor customer reaction.

Business process analysis focuses management attention on the interdependencies of departments. It forces managers to realize that their customers are other departments and the performance of their activities affects subsequent activities in the business process. In Madison, Wisconsin, the city was appalled at how long it took to repair vehicles. They blamed the repair department for being so slow. Finally, the mayor asked what caused the delay. The mechanics said that purchasing is required to buy the model of vehicle that has the lowest price on the bid date. Therefore, the city had a combination of manufacturers and models. Obviously, each manufacturer and model was made differently and had to be repaired differently and required different tools. Purchasing blamed legal for requiring them to buy from the lowest bidder. After discussing this with the city legal department, legal saw no problem in buying from a single manufacturer in order to reduce total life-cycle cost, including purchase price, repair costs, repair downtime, and salvage value.

It is important that organizations extend their definition of the business processes to include links between an organization and its suppliers and customers, with a view to reducing costs or enhancing differentiation.

With business process reporting, individual department managers are not penalized for exceeding budget "if overall enterprise costs are lowered." For example, a maintenance department exceeded its capital budget by $75,000 because certain repairs that were formerly contracted out were brought in-house. However, the change resulted in cost savings of over $500,000 in another department. The process reporting portrayed the wisdom of this choice.

KEY COMPONENTS OF AN ACTIVITY MANAGEMENT SYSTEM

New cost management systems are being built on activity information. The advantages of activity management are:

- Setting more realistic cost and performance targets derived from the strategic plan.

- Identifying wasteful activities and factors that drive cost.

- Improving the quality of estimating and do-it-yourself/buy decisions by knowing an accurate service cost (which is derived by tracing the cost of activities to services).

The seven steps to computing activity cost are as follows:

1. Activity analysis
2. Life-cycle classification
3. Determination of activity cost
   a. Tracing of organizational resources to activities with an established causal relationship
   b. Determination of the output measure of activity by which the cost of a given activity varies most directly (as in number of purchase orders, number of kilowatt hours generated, number of welfare recipients processed)
   c. Calculation of cost per activity
4. Identification of performance measures
5. Determination of cost of business processes
6. Tracing activities/business processes to reporting objective
   a. Technology
   b. Orders, projects, or contracts
   c. Customers or citizen group
   d. Services
   e. Channels of distribution
7. Calculation of service cost

Activity Analysis

Activity analysis identifies the significant activities (both service operation and support) of an enterprise in order to establish a basis for accurately determining their cost and performance. Activity analysis decomposes a large, complex organization into elemental activities that are understandable and easy to manage. The explicit management of activities gives an enterprise a better insight into how resources are employed and whether the activity contributes to the achievement of corporate objectives. This approach is in contrast to today's accounting systems, which provide visibility of total resources (expenses) employed by each organizational unit, but not of what the unit does (output).

Life-cycle Analysis

Life-cycle analysis provides a framework for managing the cost and performance of a service/process over the duration of its activities. The life cycle commences with the initial identification of a customer/citizen need and extends through planning, research, design, development, service operations, evaluation, use, logistics support in operation, retirement, and disposal. Life cycle is important to cost control because of the interdependencies of activities in different time periods. For example, the output of the service design activity has a significant impact on the cost and performance of subsequent activities. For example, a hospital emergency room said all patients would be seen within fifteen minutes of arrival or their medical bill would be free. This had a significant impact on the cost and performance of the emergency room.

When costs are not properly matched with time periods, service cost is distorted and cost control disjointed. Traditional accounting systems expense many costs associated with start-up, field operations, maintenance, service support, and retirement and disposal, which should be capitalized and matched to the services that benefit. For example, training employees on using electronic data interchange (EDI) will produce benefits over a number of years. Yet research, installation, and training are expensed currently even though they will benefit future periods.

Activity Cost

Activity cost is derived by tracing the cost of all significant resources to perform an activity. The resources consist of people, equipment, travel, supplies, computer systems, and other resources that are customarily expressed as expense elements within a chart of accounts.

Activity cost is expressed in terms of a measure of activity volume by which the costs of a given process vary most directly (e.g., the cost of scheduling planes may be expressed as a cost per plane or the cost per schedule). Measuring activity effectiveness requires knowing the amount of output (activity volume) as well as the activity cost.

Activity Performance Measurement

Performance measures are the financial and operational statistics used to gauge the performance of an organization. Under activity-based performance measurement, each activity is analyzed to determine how effectively the work is being performed as gauged by key performance measures such as quality, cost, and time. Each performance measure is simply a different attribute of an activity.

Performance measures provide an important perspective on how effectively the activity helps to achieve enterprise objectives. Performance measures are interrelated. A reduction in time, for example, will affect cost, quality, and flexibility because it changes the performance of the activity. A key to effective cost management is the implementation of changes that simultaneously improve multiple dimensions of performance.

Performance measures should be determined with respect to customer demands. The focus should be on the customer and competition, and not on some internal goal determined by management or by department heads.

Performance measures should first be set at the business process or total service level. Then performance measures can be set at the activity level. Otherwise, activity managers might achieve their performance goals at the detriment of the business process or total service.

Technology Accounting

Technology accounting is a system that aims to identify and monitor all significant **technology costs** (e.g., "smart" offices, scanning, EDI, fax equipment, and information systems) and to assign them to services that use the technology. Technology consists of more than equipment and machines; it includes the techniques of operation and the organization that makes a particular machine, computer, or equipment workable. It includes technology research, training, maintenance, operations, and updating. In essence, a technology reflects an evolution of enterprise structure spawned from external market demands and internal decisions. Since technology costs are both a significant determinant of service cost and a key factor in organization strategy, technology accounting treats service technology costs as a direct cost on the same level as direct labor and direct supplies.

Functional Analysis

Functional analysis aggregates the total cost of activities common to a function (e.g., quality). This is accomplished by classifying activities into functions. Function costing provides visibility of costs that would otherwise be hidden in numerous departments. The knowledge that the requirement for a given activity resulted from a source outside the department is valuable in understanding what drives a department's normal activities.

Business Process Analysis

A business process analysis determines the interdependencies among activities. Insight into these interrelationships provides visibility of the events that trigger the process. By controlling the initiating event, an organization can reduce or eliminate the cost of all subsequent activities. Today's management accounting systems do not portray the interrelationships among activities.

Understanding activity relationships facilitates the streamlining of business processes by identifying redundant and unnecessary activities, which increase cost without any corresponding benefit in the marketplace. The entire business process can therefore be restructured to reduce cost and improve efficiency. The procedure for analyzing a business process is to determine the sequence of activities by following the flow of information from one activity to another. The information flows represent inputs and outputs, and constrain an activity. Until information needed to perform an activity is delivered correctly and at the appropriate time, an activity cannot be effectively performed.

Business process analysis facilitates the evaluation of alternative organizational structures. It is often best to organize people and equipment into natural groups around business processes or information flows as one major U.S. railroad company has done.

Business Process and Cost

In activity management, the execution of an activity is understood to consume resources. Business processes and services consume activities.

Business process and service cost is determined through a bill of activities that itemizes the activities and the quantity of each activity consumed in producing a specific business process and/or service. A business process or service cost is derived by summing up the cost of all the activities into a bill of activities. Business process and service costing is enhanced by more direct tracing of support costs, which have traditionally been lumped into overhead and allocated to business processes and services.

Activity management is the foundation of a management system. The focus of activity management is to understand the cost and performance of significant activities and trace the activities to final cost objectives, such as business processes, services, customers, and functions. In other words, activity management determines the pattern of activity resource use. It doesn't question whether an activity should be performed or if it could be performed more effectively.

Activity management is the analysis of activities to determine the best mix of activities and the optimal level of resources assigned to activities. A discussion of some of the important elements of an activity management system follows.

Activity/Business Process Investment Management

Activity investment analysis evaluates the impact of changing an activity/ business process, such as introducing a new technology, on the cost, performance, and interdependencies of those activities/business processes. The analysis process systematically decomposes the organization's objectives and strategies into activity/business process-level goals that provide a foundation for judging the value of an investment. This facilitates measurement of the cost and nonfinancial performance effects of the investment by defining the base line set of activities/business process against which to measure change.

Activity/business process investment management embraces the concept of continual improvement by routinely challenging how activities/ business processes are performed. It decreases the probability of selecting and implementing an inappropriate investment by evaluating capital investments relative to "efficient operations" rather than to existing cost structures. It links investment opportunities to strategic objectives and couples the management accounting system with the investment analysis to facilitate corrective action.

Cost Driver Analysis

Cost driver analysis identifies activities that influence the cost and performance of subsequent activities. By reducing or eliminating the event that triggers the first activity in the chain, it may eliminate the need for all subsequent activities. For example, the detection of an incorrect invoice or real estate tax bill requires the bill to be redone or scrapped, the cause of the error to be corrected, the problem documented, and other related activities. By eliminating the cause—the incorrect invoice or incorrect real estate tax bill—the need to perform all subsequent activities is eliminated because they are executed only when an error occurs. Costs are thus reduced.

There are hundreds of activities that occur in even the smallest organization. Of all these activities, only a handful of cost drivers are critical, and have a significant impact on the success of an organization. By identifying the cost drivers of a process or an activity, an organization can most effectively control costs.

Activity Budgeting

Assessing the factors that control activity volume is an important technique for budgeting the resources necessary to perform an activity/business process. For example, one state social services agency office required the same number of workers as a second office even though the second office had twice the number of cases. At first glance it appears that the second office's performance is significantly better. However, when one looks at factors such as the number of new cases versus case continuations and at the complexity of the cases, the reasons for the difference in support department size become evident. The first office has many differentiated services that require significantly more support than the second office, which has fewer problems and a high-volume of renewal cases.

Understanding the number of activity occurrences is an effective tool in predicting the effect on support costs of different strategic decisions. For the previous example, the impact of a 10-percent increase in a department's budget depends on whether the increase comes from additional renewal cases or from new and complex cases. In a service company, the impact of a 10-percent increase in a department's budget depends on whether the increase comes from additional sales for a high-volume line or from a low-volume service line. A low-volume service line often requires significantly more support costs per unit than a high-volume line.

Non–Value-Added Analysis

Non–value-added activities result in profitless spending of time, money, and resources, and add unnecessary cost to the services. A non–value-added analysis identifies activities that can be eliminated with no deterioration of enterprise performance (e.g., cost, function, quality, perceived value). Non–value-added analysis highlights wasteful activities.

Best-Practice Analysis

A best-practice analysis compares activity/business process cost and performance between different departments, divisions, best-in-class, and/or competitors to identify the most efficient way to perform an activity. Once the activities/business processes with the lowest cost and highest performance are identified, they can be analyzed to identify the source of excellence. The results of the analysis can then be shared with other groups within the organization that perform the activity to determine the applicability to their operations.

Activity Target Cost Analysis

Activity target cost analysis determines activity/business process cost and performance goals based on market demand for a service. Target costs are derived by estimating the market price necessary to capture a certain market share and then subtracting the desired profit margin. Typically, a target cost is lower than the initial estimated cost to create a service. The challenge is to reduce the service operation cost to the target level. Activities provide an excellent basis for identifying opportunities to achieve targets. Identification of non–value-added activities and best practices provides a basis to apply value engineering and business process redesign techniques to eliminate or improve the cost and performance of these activities.

Activity Strategic Analysis

Activity strategic cost analysis uses activity cost and performance data to develop enterprise strategies. Strategic cost analysis evaluates an organization's activities, from service design to distribution, and determines where value to the customer can be enhanced or costs lowered. For example, is it better in the long run to provide welfare parents with training and a computer so that they may work and earn money at home or is it cheaper to just given them a check? Is the lack of a meaningful event profitability accounting system really costing the nonprofit organization many times the cost of such a system by having fund raisers work on low-yield events? Is the cost of having the latest medical equipment, even though it is only used 20 percent of the time, more or less expensive than losing some patients who would go elsewhere for those tests requiring the latest equipment?

Cost management systems play a critical role in allowing an organization to assess the financial impact of various alternatives and to select appropriate strategies. Information obtained from traditional cost accounting systems is usually inadequate for strategic cost analysis because it does not help the organization understand the behavior of costs from a strategic perspective. It follows that an organization's accounting systems must be designed to facilitate strategic cost analysis—a function radically different from traditional record keeping.

SUMMARY

Today's model of collecting costs by chart-of-account expense classification within organizational structure is providing insufficient visibility of key activities and of economic cause-and-effect relationships between activities.

An activity management system is used to calculate a more accurate service cost, to control costs, to integrate strategic planning into the cost management system, and to manage performance as well as costs.

An activity-based cost management system provides a set of tools for more effective management of cost and performance. The information provided by an activity cost management system enables service managers to solve problems rather than treat symptoms. This is critical because if managers don't understand the problem, they can't find the solution.

An activity management system relies on the costing of significant business activities/business processes to:

- Provide a natural base line for improvement

- Provide visibility of non–value-added activities
- Understand the underlying cause-and-effect relationships between the factors of service operation and the activities
- Identify, evaluate, and implement new activities
- Capture budgeted and actual activity/business process cost
- Measure the efficiency and effectiveness of the activity/business process

4

WHY ACTIVITIES?

The purpose of this chapter is to:

- Provide an overview of why activities are an appropriate basis for an activity management system
- Provide insight into the potency of activity management for achieving enterprise excellence

Activities are a powerful basis for managing an enterprise. Several characteristics of activities make them such a powerful management tool. This chapter examines the most important of these characteristics.

ACTIVITIES ARE ACTIONS

A management system structured on activities ensures that plans are transmitted to a level at which action can be taken. Activities are what organizations do. To make changes, one must change what people or machines do. Therefore, changes must ultimately be made to activities.

In contrast, the traditional practice of collecting costs by cost element (e.g., wages and salaries, office and equipment supplies, occupancy costs, travel, and the like) does not provide the detailed information necessary to identify needed changes. For example, consider wages and salaries in the real estate department of a fast-food franchise. Two important activities of the department are "selecting new locations/negotiating purchase" and "paying real estate property taxes."

A conventional cost accounting system, which captures the total cost of wages and salaries at the departmental level, does not provide insight into how people are utilized. To accurately trace costs to services or, in this case, store locations, it is necessary to break costs down into activities with unique cost behavior patterns.

The activities of "selecting new locations/negotiating purchase" and "paying real estate property taxes" are two activities of the real estate department with significantly different cost behavior patterns, yet both activities are part of a single salary cost account in the real estate department. The cost behavior pattern of "selecting new locations" is related to the location's distance from headquarters, whether it is a new section of the country/world or an area the organization is already familiar with, whether it is a high- or low-demand area, the size of the location needed, and whether a stand-alone, mall, corner, or strip center is desired. The cost behavior patterns of "negotiating the purchase" depends on what lawyers charge in the area, whether there will be a mortgage, what the zoning laws are, zoning changes that have to be approved, and what structure is on the current site.

The activity "paying real estate property taxes" depends on the accuracy of legal descriptions, addresses, tax rates, how often the real estate values of comparable properties are reviewed, and the degree of automation.

The cost behavior pattern of "selecting new locations/negotiating purchase" is related to the number of times the organization finds new locations. This could increase or decrease depending on the corporate strategy and capital budget, while "paying real estate property taxes" is done on a regular time schedule. Traditional practice would group these separate activities together even though they have separate cost behavior patterns. Activity analysis preserves the individual nature of these two activities.

ACTIVITIES IMPROVE SERVICE COST PROFITABILITY

An age-old quest of most organizations is to determine the "true" cost of providing a service. Overhead service cost allocated on the basis of sales, direct labor, equipment use, or total direct costs distorts service cost because it erroneously assumes that the usage of these overhead factors is proportional to sales, direct labor, equipment usage, or total direct costs. The cost behavior pattern of the activity "issue purchase orders," for example, depends on the number of purchase orders issued. Using sales to allocate the cost of running the purchasing department overcosts services with high sales, and undercosts services with low sales. In reality, a service with low sales may require just as much or even more purchasing department activity as a service with high sales.

Activity management challenges the goal of determining the "true" cost of providing a service. After-the-fact actual cost systems are considered to violate the principles of excellence. Using activity management to determine the "true" cost of providing a service during the pre-introduction planning phase is considered positive. The idea is to stress **preventing** rather than collecting costs.

To illustrate this point consider the cost of providing automated tellers. A bank that has invested in installing automated tellers may wish to know the "true cost" of the service on a monthly basis. Knowing the true cost monthly provides little value since the investment has already been made and the customers expect this service. The bank would also have difficulty in charging extra for this service since prices are set by market factors.

Alternatively, a bank may, as part of its annual budgeting process, want to know the current cost of providing automated tellers for the following reasons:

1. To measure continuous improvement

2. To provide a basis for instituting process controls

Continuous improvement occurs when an organization lowers the cost of providing the activity. Suppose, for example, that the cost is $5 per transaction. By improving the preventive maintenance on the computers, it is possible to lower total operating cost by $.20. Thus, the new activity cost is to be $4.80 per transaction.

The next step is to institute process controls to ensure computer breakdowns are decreased by the new procedures. Process controls would be implemented to monitor the tellers' availability and computer breakdown occurrences.

There would be no need to determine the actual cost of the tellers, since each activity/business process would have its separate process controls to ensure performance is at the expected level. If all activities, including breakdown maintenance, are managed, we know the cost of the automated teller will be $4.80.

Planning activity accounting improves the accuracy of service costing by tracing activities to services on the basis of usage. The number of purchase orders, for example, would be directly traced to each service, thus creating a more accurate costing of the service, because now each service is charged with the number of units of purchasing activity that it uses.

The cost of processing purchase orders is traced to services on the basis of the number of purchase orders required to provide a service. Those purchase orders may be for supplies and equipment (e.g., engine parts for a waste management truck/army depot vehicle). Services with a significant number of purchased supplies or equipment would receive a higher proportion of the cost of running the purchasing department than services with few purchased supplies or equipment, since additional purchasing activity is required.

Under traditional cost accounting, some organizations include information systems costs in overhead and allocate these costs to services on the basis of direct labor, equipment usage, total direct costs, and sales. Other organizations don't even bother to allocate these costs to services, and include them in general overhead. If direct labor was used to allocate overhead, services with the largest proportion of direct labor absorb the bulk of information systems costs. However, services that have been operational for some time have had most of their bugs eliminated and thus require less information systems support. New services, in contrast, typically have more operational and quality-control problems that require a number of information systems changes until the service is running smoothly.

Information systems charges are more accurately related to factors such as the amount of time the new service has been in operation, service complexity, and use of standardized procedures. It would make more sense to trace information systems costs to the departments, services, and/or locations using the service. For example, a hotel wants to keep track of the preferences of its frequent guests. The information systems costs should be traced to their frequent guests and the program, and not just allocated as part of overhead to all guests.

Other activities, such as management and administration, are not directly traceable to services. These costs should be excluded, or allocated if the organization wants a fully absorbed cost.

Activity management differentiates services produced in small and large batches. For example, creating one thousand paper party plates with standard balloon designs printed on them requires different resources than creating fifteen paper party plates with personalized design. Activity management traces the costs of setup-related activities to the service order that creates the demand for those activities. The cost of setup (e.g., setting up the equipment to print a design on paper plates in a party store) activities is then spread to the services generating the batch. Thus low-volume services (e.g., personalized design for only fifteen plates) incur a relatively high setup cost per unit (e.g., per plate), whereas high-volume services (e.g., one thousand plates with standard design) incur relatively little setup cost per unit (e.g., per plate).

In contrast, traditional cost accounting allocates batch-related costs to all services produced during the accounting period on an erroneous volume-related basis. Traditional accounting would say the setup charge per plate was the same for both the large-volume batch and the small-volume batch.

ACTIVITIES DRIVE COST

Cost drivers are factors that constrain an activity or cause cost to increase or decrease. Typically, cost drivers are a consequence of previous activities. Too often cost control is focused at the point of cost occurrence without adequate consideration of cost drivers. Consider the purchasing department of a transportation company that buys the lowest-cost equipment because its bonus system is based on low cost. Meanwhile, operations may have high operating costs and high maintenance because lower-quality equipment was purchased.

Typically, an organization would control operating cost through a fleet manager and maintenance costs through a maintenance manager. Yet much of the cost was built into the system once the type, quality, and size of transportation equipment was determined. Therefore, to focus primary attention at the point of cost occurrence could fail to address the cause of the cost, and permanent prevention of the cost becomes impossible.

In all cases, the company should address the root causes of the costs before attempting to improve its efficiency. In other words, correct the source of the cost (e.g., management and purchasing) rather than treat its symptoms (e.g., high operating and high maintenance costs).

Determining the amount of time a phone, gas, water, or electric repair person spends on various activities—such as installing new service or making repairs between the home, office, or factory and the main line—provides a basis for understanding what causes repair cost. Excessive repair time might indicate poor line design, low-quality installation materials, poor installation procedures, inadequate installation training, and/or a lack of self-inspection after installation. Similarly, a great deal of new line problems might suggest that something has changed since the design had been created, such as a greater number of earthquakes or tropical storms resulting in an excessive number of repairs. In any case, the economic causes of these various repair activities are significantly different. Activities highlight the areas that drive cost, such as service design, and indicate where action is required. The traditional system does not provide this insight.

ACTIVITIES FACILITATE EVALUATION OF ALTERNATIVES

Determining the best possible cost and performance of an activity permits a comparison with different divisions/departments and other organizations within the industry that perform the same activity. For example, the federal government calculates for states the ratios of processing costs per welfare and social security disability recipient served. Nonprofit organizations calculate operating costs against dollars raised. The most cost-effective operations can then be studied to specify a set of best practices that can aid other divisions, chapters, departments, or states in improving operations.

Activity management assesses an organization's activities to determine if they are being performed cost effectively in comparison to alternatives both inside and outside the organization. Activity management enhances the understanding of new process technologies. The introduction of a new technology (e.g., the electronic data interchange (EDI) or point-of-sale scanning) changes the factors of service operations and the performance of activities. Activity management identifies the impact of these changes by focusing on how the activities are performed.

Consider the processing of payroll checks. Currently an organization may process payroll checks manually. An activity management system would routinely calculate a cost per payroll check, identify the time it takes to process a check, and evaluate the quality of the process (e.g., number of errors per check run). An alternative method is to acquire a computerized payroll system. The cost and performance of the manual system would be compared to the computerized system to determine the value of the change in terms of its impact on profitability and performance.

Similarly, the manner in which different offices process a payroll check can be compared to determine which office has the best performance. This site can then be studied to determine why it has the best practice and share the results with the rest of the organization.

ACTIVITIES FOCUS CORPORATE STRATEGY

Activities are what an enterprise does. Strategic goals represent what the enterprise wants to achieve. Knowing the corporate goals enables an organization to determine what it is doing (activities) and whether its activities are helping to achieve those goals.

The mix of services management has chosen to provide and the current activities must be continually evaluated to ensure that the activities contribute to the achievement of the organization's objectives. Poor structuring of organizational activities/business processes leads to missed deadlines, unfinished projects, disappointed customers, and wasteful costs.

A common organization objective is to be a low- or lowest-cost producer. However, managers who claim to hold this position rarely know how accurate their own service costs are, much less how they compare with competitors' service costs. Even not-for-profit organizations such as hospitals and governments need to know how much it costs to provide a given service compared to other hospitals and government agencies. They also need to know the external cost of buying an activity. For example, in the United Kingdom private enterprise sells stamps and manages the equivalent of the Federal Aviation Authority rather than the government performing these activities.

ACTIVITIES COMPLEMENT CONTINUOUS IMPROVEMENT

In daily operations, many activities are non–value added and secondary to the organization's mission. Visibility of these non–value-added and secondary activities provided by the activity management system is a basis for continuous improvement.

Activity analysis provides information to identify redundant and wasteful activities, together with the factors that drive cost. Understanding activities provides a basis for determining whether to continue performing or to restructure an activity/business process. Continuous improvement has several objectives:

- Elimination of waste (non–value-added activities)
- Improvement of performance of value-added activities
- Reduction of lead time for introduction of new services
- Decreasing lead and cycle times for operational activities/business processes

- Improvement of quality
- Minimizing process variance by correcting the root cause of the variance
- Simplification of activities/business processes

Continual process improvements do not come automatically with experience or the passage of time. They require constant management attention in all matters to achieve productivity gains and cost reductions. Too often service cost, and consequently price, drift out of line with competitors. Services often become unprofitable without management's realizing the reason for the problem. Management might not take appropriate action until it's too late.

There are several inhibitors to continuous improvement. First, there is an overemphasis on direct wages and salaries and other direct costs. It is much more important to concentrate on total enterprise costs. Overhead and other support costs can throw an organization's cost structure out of line. Support activities tend to over-accumulate in good times when there is no pressure for tight performance and the exercise of common sense.

Second, inflation works against continuous improvement. Inflation can provide a false sense of security that often allows organizations to pass higher costs to consumers and avoid addressing fundamental cost problems. It is easy to raise prices when cost automatically increases with inflation. This, in turn, leads to lack of discipline in controlling cost. Think of all the local governments that lived off increased property taxes due to increasing property values. When property values decrease, discipline must be restored.

Activity management provides information crucial to continuous improvement. It yields a wealth of information on operating activities that managers can use to eliminate waste.

Activity management supports continuous improvement by managing the processes. Consider the traditional procurement process. The key activities include:

- Schedule the service
- Process purchase requisitions for needed supplies
- Issue purchase orders
- Process supplies-received vouchers
- Pay vendors

The buyer receives a weekly printout of the service operation plan and supplies requirements, checks the inventory computer records, and compares the requirements with the quantity on hand. If there is a shortfall, a purchase requisition may be created and the buyer calls the vendor to place a purchase order.

When supplies are received, they are inspected and moved to the supplies storeroom for further issue to the service as it is performed. A "supplies received" voucher is completed. The supplier issues an invoice, which is entered into the purchaser's accounts payable system. The supplier issues a statement of all outstanding invoices monthly, which is matched against the purchaser's outstanding invoices. The purchase order is matched with the supplier invoice, and the vendor is paid during the next check-processing cycle.

An activity management system would identify and analyze these activities. The activity analysis provides insight into how to restructure the process. For example, a purchasing department study might conclude that all the activities other than scheduling services and paying suppliers are non–value-added and could be eliminated. Furthermore, other value-added activities can be improved. Consider a new procurement process that is triggered by the weekly service schedule. The weekly schedule is sent to the supplier, who delivers supplies daily in accordance with the schedule. The supplier is paid weekly on the basis of units shipped. As a result, activities other than scheduling services and paying suppliers are eliminated.

ACTIVITIES ARE COMPATIBLE WITH TOTAL QUALITY MANAGEMENT

Total quality management (TQM) strives for perfect quality in every activity/business process an organization performs. It emphasizes the importance of quality in every aspect of operations. TQM has two objectives: (1) to produce a service right the first time and (2) to work for continuous improvement. TQM emphasizes the need to treat all service functions as processes (activities) and to strive to improve the various activities/business processes. The traditional service cost model—which separately collects wages and salaries, supplies, and other costs by service, rather than by activity—is not compatible with the TQM philosophy. The effect of a process change on a service cost cannot be easily determined. Activities are processes and are therefore compatible with TQM.

ACTIVITY MANAGEMENT IS COST-EFFECTIVE

A management system must be only as complex as is necessary to achieve the required benefits. It should not be so simple that it fails to provide enough information to support enterprise excellence. To paraphrase Albert Einstein: A management system should be as simple as possible, but no simpler! Managers who simplify service operations and eliminate waste do not wish to introduce a service costing system that identifies what happened in the past. Knowing a variance, after the fact, can only help to prevent a repeat problem. To prevent a variance from occurring in the first place is the only logical way to manage. The key to excellence is to plan well, implement process controls, and then to have a simple after-the-fact reporting system to ensure that the plans and process controls are indeed working.

Activity management facilitates the understanding of a complex service environment by breaking it down into individual activities/business processes. The planning of an organization's activities/business processes provides a basis for identifying needed changes. After the planned changes are identified, install process controls to ensure the activity is executed perfectly in accordance with the plans. At this point, a simple after-the-fact actual cost system of activities/business processes can be implemented.

Activity management can be applied to an entire organization, various service operations, a department, or a work cell. The activity focus permits a flexible cost management system that decouples the organization's structure from the functions performed. The decoupling of activities from the organization facilitates an adaptable and flexible **cost accumulation** procedure to support multiple reporting objectives (e.g., activities, business processes, services, functions, customers, channels of distribution, citizens).

An activity management system is typically first implemented as a separate management system rather than a replacement for the financial system. This avoids the need to change the accounting model, which is acceptable to auditors and external agencies. For example, today the activities of accounts payable, payroll, and human resources are seldom treated as part of service cost. However, these activities are traceable to services through activity measures such as the number of different supplies used in a service (purchasing department), number of employees (payroll department), number of new hires (human resources department), or number of new support services (MIS). Rather than being traced to services through the same modified financial system used to support external financial reporting, these activities can be traced as part of a separate management accounting system.

ACTIVITIES ARE EASILY UNDERSTOOD BY THE USERS

Activities are "natural" identifiers because they are easily understood by such diverse groups as marketing, sales, operations, administration, MIS human resources, engineering legal, customer service, quality accounting, and top management. Activities such as processing payroll checks, issuing purchase orders, expediting orders, and testing new services are universally understood throughout the organization. Thus activities provide an effective medium for communication between accounting and operational personnel because they correspond to familiar service terms and events.

Conversely, much of today's management information is presented in financial terms rather than in user-friendly terms. For example, when costs are allocated among departments, users do not understand what composes the charge, and consequently cannot relate it to their activities and tasks. Similarly, variance analysis comprises a significant section of a college course on managerial accounting. It is no small wonder then that nonaccountants have a difficult time understanding the components of variance analysis. As a result, they often question the fairness of the charge and feel they have little information with which to control cost.

ACTIVITIES/BUSINESS PROCESSES LINK PLANNING AND CONTROL

Feedback is essential to control. It is crucial that planning (e.g., strategic, decision support, investment, and so on) and control (cost management) be linked, because management needs information to make necessary adjustments to achieve the plan or to make modifications to the plan. Anticipating problems is essential.

Today much of the information provided to management is derived from different information systems. Inconsistency among systems complicates the management process of planning, monitoring, and calling attention to problem areas in order to achieve anticipated results. Without a consistent planning and operational control system, it is difficult for managers to achieve their plans.

Activity management provides a logical framework ensuring that the control systems represented by the cost management and performance measurement system is consistent with the planning systems. Activities form the common denominator that links the planning and control processes. In an activity management approach, the organization's decision support system and cost management would be activity based.

Knowing an activity/business process cost assists in planning and budgeting. Each organizational unit is analyzed to determine the current activities and cost per activity output. This information represents the current level of service. The impact on the budget of changes in service level (workload) can thus be identified and incorporated into budget updates and used to analyze performance.

ACTIVITIES INTEGRATE FINANCIAL AND NONFINANCIAL PERFORMANCE MEASURES

Increasingly, competitive advantage accrues to organizations that manage nonfinancial performance by compressing lead/cycle times and improving quality. Unfortunately, today, too much attention is focused on short-term financial performance—profit margins, return on investment, revenue in excess of expenses for nonprofits, expenses in excess of budget for government entities, and similar measures. An activity management system provides a vehicle for evaluating the total performance of an activity/business process, including cost, time, quality, and flexibility.

In activity management, performance is measured as the cost per output, time to perform the activity/business process, and quality of the output. Process controls are monitored to ensure that the planned levels of performance is achieved. Also, the people responsible for each activity/business process are made accountable for continually improving the performance of their activity/business process.

ACTIVITIES HIGHLIGHT INTERDEPENDENCIES

Activities are interrelated over time. For example, a service cannot be performed until it has been determined how the service is to be performed. Because most costs are determined by decisions made early in the life-cycle process, it is important to understand the interrelationships among activities. If a restaurant menu is designed to have over one hundred entrees, then both number of other departments and costs will be affected. There will necessarily be increased costs for the purchasing department, higher storage costs, more spoilage, advanced skill requirements and compensation for chefs, and longer food preparation time due to increased diversity.

Today's cost accounting systems do not portray the time interrelationships among activities. Costs are accounted and controlled as they are incurred. An understanding of the inputs and outputs of activities clarifies the linkage among activities. This visibility provides insight into the performance of an activity/business process by highlighting its link to the activities that cause it to be executed, so that corrective action can be applied to the original cause of cost.

ACTIVITIES FACILITATE LIFE-CYCLE MANAGEMENT

Life-cycle accounting is defined as the accumulation of cost and performance for activities/business processes that occur over the entire life cycle of a service, from inception to abandonment. The life-cycle concept is significantly different from conventional practices, which expense many costs in the current period rather than match them to future services.

Life-cycle accounting requires the separation of accounting practices and risk. Today, risk is managed by expensing costs as incurred. The conventional cost accounting model distorts service costs by expensing a major portion of a service's cost before service begins. It is a common, conservative practice to expense marketing research, site selection, initial marketing and brochure design, development, and all other service preproduction costs as incurred.

Accounting for risk by conservatively expensing activities for which a future benefit is planned makes it difficult to measure the success or failure of those expenditures. Significant investment is made in these activities, but the conventional model does not measure the return on that investment. The conventional model also encourages people to consider many of these expenditures as discretionary when success in today's marketplace requires continuing investment in research, development, and marketing.

A *Wall Street Journal* article stated that "U.S. contractors are largely mired in decades-old practices fostered by a competitive-bid process that critics say discourages innovation and emphasizes cost over quality." As a result of this lack of research and development, the U.S. share of major construction contracts worldwide fell from 50 percent in 1980 to 25 percent in 1988. The Japanese have come up with construction robots, as well as "mastered techniques for tunneling and invented devices that safely separate a building from its foundation in case of earthquakes," according to the *Wall Street Journal*. The technological advances have enabled the Japanese to cut cost by shortening time of construction. "Mighty-Hand," a construction robot developed by Kajima Corp., can install a precast concrete wall in less than twenty minutes, compared with the hour it takes when installed by conventional methods. Kajima built a six-mile automobile test track for Nissan in ten months versus a normal period of eighteen months by using a new computer-controlled paving machine. In the same way manufacturing companies are using "design for manufacturability," some builders are using "design/build" systems, in which contractors and architects work together in order to save time and money for owners. These examples show the importance of continuing investment in research and development in order to maintain and increase market share.

Most agree that designing a service for ease of production is most efficiently done during the research, design, and development stage of a service's life. Problems are much more easily and efficiently resolved at this time than once the service is being produced.

These service preproduction costs directly affect current earnings under the conventional model, encouraging managers to place many services into service production prematurely so as to reflect positive short-term performance. Finally, expensing many of these service costs as incurred means that the actual cost of a service is unknown and the service may in fact be selling at a loss while the organization reports a profit. For example, the federal and state governments could in fact be running prisons at a cost much greater than they realize. If they knew the life-cycle cost, they might decide to contract these services out to independent companies.

An example of activity-based life-cycle management can be seen in the treatment of all the costs related to remodeling a freezer section for frozen juices in a grocery store. Activity management traces the support and administrative costs of this remodeling to the services for which the change is being made (frozen juices). Traditional service costing, however, allocates all this support and administrative support cost to a volume-related measure such as sales of the entire store or sales of total frozen foods. This approach allocates an equal amount of support or administrative cost to each dollar of sales. Frozen food lines with the most total dollar sales incorrectly pick up most of the new freezer costs. Indeed, the process of attaching costs to services based on some arbitrary measure such as direct labor, direct costs, or sales leads to an incorrect analysis. In reality, the new freezer for frozen juices should be traced totally to frozen juices and not to all frozen foods nor to sales for the entire store.

Even though this analysis may show that frozen juices are unprofitable, stores should ask their customers about their preferences and use activity management techniques to reduce the cost of providing frozen juices.

ACTIVITIES IMPROVE DECISION SUPPORT

Activity management provides information that gives a realistic picture of the impact of a variety of decisions on current activity consumption. This assists managers in determining service line mix, pricing, developing a do-it-yourself/buy strategy, assessing new technologies, and making other important decisions.

Consider a financial organization that decides to get into the credit card business in order to have a more complete line of services for its customers. The new service requires legal advice, card design, procurement, marketing, financial analysis, and other activities. Although introducing this new service may not require hiring new advertising, purchasing, or accounting personnel, it does affect their workload. Over time, as new services are added, the demand for these activities increases to the point where new staff is required. Without visibility of activities, the relationship between these new services and profitability would be obscure.

To be profitable, the new service must show a greater total revenue at the end of its cycle than just the total of **all directly traceable** costs. Revenue must cover research, design, initial marketing, and other start-up activities. Traditional systems that use volumes (direct wages and salaries, total direct costs, equipment usage, or sales) for absorbing over-head spread these costs over all services, including the existing services. The traditional cost system therefore reports that the low-volume specialty services are among the most profitable services sold by the division, which is a direct conflict with reality.

An activity management system, however, would trace costs to services on the basis of actual activity usage. The resulting service cost would show that low-volume services such as handling hazardous waste—as opposed to non-hazardous waste—are more costly than had been previously thought. Using this information, management can consider a range of alternatives—such as dropping certain services, increasing their price, changing their design, changing who does the service (e.g., bring in a sister company to perform the specialty service), or other techniques to lower cost.

SUMMARY

Activity analysis is the set of techniques used to identify the significant activities of an enterprise and analyze their cost and performance in detail. Activities are the heart of an activity management system. Analyzing an organization in terms of activities/business process ensures that plans are transmitted to a level at which action can be taken, facilitates goal congruence, highlights cost drivers, supports continuous improvement, and enhances decision support systems.

5

ACTIVITY ANALYSIS

The purpose of this chapter is to:

- Describe several approaches to activity analysis
- Provide guidelines on aggregating and decomposing activities
- Describe and contrast common techniques for gathering activity information
- Present a seven-step activity analysis methodology

Activity analysis identifies the **significant activities** of an enterprise in order to establish a clear and concise basis for describing business processes and for determining their cost and performance. A structured method of analyzing the outputs of an organization and identifying the processes that generate the output is known as **activity analysis**. It fosters a common understanding of how an enterprise functions in order to improve enterprise performance, including profit, quality, and timeliness. Specifically, activity analysis provides valuable information about an organization such as:

- What is done
- How much work is done (workload)
- How the work is done
- Cost of doing work
- Quality of work
- Time to perform work
- Output of work
- Customer/supplier relationships
- Service relationships

Activity analysis leads to activity management. **Activity management** supports excellence by providing a formal management system that compels people to understand their work and how it contributes to achieving strategic objectives. ABM changes traditional management practices to guide managers to emulate best practices and establish process controls to ensure consistently good performance. ABM supports the quest for continuous improvement by providing managers with new insights into customers of activities and business processes and by permitting managers to adopt management practices that encourage greater added value by all associates. ABM is the effective planning of the enterprise's activities and the achieving of consistency in performance of activities to achieve its objectives. The intent is to plan what an organization should do (activities/business processes) to achieve the organization's objectives, and then institute process controls to ensure activities are performed perfectly. This management approach converts underplanned and externally determined daily operations to goal-oriented and systematically planned ones. Activity management reallocates time and systemizes work methods to improve the effectiveness of activities/business processes even in a dynamic environment. Activity analysis supports multiple objectives including:

- Customer satisfaction
- Organizational restructuring
- Business process redesign
- Improved quality of services
- Time reduction
- Improved planning and budgeting
- Continuous improvement
- Gainsharing
- Employee involvement

ACTIVITY ANALYSIS OVERVIEW

Activity analysis is used to decompose a large, complex organization into elemental processes (activities) and the outputs of the activities that are understandable and manageable. Activity analysis is based on the observation that an entire system is too large to manage, but its individual activities are not.

An activity analysis develops an understanding of the way an organization currently functions. Activity analysis leads to activity planning, which determines the resources (and hence skills and staffing levels) required to support a given level of service, and indicates how business processes can be streamlined by eliminating redundant and wasteful activities/tasks.

All organizations must meet their objectives to survive. Their expenses must be in line with their revenues. The government, whether federal, state, or local also needs to balance its budget. Otherwise, future income must be devoted to pay for debt resulting from past expenditures. The consequence is spiraling debt, a lower standard of living, and decreases in service. Prudent management is necessary to ensure that money is spent by government to most effectively assist its citizens.

One objective of activity analysis is to improve enterprise performance by emulating the best practices of an activity/business process. Such a determination of best practices is possible only if activities are consistently defined. A comparison of cost and performance in several organizations that perform a common activity can identify useful similarities in the practices of those organizations. Such a comparison is impossible without a consistent definition of the activity.

AGGREGATION AND DECOMPOSITION

What an organization does (activities) can be viewed from a number of different levels. This is discussed in the next section.

The process of combining activities into functions or business processes is referred to as **aggregation**. Aggregating activities common to a function/business process provides a basis for directing management attention to high-cost areas that might otherwise be obscured in numerous individual activities. Functions are analogous to the forest that one views instead of the trees (activities/business processes).

The process of breaking down an activity into tasks and operations is referred to as **decomposition**. Essentially, it involves looking inside the activity to model the detailed workings of its internal tasks. Tasks, being the work elements of activities, are at the appropriate level for introducing change. Performance improvement is best achieved by decomposing activities into tasks and then restructuring the tasks.

WHAT IS ANALYZED?

Activity analysis defines the significant outputs of an organization and the activities (processes) that create the business processes. An activity (process) is a series of repeatable, robust tasks that can be continuously improved and the variability removed. The key points of this definition is that the activity is a process that is:

- *Repeatable* Repeatability occurs when a process is done more than once. Repeatability facilitates establishing "best practices" and is the opposite of ad hoc.
- *Robust* Robustness occurs when a process is adaptable to changes in the environment in which the activity operates. A robust activity minimizes the adverse effects of unutilized capacity.
- *Consistent* Consistency occurs when a process output is identical because the process is repeated in the same way.
- *Continuous improvement* Continuous improvement occurs when a process performance is better than its previous performance.

The focus is that the activity is a process that can be improved. This is not to be confused with a business process, which is a series of activities where the output of the first activity becomes the input of the next activity and so on.

To ensure a good process definition, the activity analysis should identify the following information:

- *Activities*: what the enterprise does—a collection of specific tasks that make up the job assignment; their relative timing and importance in achieving organization goals
- *Input/output*: the transactions that trigger the activity (input) and the service resulting from the activity (output)

No matter which activity analysis technique is used, the same basic information must be obtained, such as the nature of the activities, inputs, outputs, methodologies, and technologies. Some of the important information that should be associated with an activity includes:

- Organization unit (cost center)
- Business process that the activity is part of

- Resources needed to provide the service

    Wages and salaries of employees that do the activity

    Labor hours

    Labor grade

    Technology required to do the activity

    Machine type (e.g., scanners, computers, fax machines)

    Number of machines (e.g., phones, copiers, computers)

    Capacity (storage)

    Unit of capacity (e.g., number of phone lines, megabytes of memory)

    Quantity per unit of capacity (number of calls/phone line)

    Facilities (e.g., office, hangar, store, warehouse)

    Supplies

- Traceable administrative overhead expenses
- Time

    Elapsed (e.g., order receipt to order delivery)

    Process (e.g., time to process insurance policy)

- Value-added/non–value-added indicator
- Quality measure
- Inputs/outputs

    Customer/supplier

    Description of input/output

    Frequency

    Unit of measure

    Sources of input and destination of output

    Volume

It is important to determine activity workload patterns. The pattern of activity occurrence determines whether most inputs arrive at certain times of the day, month, or year. Understanding the patterns of activity occurrence is important for setting service levels and determining activity/business process capacity.

The evaluation of activities should not be limited to cost alone but should also include performance measures. Performance includes both system performance such as technical characteristics (storage capacity, store size, and air conditioning capability) and system effectiveness (availability, dependability, and the like). The focus of the activity/business process analysis is on system effectiveness.

Performance measures should be defined for every significant activity/ business process. The aim of performance measures is to monitor how the activity/business process is performed in terms of the quality of its output, timeliness (ability to deliver the output at the scheduled time), and flexibility (ability to cope with changes in volume, scope, mix, technology, and requirements).

The resources (factors of service operations) used to support the execution of an activity are assigned during the activity analysis stage. Activity costing determines the resources such as capital, people, travel, occupancy, supplies, scanners, bar coding, application programs, and personal computers used to support an activity.

Activities are analyzed as they exist at the time the analysis is performed, not as they should exist, not as they existed in the past, and not as they exist in similar organizations. If the activity analysis does not reflect the reality of the business, it will be impossible to construct a viable improvement program.

Activity analysis is concerned with facts—information about activities, not individual employees. A first-rate activity analysis must be the result of a thorough analysis, or it cannot be depended upon as an objective source of activity information.

ACTIVITY ANALYSIS METHODOLOGY

An activity analysis is a communication tool that provides a set of structured information about what an enterprise does. The activity definitions must provide a logically consistent and demonstrably accurate representation of the totality of the enterprise to be a useful part of the decision-making process.

The following sections describe the principal steps required to perform an activity analysis. These steps should be regarded as guidelines, because the specific organizational environment in which the activity analysis is performed may demand differences in approach.

STEP 1: DETERMINE ACTIVITY ANALYSIS SCOPE

An essential prerequisite to activity analysis is a definition of the specific problem or business decision to be analyzed. A clear statement of the problem ensures that the analysis is applied to an area of potential improvement. The problem definition leads to selecting the segment of the organization to be analyzed. Typical problems to be solved include:

- Customer satisfaction
- Market share expansion
- Cost reduction
- Business process improvement
- Time reduction
- Quality improvement
- Service profitability improvement
- Reorganization
- Increased flexibility
- Customer profitability
- Service breadth issues
- Decreased redundancy

Activity analysis should start with a pilot program that covers only a segment of the organization. Typical segments include an entire operating unit, a department, a channel of distribution, or a business process. This limits the range of activities specified in the activity analysis so that the information can be efficiently gathered. For example, an organization faced with competition that uses rapid service introduction as a competitive strategy may apply activity analysis to the process of introducing new services in order to highlight unnecessary and redundant activities. The only activities analyzed would be those affected by the new service introduction process.

At the scope identification phase, it is important to commit to changes that will be implemented. Activity analysis identifies improvement opportunities. They will remain opportunities until management commits to releasing people, redeploying people, disposing of equipment and inventory, or investing or dropping service lines. Too many organizations stop at the analysis phase and do not take action. It is easier to analyze than to act. The steering committee and implementation team must agree to the necessary sustaining actions. There must be an explicit commitment to employees in terms of empowerment, changing performance criteria, providing job stability, and/or sharing in productivity improvement.

An important start-up activity is to collect background information including:

- Organization charts
- Office layout graphs
- Fixed asset register
- Information systems statistics
- Previous activity information
- Job descriptions
- General ledger
- Information flowcharts

This information will be used throughout the activity analysis phase.

STEP 2: DETERMINE ACTIVITY ANALYSIS UNITS

An organization chart and headcount summary provide a starting point for the process of understanding activities. The purpose of the organization chart and headcount summaries is to ensure that the structure of the organization is fully understood and that the whole organization has been covered. The organization chart is checked by senior management to ensure that it is current and accurately reflects the existing operational structure.

If an organization is so small that one person does a variety of activities, then it might make sense to call that person the activity. For example, if one person prepares payroll, hires, administers benefits, does salary review, and so forth, then the organization might change these activities to tasks and just call the activity "manage, human resources."

STEP 3: DEFINE ACTIVITIES

Step 3 in the process is to define activities by selecting an activity approach, determining activity definition criteria, and deciding on collection techniques. This step involves analyzing historical records, analyzing organization units, analyzing business processes, analyzing business functions, performing engineering studies and reconciling activity definitions.

Selecting an Activity Definition Approach

The decision to use an organizational, business process, or functional approach to defining activities depends on the desired purpose of the study and the resources and time available. The advantages and disadvantages of each approach are summarized on pages 115 to 126.

Activity Definition Criteria

As defined previously, an activity is a process that produces an output. An example of an activity follows:

Input	Activity	Output	Output Measure
Vendor Invoice	Pay Invoice	Vendor Check	Number of checks

Input Supplier	Activity Customer
Vendor	Vendor

Resources	Task
15 min of AP clerk	Locate PO
3 min of AP computer system	Find supplies receipt notice (RN)
5 square feet of space, furniture depreciation	Receive vendor invoice (VI)
	Match PO/RN/VI
	Enter data into computer
	Edit and correct data
	Expedite payment
	Consolidate multiple payments to vendor
	Computer generated payment
	Manual payment
	File documentation

There are several rules of thumb for determining whether a definition of an activity is sufficient. These include:

1. Use Verb + Objective (optional) + Noun to characterize the activity as a process:
   Verb is the action
   Noun is the result
2. Activity must have a discernible and homogeneous output

3. Typically, an activity is done primarily by an individual person (minor steps done by other people are tasks)
4. Activities must represent a significant level of expenditure
5. Activities must support process management
6. Ignore your organization's services when defining activities. A service should never influence the activity definition
7. Keep it simple!

Examples of good and poor activity definitions follow:

Good	Poor	Explanation
Deliver mail $35/delivery	Mail $116/batch of claims	Not verb/noun Workload is not a batch of claims
Pay employee $10/employee	Payroll $1,500/payroll run	A function Workload is not a payroll run
Operate cash register $1.30/customer	Operate cash register $8.20/hour	Too global Hour is input measure—not a workload measure
Contact customer $85/contact	Visit customer $85/trip	The objective of the activity may not be to visit customer, but to contact customer; decision to visit customer can be changed

Data Collection Techniques

There are several methods for collecting activity data. The most common methods include:

- Ask employees
- Watch employees
- Randomly sample work
- Record work

Each activity definition method uses measurement tools with its own unique advantages and limitations. The primary techniques include:

- Interview
- Observation
- Workshop
- Self-analysis
- Activity sampling

In selecting the appropriate data-collection technique, the two key criteria to consider are the degree of precision and the cost of measurement. The more precise measurement techniques require considerable training to apply and, as a general rule, require more time to collect the data. Additional training and analysis time increase the cost of measurement.

Activities should be defined with a verb and a noun. Activity names may be persons, places, or things that play a role in respect to a particular activity. Do not use generic labeling terms such as data, activity, or output. These terms lack the specificity required for activity analysis.

In performing an activity analysis, it is important to use a structured approach. The use of worksheets and work distribution charts helps to analyze time and activities, and ensure a consistent analysis. A sample worksheet follows:

No.	Activity	Duration	Input	Output

A work distribution chart summarizes all the activities performed by the employees in a given department. It provides a basis for verifying that all major activities have been recorded and examines the distribution of time to activities.

The following sample work distribution chart summarizes the appropriateness of each data collection technique to the activity analysis approach selected.

Employee 1	EH	Employee 2	EH	Employee 3	EH	Employee 4	EH	Total hours	% of Total
Check credit	20	Check credit	20	Check credit	6	Check credit	4	50	31.3%
Invoice customer	12	Invoice customer	12	Invoice customer	4	Invoice customer	15	43	26.9%
Update records	4	Update records	7	Update records	16	Update records	10	37	23.1%
				Check supplies	12	Check supplies	6	18	11.2%
Order supplies	4	Order supplies	1					5	3.1%
				Research problems	2	Research problems	5	7	4.4%
Total hours	40	Total hours	40	Total hours	40	Total hours	40	160	100 %

EH = Employee Hours

3a: Analyze Historical Records

An analysis of historical records involves the use of service operation statistics compiled over a period of time, perhaps a month or year, to determine what a department does and how long it has taken in the past to process the input of an activity. A starting point for this process is any past activity analysis. In certain cases, an organization might have recently undergone a one-time analysis of its operations as part of a zero-base budgeting, office analysis, or special project. Alternatively, some individual organizations maintain private labor reports or other local reports that identify activities. Finally, a study of information systems statistics provides insight into activities. Computer operating systems maintain statistics on transaction codes and record volume. This information is an excellent source of activity volume.

3b: Analyze Organizational Units

Activities can be defined by studying the organizational units that perform or manage a functional area to determine how each unit completes its specified objectives. This approach relies to a large extent on various people's knowledge of the organization's operations.

An organizational analysis normally uses a subjective estimate of experts to define activities. The method queries the most knowledgable experts (e.g., department heads or key associates) to identify current activities and the resources allocated to accomplish them. The activities and time allocations recorded are based on the judgment of the experts. The primary data-collection techniques include interviews, questionnaires, panels of experts, and observation. The disadvantage of an organizational definition is that it requires a significant number of iterations and rethinking as business processes and functions are defined.

An organizational analysis is an iterative process of studying individual organizations to develop an initial list of activities, and refining the activity definition with subsequent analysis. The seven key steps in an organizational analysis include:

- Analyze job classifications
- Review computer records
- Interview key personnel '
- Observe activities

- Review diaries and logs
- Consult panel of experts
- Review checksheets

Analyze job classification

An organizational definition of activities starts with an analysis of job classifications. From the organizational chart, the number of staff assigned to each job is extracted in order to calculate the number of full-time equivalent employees. The total hours are broken down by job classification into normal and overtime. The analysis determines what each job classification does and how much time is apportioned to each activity.

During the process, a functional description of each organizational unit is developed to identify its mission. Next the staffing level, including job grade/classification is determined. Typically, this information is obtained from staffing charts and job descriptions and validated through interviews with department managers. The activities performed by each job category and the percentage of time spent by each job category on a specific activity are defined.

Review computer records

The interview is supplemented by a review of the current computer systems that support activities. The review determines the availability and level of data available from the computer system and identifies the frequency of data collection and the integrity of the data.

Interview key personnel

The interview technique asks the people doing activities (interviewees) what they do. This process obtains activity information by questioning the people most directly involved. The most important advantage of the interview technique is that the direct person-to-person contact usually provides the best understanding of the job. The drawback is that the employee may provide incorrect information. Countless studies have demonstrated that when people's descriptions of their jobs are compared with an actual record of what they do, large differences appear.

The interview process consists of four main steps:

1. Determining who to interview
2. Educating the interviewee

3. Conducting the interview
4. Providing feedback to the interviewee

Determining who to interview. The interview process starts by determining who to interview. The primary objective of the interview process it to determine what the organization does. The interview process should interview as few people as possible to satisfy this objective. A secondary objective is to gain commitment from the people in the organization to the final activity definition. Often, additional key people are included in the interview process to gain their support rather than to improve the definitions.

The interview process should always begin with the department manager. Often managers are promoted because of experience and technical skills, and are an excellent source of information. However, the interview process should start with the manager even when he or she is new to the department because it is politically important to gain his or her support. The manager, with guidance from the interviewer, should then suggest additional people to interview.

One method of determining who to interview is to select significantly different job classifications from the organization analysis worksheet. The manager should suggest the most knowledgable person with the job classification. Alternatively, select an employee who has been working in the department for a long time and has performed numerous jobs.

In any case, at least two people should be interviewed to isolate any perceived differences.

Once the people to be interviewed are identified, an interview timetable is prepared. The interview timetable lists the people to be interviewed and the time, place, and date. It is important to clearly schedule the interviews because people are taking valuable time from their daily activities. A rule of thumb for preparing the interview schedule is to allow up to two hours per interview and one to two hours to write up the results immediately after the interview. Avoid doing interviews back-to-back without the write-up time, otherwise it is difficult to remember the fine points of each interview. Normally an interviewer can conduct 2 to 3 interviews per day.

Educate the interviewee. Activity analysis can be very threatening to the people being interviewed. If a person being interviewed does not know why they are being interviewed, they will often assume the worst. Therefore, explaining the objective of the activity analysis to the interviewee is very helpful in gaining their trust.

Another techniques to allay employee fears is to provide articles and written materials about Activity Management. An employee can see from the written material that the techniques have been applied successfully at other organizations.

Conducting the interview. The interview situation should be relaxed. The interview should take place in the employee's office or in a neutral conference room. A round table is preferable to avoid a confrontational situation. It is also ideal to have a well-respected member of the department other than the manager or supervisor present to ease the nervousness of the interviewee, and ensure the correct interpretation of questions and answers.

It is ideal to have one project leader involved in all interviews. An important objective of activity analysis is to have consistent definitions. Consistency is facilitated by having the same person present at all interviews.

Typical questions an interviewer might ask include:

- What do you physically produce when you do your work?
- What do you do?
- What are the different things that your organizational unit does?
- What parts of your organization support other organizations or projects?
- What would cause you to add more staff?
- Why do you do your work?
- Why is one output different from other outputs?

Providing feedback to the interviewee. Always write up the results immediately after the interview. A copy of the interview notes, completed questionnaire, and worksheet should be sent to the interviewee to check for accuracy and completeness. Also, another team meeting should be held after the initial activity definition is complete to share results with the entire department.

A questionnaire is the least expensive method of gathering activity information but provides the least consistency. A questionnaire is effective when used in conjunction with an interview. It allows the respondent to consider the questions that will be asked and to gather any necessary information prior to the interview. Generally speaking, questionnaires are most successful when completed by white-collar, managerial, and administrative employees.

An interview checklist serves as a guide to ensure that all critical information is analyzed. A sample interview checklist that was developed as part of one organization's activity management project follows:

1. Verify organizational structure.
2. Request a current staffing chart.
3. What are the major classifications of people?
4. What direct/indirect services does your department provide?
5. What are the major functions of your department?
6. Request any flowcharts or pictures that help illustrate how functions are performed.
7. Review service list.
8. Are all the services/functions included?
9. Rank services in terms of their importance.
10. What are the most labor-intensive, costly, time-consuming operations/services?
11. What are the bottlenecks? What are the causes of the bottlenecks?
12. How do you track the amount of activity in your area?
13. What is your current workload?
14. How do you keep track of your cost/labor?
15. Do you have a workload forecast? How was it developed? How does it vary from time to time and why?
16. Do you have a personnel loading and forecast? How was it developed?
17. What computerized reports and databases are used? What information is input into the system, and how is it done?
18. What information and other support do you need from other organizations that would improve your operations?
19. How do other organizational units increase your workload?

The interview process provides an initial list of significant activities performed by job category. The employee occupation code is a key indicator of the types of activities performed. For each occupation code, the key activities and percentage of total time spent on activities is assigned by departmental managers. The percentage of time spent on each activity varies primarily when the activity changes or the level of activity volume changes.

Through the interview process a preliminary definition of activities is developed. The final output of this step is a listing of activities with a narrative text that describes each activity. The magnitude of the activity is based on estimates of time spent on each activity. For example, a study of occupational codes for a supplies control department revealed the following:

Labor Grade	Type	Hours
2540	Administrative	100
2900	Administrative	300
9050	Operational	1,500
9075	Operational	600
	Total	2,500

Interviews with managers and supervisors determined that the following key activities were performed by the supplies department:

- Receive incoming supplies
- Deliver incoming supplies
- Control outgoing supplies
- Store supplies
- Manage and administer employees
- Train employees
- Other

These activities were selected because they represent a significant portion of the department's time and cost.

It is important at the outset of the interview process that a standard definition of an activity be established. Different people define different activity models for the same subject area differently simply because they adopt different points of view. Therefore, the activity definition perspective must be clearly understood by all members of the activity analysis team so that a consistent definition of activities evolves.

One useful method of ensuring a consistent definition of activities is to use an **activity dictionary** to determine typical activities in a department. An activity dictionary provides a consistent starting point for defining activities by listing generic activities according to functions performed in a "typical" organization within an industry. It provides a base line for defining an initial list of activities for any service environment, from the smallest to the largest. The generic activities relevant to a greater or lesser extent depend on the individual organization.

An activity dictionary provides a list of typical activities within a function. Examples of functions include:

- Marketing and sales
- Service operations and quality-control
- Research and development
- Finance and administration
- Logistics and field support

The activity dictionary identifies the important activities that are performed by job classification within a function. Each activity is presented in the form of a short statement of **what is done** (not how or why). The type of data normally included in an activity dictionary includes:

- Activity
- Activity description
- Inputs (triggers)
- Cost drivers
- Output measures
- Performance measures
- Business process
- Input supplier
- Activity customer
- Tasks
- Resources
- Function activity relates to

The activities in the dictionary are tailored to the specific organization under consideration. Whether the generic activity is appropriate to the organization being studied is based on frequency of performance, cost, and time spent on each activity. Additional organization-specific activities that are not part of a generic dictionary must also be defined.

It is important to be careful when using an activity dictionary. Some important points to remember include:

Do	Don't
Use by interviewer	Use by interviewee
Use as guide to structuring activity	Use verbatim

A method of validating an initial definition of activities is to determine how activities are used in the decision-making process. The interview team must have a preliminary understanding of the decision-making system so that model scope, objectives, and viewpoint can be established to define activities based on typical uses of activity information.

Observe activities
The interview process should be augmented by a physical observation of the unit being analyzed to identify recurring activities. The observation process is different from a detailed time-and-motion study. Observation is the nonscientific process of watching the activity being performed.

Review diaries and logs
Logging is a semi-formal technique of recording what an employee does. The employee records the daily activities in a log or self-reporting diary. This method enables the analyst to gather information on the activities performed and the percentage of time spent on each. However, it requires considerable diligence on the employee's part, and many employees simply lack the skill and discipline to record their activities in clear, concise language.

Consult panel of experts
Where the department being studied is in an unstable environment or where activity analysis is being applied to newly created activities, a panel of experts can develop a consensus definition of activities based on their experience. Activity information can be obtained by assembling a group of employees from the area being analyzed or supervisors from other divisions performing similar activities to develop a consensus list of activities.

Review checksheets

A checksheet records the number of activity occurrences. It is used to gather activity data based on sample observations in order to detect patterns. Checksheets answer the question, "How often do certain events happen?" Activity checksheets are normally used as part of an activity sampling technique.

Ratio delay studies

Calculate the amount of time a process is delayed in relation to the amount of time the process is being performed. This approach gives insights into non-value delay time.

Finally, consider **storyboarding**. This is a technique invented by either Leonardo da Vinci or Walt Disney. Mark Moelling formerly of Johnson & Johnson has used it very successfully in getting departments to define activities quickly. He uses various-colored post-it notes to differentiate between activities, tasks, and business processes. He has several key people from a department define activities, tasks, and business processes. If they find that they have a task instead of an activity, they can just move the post-it notes around as they refine the department's activities. Storyboarding is a quick and successful way to define activities and tasks.

3c: Analyze Business Processes

The business process approach to activity definition studies the business processes that transcend organizational boundaries (e.g., service design, supplies procurement, service operations, planning and customer service) and defines them in terms of major activities. The business process of procuring supplies, for example, is composed of activities such as the issue of purchase specifications, the selection of vendors, the issue of purchase orders, the receiving of supplies and/or people, the storage of supplies, and the payment of vendor accounts. These activities occur in a structured sequence and are interconnected by a flow of information.

A business process analysis traces inputs to outputs. Until information to perform an activity is delivered to the activity in a timely and correct manner, an activity cannot be effectively performed. The procedure is to determine the sequence of activities by following the flow of information/transactions/physical service from one activity to another. The output of one activity becomes the input to another activity. When the inputs and outputs of individual activities are connected, a business process emerges.

A flow chart is a common tool for analyzing business processes. As a pictorial representation of all the activities in a business process, it is an excellent graphic technique for examining how activities in an organizational process are related to one another. A flow chart uses standard symbols to represent the type of processing, as illustrated here:

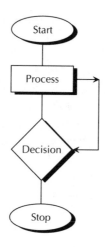

This approach is particularly applicable to continuous process operations (e.g., claims processing, collecting waste, dropping bombs, issuing food stamps). Activities are defined by observing the physical flow and the change in the service.

The advantage of this approach is that it is possible to graphically link all inputs and outputs among activities and identify interdepartmental communication routes. The disadvantage of the approach is that lateral or general activities like supervising and secretarial support may be missed. A limitation of the business process approach is that hidden processes such as general management, expediting, nonconformance, and others may not be identified and included in the analysis.

A business process analysis usually results in a revision of the initial activity definition developed by interviews. Organizational units might aggregate activities that are an important part of a business process. Often key activities, inputs, or outputs are missing. This results in disconnected business processes. The activity gaps require a reanalysis of the affected activities.

The final output of a business process analysis is a set of diagrams or flowcharts that represent the interrelationship of activities and their information flows. An important tool used to define business processes is the Plan–Evaluation–Review–Technique (PERT) chart, which portrays the relationship between activities and their timing.

Plan–Evaluation–Review–Technique (PERT) Chart: Underwriting a Mortgage

		Time (days)		
1	15	1	18	1
Complete application	Order & receive credit, appraisal, survey reports	Approve loan by committee	Prepare mortgage documents	Disburse funds

As you can see from the above example, the loan mortgage process starts with completing an application, ordering credit, appraisal, and survey reports, approval by the loan committee, preparing mortgage documents, and finally disbursing the funds. As the figure shows, the longest amount of time is taken by preparing the mortgage documents.

3d: Analyze Business Functions

The functional approach to activity definition breaks down each major function (e.g., secretarial, quality, security) into activities. For example, the function of purchasing may be broken down into activities such as finding suitable suppliers, negotiating prices, agreeing on quality standards, and maintaining records. This approach allows common activities (e.g., secretarial services) to be considered across the whole business. It treats common problems as part of a single analysis.

The description of a function should be as precise as possible when answering the question, "What does it do?" The description should contain a verb and noun only. The verb should be active and should have a direct object. The noun should be measurable. For example, the function of maintenance could be defined as "maintain equipment." The overhaul of the equipment is a specific activity that is a subset of the maintenance

function. The maintenance is performed for the equipment, and is a major
item. An example of a functional activity analysis follows:

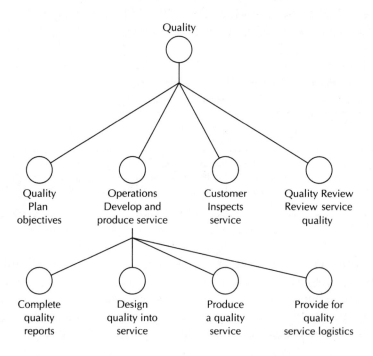

There are two primary methods for reporting functional activities. The
first is to treat them separately from the organizations performing the
activity—that is, count them only once. The second method is to include
the activity in the organization performing the activity and report it as a
"ghost" function. A ghost function means that each department analyzed
has, for example, its secretaries included in its total cost. However, the
activities can be summarized across the whole business—that is, in more
than one format.

3e: Perform Industrial Engineering Study

An industrial engineering study is a precise but expensive method of
defining activities. In this approach an industrial engineering team uses
standard work analysis techniques such as timed observation to assess an
organization's significant activities.

An important engineering method is time observation. This is a method of gathering activity information by watching employees perform their daily activities. It is particularly appropriate for office or clerical jobs that are repetitive, are of short duration, and have observable work cycles. If some elements of the job occur at infrequent or irregular intervals, observation is not practical. Managerial and administration jobs are not suitable to this approach.

3f: Reconcile Activity Definition

Although all the activity definition approaches have different starting points, they are merely different methods of defining the same set of activities, and therefore require reconciliation. For example, the business process of procuring supplies consists of activities that are a subset of various organizational units involved in the supply procurement process.

When choosing an approach, one must define the desired purpose of the analysis. For example, a functional analysis is rarely appropriate for analyzing a possible restructuring of a business. Only when the relationship between various departments is determined can alternative organizational structures be suggested.

Additionally, it is important to make use of existing information. For example, an activity analysis might have been previously used as a process improvement, system design, office modernization, or quality project. It is prudent to use the existing information and then to supplement it with further activity analysis.

It is advisable to begin an activity analysis with an organizational review of each department followed by a business process or functional analysis. The activity definition is completed after the subsequent analysis. The secondary activity definition techniques are used to fine-tune or reconcile the activity definition.

STEP 4: RATIONALIZE ACTIVITIES

The key to meaningful activity definition is to structure an activity list that provides a sufficient, but not excessive, level of detail. The more simplified the activity list, the easier it is to manage and positively influence business decisions. An overly detailed activity analysis invalidates many of the benefits of an activity management system. Such systems are complex and not focused on key decision variables. They therefore tend to be expensive and ineffective.

One organization developed a list of over 1,700 activities for a single department. Needless to say, this is a bit much to manage. What they really defined was 1,700 tasks, not activities. Remember to focus on the *significant* 5–10 activities per department.

An excessively simple system, however, does not provide the level of detail necessary to properly account for activity cost behavior. The degree of simplification is influenced to an extent by the complexity of the organization, but it is far more likely to be affected by the type of organization and the type of customer. Separating activities with different cost behavior patterns results in more accurate service costing and improved decision making. The cost of measurement will be higher, however, because two sets of measurements must be made.

Often the information flows between activities within an organizational process provide insight into how to decompose activities. A flow of information or outputs delineates activities. When an organizational process analysis identifies a new information flow that cannot be accounted for by previously defined activities, the activity should be decomposed. Similarly, when an organizational process analysis identifies no flow of information between two previously defined activities, the activity should be aggregated.

Although the activity management system requires tasks to be aggregated into activities, performance improvement requires an activity to be broken down into tasks, operations, and elements. Activities/business processes often are too global to identify where changes should be implemented to improve activity performance; only tasks/operations/work elements can be modified.

Rationalization Criteria

Aggregation of activities with very different economics is best avoided. For example, it would be desirable to keep advertising and promotion separate, since the relevant cost driver for advertising may be total organization market share, whereas promotional costs are often specific to a service or customer.

One must guard against aggregating dissimilar activities. Otherwise a single activity measure will inaccurately reflect the cost behavior pattern.

As a consequence, a service cost based on the amount the service consumes of each activity is not a valid indicator of the total resources apportioned to the activity. An invalid activity measure makes it impossible to predict and manage the correct amount of resources necessary to produce a given amount of output.

For example, when the activities of designing a new service are combined with those of custom design for a specific customer, the cost behavior patterns are significantly different. The design costs for new services benefits the service over its entire life cycle and should be capitalized. The costs associated with custom design for a specific customer benefit only a specific order and should be directly charged to that order. Two separate and distinct activities should be established.

The most common problem facing the activity analysis team is not decomposing activities but aggregating them. It is human nature for people to explain what they do at a significant level of detail; that is, they articulate their tasks. All the individual tasks necessary to perform an activity should be combined and treated as part of a single activity.

To summarize, when decomposing activities, one must break down each major activity to the level of detail where costs are proportionately distributed among activities with homogeneous inputs and outputs. The magnitude of the activity is based on estimates of the time and resources apportioned to each activity. The process requires a balance of costs at a level of detail that is fine enough to be manageable, but not so fine that it becomes complex and expensive to operate. It is tempting to decompose an activity too far. There are several tests to determine whether an activity has been decomposed to a low enough level:

- If an activity is part of a decision-making process, then it is an ideal candidate for decomposition. The decision scope and objectives aid in determining which activities to decompose.
- If knowing the cost and performance of a further decomposed activity would not make any difference to the decision model, then the activity probably should not be decomposed any further.
- If an activity corresponds directly to a repetitive action in the enterprise that is already at its lowest level, then the activity should not be decomposed further.
- If an activity cannot be modified, then it is of little value to decompose it further.

- If at least one input and one output for each activity cannot be detailed, then the definition of the activity must be redefined.

- If there are multiple primary outputs from an activity, the activity should be decomposed into a number of different activities or thought of in terms of sub-activities. It is permissible to have by-services (services that are of little value that are produced as part of the main service; e.g., selling liquor on a plane might be considered a by-service since it has little value in relationship to the plane ticket itself).

- If an activity cannot be associated with a business process, an alternative activity definition should be sought.

- If the inputs and outputs of an activity are identical, then there is a strong possibility that they are tasks and part of the same activity. For example, two activities identified by the accounts receivable department are:

  Check customer credit

  Approve/disapprove customer credit

  Both of these supposed activities are triggered by a customer order, processed by the same person, and the output was an approval or rejection. Therefore, they are tasks rather than activities.

- If an activity has multiple inputs and outputs, then it should be decomposed into different activities or some inputs/outputs might be ignored if they are not material.

- The activity must add value to be of benefit to an organization.

- The activity should always be something that could be subcontracted to a separate organization.

STEP 5: CLASSIFY ACTIVITY AS PRIMARY OR SECONDARY

Each activity should be classified as primary or secondary. A **primary activity** is one whose output is used outside an organizational unit. Activities used within a department to support the primary activities are **secondary activities**. Activity classification is necessary to apportion the cost of secondary activities to the primary activities for service costing and to manage the ratio of secondary activities to primary activities.

STEP 6: CREATE ACTIVITY MAP

An activity map identifies the relationship between functions, business processes, and activities. Creating an activity map is the first step in analyzing alternative organizational processes and activities to perform a function. Activity management maps the organization's activities and describes the cost structure in terms of activity consumption. An example of an activity map follows:

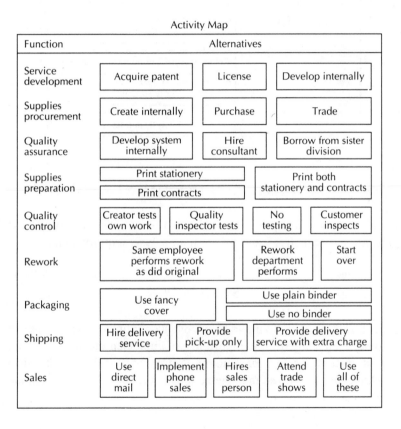

After organizational processes and activities have been mapped to functions, the next step is to map activities to business processes. This step is illustrated in the following figure:

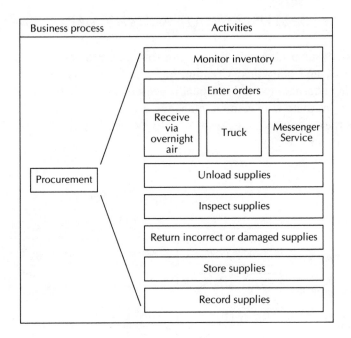

STEP 7: FINALIZE AND DOCUMENT ACTIVITIES

The final step is to compile a composite list of activities that supports the organizational objectives and functional analysis requirements.

SUMMARY

As organizations begin to move from cost accounting to cost management to activity management, the importance of implementing an activity management system becomes paramount. Activities provide valuable insight into what causes costs, so management can take the initiative to eliminate or minimize these costs.

6

ACTIVITIES OF AN ENTERPRISE

The purpose of this chapter is to:

- Define the functions in an organization. A consistent and comprehensive activity definition is essential to ensure an effective activity management system that permits comparison of divisions and departments of organizations.
- Serve as a basis for introducing changes to activities/business processes to facilitate quality improvement, time reduction, cost reduction, and performance improvement. Today, special attention to these issues, through activity management, is justified more than ever before.

In order to exist, any enterprise, regardless of size, must perform certain essential functions. An individual employee in a small organization might perform numerous activities, or the organization might contract the activities to outside professionals. Large organizations (e.g., governments) require hundreds or even thousands of employees to support all the needed functions.

All the different activities of an enterprise must be coordinated to operate effectively; this requires organization. The organizational structure is the means by which an enterprise coordinates the activities of different elements—supplies, labor, energy, physical assets, time, and money—to achieve the organization's objectives. Organization is the grouping of activities/business processes to facilitate the flow of information, accomplish work, and control the processes. The groupings vary from organization to organization and enterprise to enterprise, but they always include the basic functions described in this chapter.

Traditionally, there are five major groupings of functions in an enterprise:

1. Marketing and sales (e.g., the post office's overnight mail)
2. Service Operations and quality assurance (e.g., producing a charity's literature concerning its cause and ensuring it is correct and complies with the law)
3. Research and development (e.g., new phone service)
4. Finance and administration
5. Logistics and field support (e.g., field backup for police)

MARKETING AND SALES

The marketing and sales function appears in organizations in different forms. An enterprise may have a single marketing function that includes marketing or sales, or it may have two separate departments. The mission of the marketing function is to direct the flow of services from the producer of services to the user.

In simple terms the marketing function determines the consumer's or user's needs and informs the market of the organization's services. The sales function consummates the transaction. It tells service operations what to produce and when and where to ship. It provides the necessary customer service to resolve any problems with the service. In the Department of Transportation, an equivalent to a marketing function is performed by the engineers who tell the legislature that money is needed for additional roads. The sales function is fulfilled by the people who sell this idea to the legislature and the voters.

Various types of marketing organizational structures exist. Many marketing departments are organized by service lines. Others are organized geographically so that a given department is charged with marketing in a specific region. Still others are organized by major customer accounts. These different groupings do not in any way change the basic mission of marketing nor the activities performed. They merely change the assignment of responsibility for performing the activity.

Marketing determines the demand for existing services and identifies the need for new services. This is done by the **market research** subfunction. The market research group evaluates market needs and translates them into requirements such as the features required for a given service. Market research reexamines the service's intended and actual uses, identifies the features or specifications for the perceived demand, and verifies those features that are absolutely essential to the marketability of the service.

A second mission of marketing is to communicate to potential buyers what services the organization has to offer and at what price. Advertising and promotional activities are key communication activities. Through such efforts market share can be maintained or expanded.

Still another marketing activity is forecasting and planning the number of units of services to be produced to support demand. Unit Costs and projections are closely intertwined.

Finally, the marketing function processes orders, handles requests for service literature, maintains a distribution network, and schedules delivery dates.

The main activities in the marketing function include:

Activity	Decision
Specify service/service line	Number of variations
	New service introduction
	Service abandonment
	Service modification
Provide customer service	Range of guarantees
	Pricing of service activities
	Service cycle time
	Hours of operation
Develop distribution channels	Number of distribution channels
	Types of distribution channels
Determine discount policy	Discount policy
	Special orders
Promote sales	Type of promotion
	Frequency of promotion
Process orders	Processing sales/service order
Determine service programs	Selling/providing service

Customer service is a subfunction of marketing that resolves service problems after shipment to the customer. The activities associated with customer service resulting from service problems are non-value-added because they are wasteful and damage customer satisfaction. As the term is used here, it does not include customer service used to listen to the customer to determine new ideas for services. These costs are significant where there is warranty cost, defect cost, repair cost, and cost of sales, in addition to the cost of the customer service department. The redesign of a service that is introduced, along with cost-reducing changes, simultaneously reduces warranty cost.

Field testing is normally a customer service activity. A network of field service representatives conducts field tests of pilot service operations (e.g., a new menu item at a pizza restaurant). In many instances, when service changes are extensive or laboratory testing cannot determine the reliability of a new design, field testing under actual user conditions is absolutely mandatory.

SERVICE OPERATIONS AND QUALITY CONTROL

The service operations function involves procuring necessary supplies, transforming supplies into finished services, and shipping the finished service to customers. The quality-control function ensures that all supplies entering the office and all finished services leaving it conform to predetermined specifications.

The service operation function consists of direct service operation activities that can be organized in different ways, depending on factors such as volume of services, diversity of operations, single- or multi-office operations, proximity of the offices, and so on.

Service Operations

The **supplies management** function regulates the movement of supplies and finished services through the facility. The key supplies management activities include:

- Schedule service operations
- Coordinate service changes
- Receive and ship supplies and services
- Purchase supplies
- Control supplies inventory
- Expedite orders
- Certify vendors

Service operations scheduling informs the service operations what equipment (e.g., computers, scanners, airplanes, trucks, trains, fire engines) is needed to produce a given service. It plans the sequence of operations and determines economic quantities. Service operations scheduling checks inventory and employee availability, and triggers the procurement of equipment, personnel, and supplies. It plans the dates when finished services will be available for shipping or installation.

Receiving and shipping are the two points within the facility through which all supplies pass, both when entering the facility and, in some cases, when leaving it.

The procurement function, often called purchasing, involves the purchase, receipt, inspection, and storage of supplies. It plays an important role in selecting vendors and subcontractors, and in negotiating prices and lead times. Purchasing notifies service operations of the lead times, and service operations, in turn, uses them to plan service operation schedules.

The inventory control group determines how much or how many of a supply or service is on hand and where it is stored.

The service operation engineering subgroup (called by different names depending on the service being provided) includes the following:

- Industrial engineering (e.g., conduct time-and-motion studies of postal carriers)
- Service operations engineering (e.g., decides how to process claims in an insurance organization)
- Office/facility engineering (e.g., decides office, store layout)
- Equipment design (e.g., decides equipment configuration)

Industrial engineering determines the labor content of the service operation processes and specifies the best service operation methods. It conducts time-and-motion studies and develops service standards. Service operation engineering decides how much of the service can be produced in-house; and what needs to be subcontracted. It determines which processes and equipment to utilize and which kinds of computers, scanners, bar coding, and computer-aided design (CAD) equipment are needed. The equipment design section designs any special equipment, software, and fixtures (e.g., airplane, truck, or auto maintenance equipment). Office engineering, or facilities, assigns floor space to specified people and activities. It is responsible for the design of dedicated electrical lines for computers and communications, special security, shredding of confidential documents, and removal to storage. Office engineering often includes building and grounds maintenance.

The quality-control function is charged with ensuring that all services leaving the facility conform to predetermined marketing and customer specifications. Incoming inspection and vendor control ensure that all incoming supplies and purchased items conform to specifications. Quality control also monitors all office activities to make sure that they consistently produce acceptable services. It provides the necessary measuring instruments, handbooks, and calibration, and determines the in-process inspection points. It is responsible for final service testing.

Finally, the service operation function is responsible for service operations. Here the service is created and made into a finished service, packed if necessary, and shipped (e.g., via overnight air delivery if necessary) or held for pickup. Design errors, poor estimates, and wrong assumptions eventually surface in the service operation area.

The main activities of a service operation and quality-control function include:

Activity	Decision
Supplies management	
Plan service operation	Schedule equipment/employee
Coordinate changes	Schedule operations
Receive supplies	Receive by department/organization
Control service operation routing	Check inventory
	Sequence steps
Schedule receipts	Schedule supply receipts/personnel
Control inventory	Manage physical inventory/inventory records (e.g., medical drugs)
Supplies procurement	
Plan procurement	Analyze supply specifications
	Value engineer service
Select/evaluate vendor	Select vendor
	Assess vendor
Negotiate price, delivery	Negotiate with vendor
Ensure quality	Assess quality control of vendor
Complete purchase order	Issue PO
Certify vendors	Ask how to improve quality
	Audit vendors
Coordinate vendors	Expedite orders
	Track POs

Activity	Decision
Distribution	
Manage finished services	Control finished services
Deliver finished service	Select methods of delivery to customer/citizens
Package service	Package finished service
Support in field	Support customer on site versus only at office or both
Manage spare parts	Carry spares (e.g., computers)
Select dealers	Select dealers (e.g., computer dealers)
Service engineering	
Industrial engineering	
Determine time standards	Specify labor content
Select methods	Determine best methods
Justify investment	Evaluate/select equipment
Complete special projects	
Prepare customer quotations/ proposals	
Service operation engineering	
Conduct do-it-yourself/buy analysis	Subcontract
Plan procedures	Select procedure
	Select equipment
Facility	
Allocate floor space	Design facility/office
	Plan facility and office layout
Control environment	
Maintain grounds and building	
Set up equipment	Select type of furniture, equipment
Design equipment	Decide which computers, scanners, faxes, delivery trucks
Quality control	
Set quality specifications	Set customer specifications
Inspect incoming supplies and personnel	Control quality of incoming supplies and personnel
Inspect in-process operations	Establish in-process inspection points/guidelines
Inspect finished service	Control quality of finished service
Control equipment	Control databases/scanners/POS (point-of-sale)
Maintain/operate inspection equipment	Set maintenance policy for inspection equipment
Evaluate/qualify vendor quality	Select/qualify vendor
Certify service	Determine cost and time to obtain service certification

RESEARCH AND DEVELOPMENT

The research and development (R&D) function develops new ideas for services. This function designs new services and modifies existing ones. Research and development provide the link between marketing and service operation. The needs of the market-place are used to determine the direction of research and the services to be produced. Customer and citizens wants, as perceived by marketing/legislature, are translated into the designs.

Examples are new menu items, hotel services, insurance policies, financial services, types of mortgages, phone services, bank products, types of movie or TV program, types of homes, hospital services, software, retailing concepts, rides in amusement parks, fund-raising events, drawings, military equipment or citizen services. Then specifications are used by service operations to create the services.

The R&D function is expected to stay at the cutting edge of technologies relevant to an organization's industry, whether it be telecommunications, real estate, transportation, nonprofit fund-raising, or government services. In particular, it is expected to maintain the capability of solving special technical problems and to actively participate in the initial phase of new service development. During that phase it must validate a new service concept and develop broad guidelines for service engineering—all within market-determined cost and performance targets.

R&D includes the following activities:

- Basic research
- Applied research

The service development function translates service specifications into a service design. It continues to develop and refine the design until it falls within the limits of cost, performance, and service producibility. Finally, it creates the documentation necessary to support planning, including the specification sheets, bills of activities, and drawings.

The testing laboratory is set up to determine the practicality of the new services identified by the R & D group (e.g., new procedure in a hospital). The degree of sophistication of the laboratory may vary with the nature and complexity of the organization it services, but it is always an inseparable part of the research and development cycle. Laboratory personnel usually design and build the test programs, perform the testing, and collect test data. They assist with the design of the tests, selection of test programs, and interpretation of test results.

The technical administration function is an administrative and service function within research. It includes the complete spectrum of services where all the necessary designs, documents, and drawings are developed and maintained, bills of activities are structured, and service numbers are issued. Original drawings, documents, original bills of activities, service structure records, and final test reports are maintained and distributed to all who need them.

The technical administration group manages the development and maintenance of research software and computer hardware, and maintains the library.

The research development function includes the following activities:

- Develop new services
- Modify services to improve and meet customer requests
- Test new service concepts
- Administer research function

The main activities of a R&D function include:

Activity	Decision
Develop new service	When, how, what new services
	Pricing
Modify existing services	Number of services
	Number of service modifications
	Pricing
Perform basic research	New service requirements
	Pricing
Develop procedures for new service	New procedure requirements
	Pricing

FINANCE AND ADMINISTRATION

The finance and administration function gathers and processes financial and performance data. The finance function provides the financial planning required to manage the cash flow to meet organization financial obligations. Loan payments, dividend payments, and disbursements for personnel and services purchased are coordinated by the finance department. The financial function issues all recurring financial reports; manages payroll, accounts payable, and accounts receivable; and prepares plans. It administers the budget, and provides guidelines and assistance during the budget cycle.

An important subfunction of finance is managerial accounting. Managerial accounting compiles the service operation expenses and maintains service cost data.

The **management information system (MIS)** is responsible for acquiring and maintaining the computers and peripheral equipment, and for developing and maintaining the software programs used to support the computer facility and the application programs. The computer is usually used to process data within the management information system, which can include such items as analysis of quality deviations or headcount and skills bank. It might even be used to run the entire scheduling plan. For example, in a transportation company, the computer program might start with the sales forecast and end with such items as the city pairs; number of needed planes, trucks, or railroad cars; and required personnel.

The finance and administration group often includes the function of labor relations and human resource management. It is responsible for items like personnel recruitment, employee training, performance appraisal administration, compensation management, employee counseling, vacations, health plan administration, and so forth. It also provides assistance in labor contract negotiations and administration.

The main activities of a finance and administration function include:

Activity
Accounting and Finance
Managerial accounting
Acquire data
Create and maintain bill of activities
Report to management
Accounts Payable
Answer inquiries
Receive invoices
Pay vendors
Manage cash

Activity (Continued)

Accounts Receivable
  Issue invoices and credit memos
  Check credit and maintain credit files
  Receive/process remittances
  Manage cash

Payroll
  Maintain and collect employee data
  Issue checks

General ledger
  Close books
  Coordinate budget
  Report to shareholders & government agencies
  Conduct internal audits

Organization management
  Legal decisions
    Create and review contracts
    Create and review acquisition documents
    Handle lawsuits
  Public relations
    Inform stockholders/citizens about operating
      results
    Answer stockholder/citizen questions
    Inform about new services
  Treasury
    Make and pay off loans
    Make investments
    Prepare stock offerings
  Tax decisions
    Plan federal, state, international taxes
    File income taxes
    File property taxes
    File sales taxes
  Planning
    Create strategic plan
    Create operating plan
  Insurance decisions
    Purchase insurance
    File claims
  Benefits and salary administration
    Manage medical benefits
    Manage pensions
    Manage vacations
    Manage salary reviews

Activity (Continued)

Management information systems developments, operation, and maintenance
Operations
  Buy hardware
  Maintain hardware
  Develop and administer security requirements
  Hire and manage personnel
 	
Applications
  Software
    Buy and update operations software
    Buy and update managerial software
      Bill of activities
      Activity-based management
      Activity budgeting
    Buy and maintain EDI software
    Buy and maintain databases
 	
General management
  Plan for future
  Review salaries
  Develop staff
  Solve problems
 	
Human resources/personnel
  Report to government
  Maintain employee data
  Administer benefits
  Train employees
  Negotiate and administer union contracts
  Recruit new employees
  Manage retirement program

LOGISTICS AND FIELD SUPPORT

Logistics are all activities connected wth getting the finished service to the customer. For example, an insurance company mails the claim, an explanation of benefits, and the policy to the policy holder; a consultant delivers a report in person; a lawyer or doctor expects the client to visit his or her office; a warehouse uses planes, trains, trucks, boats, and mail to deliver products to customers.

Field support activities are included in the installation training and repair activities of an organization. It also includes training for updates and may include handling customer complaints.

SUMMARY

In order to exist, all organizations must perform certain basic organizational functions. Each function has a specific mission around which activities are structured. The manner in which an organization accomplishes its activities (tasks) to achieve its mission will vary dramatically among organizations, but there is a degree of commonality at the activity level. Tasks differ dramatically between different organizations as they seek to maximize the efficiency of information flow and the accomplishment of activities/business processes.

Developing an understanding of the typical activities in an enterprise provides an excellent foundation for structuring an activity management system.

7

ACTIVITY COST

The purpose of this chapter is to:

- Describe how to calculate an activity cost
- Explain the role of used and unused capacity rather than variable and fixed costs in the decision-making process
- Describe how activity cost is used in the decision-making process
- Describe how to select an activity (output) measure
- Identify important activity cost considerations
- Describe an activity measure and distinguish it from a cost driver
- Discuss how activity measures are used to influence behavior

An activity cost is the total cost of all traceable cost elements required to perform an activity. Costs are considered traceable when the cost element (e.g., salaries, supplies) can be traced directly to an activity, business process, or other cost objective. A cost is **allocated** when it is charged to another activity/business process or cost objective on a basis other than direct traceability. The rationale for allocating costs is to ensure that business decisions include all costs.

Activity cost is expressed in terms of an **activity (output) measure**, by which the cost of a given activity varies most directly. Examples of activity measures include number of reports, number of purchase orders, number of sales presentations, number of deliveries and number of payroll checks. The activity volume represents the number of occurrences of the activity. Finally, activity costs are traced to cost objectives such as services, business processes, functions, and orders on the basis of usage of the activity.

An activity is a homogeneous grouping of cost because resources are assigned to produce a specific output. **Homogeneity** means that variation in an activity is explained by a single activity measure. For example, the activity of manually processing a payroll check is homogeneous since the number of payroll checks (activity measure) dictates the level of resources applied to the activity. As long as the output or method of performing the activity is not changed, the necessary resources will vary in proportion to the activity measure. Thus, **homogeneous cost** is a cost in which each activity has a similar cause-and-effect relationship to the cost objective.

The conventional approach of capturing costs at the cost element level aggregates multiple activities for a single cost element. To know the total travel expenses of a department, for example, does not provide any insight into the activities that generate the need for travel. To control travel cost one must first understand the factors (e.g., activities) that drive the need for travel.

The conventional approach to managerial accounting considers only the total cost of an activity without regard to its output. Measuring activity effectiveness requires knowing the amount of output (activity volume) as well as the cost factors traced to an activity. The selection of the activity measure is critical since it makes visible the factors that influence activity volume and subsequently cost. The factor also allows management to perform ''what if'' analysis.

Expressing the cost of activities by unit of activity output provides a means to accurately trace costs to services, business processes, functions, customers, projects or other cost objectives. For example, to properly trace costs to services, one must determine how much of each activity is consumed in the service. Consider a complex service that requires an average of twenty purchase orders, as opposed to a simple service that requires one purchase order. An accurate service cost is possible only when the complex service absorbs a greater proportion of the purchase order activity than the simple service.

Knowing the cost per activity is also important in managing cost. The cost per activity output is a performance measure. To judge the effectiveness of the purchase order activity, one must know the number of purchase orders processed. For example, the current cost to process 6,000 purchase orders is $120,000 or $20 per purchase order. If, as the result of improvements in the purchasing department, the organization is able to process 10,000 purchase orders for the same cost, the new cost per purchase order would be reduced to $12.

Knowing the cost per activity is important, because it facilitates a comparison of the cost of processing purchase orders within different divisions in order to identify the most cost-effective operation. The most proficient operation can then be studied to specify a set of best practices that aid other organizations in improving work methods. For this reason, activity cost is expressed as a measure of activity volume by which the costs of a given process vary most directly.

Sometimes, an activity may have to be broken down into subactivities. For example, the activity "hire associates," might be divided into the following subactivities: "hire nonexempts," "hire local exempts," and "hire exempts in the field." These subactivities might be costed out separately if their tasks are substantially different. For example, "hiring nonexempts" might include tasks such as reviewing applications and calling former applicants. "Hiring exempts local" might include the tasks of placing newspaper advertisements and/or hiring an agency. "Hiring exempts in the field" might include the tasks of placing newspaper advertisements, hiring an agency, traveling to the field, and having the applicant travel from the field. Although the organization might use just one activity for costing, it may need to review all three subactivities for improvement purposes.

ACTIVITY COST BEHAVIOR PATTERNS

An activity's cost behavior pattern is defined as the variation of an activity cost with changes in activity volume. It is used to predict the level of resources (cost) necessary to support a given level of activity volume. In other words, there is a close bond between an activity's cost and the number of its occurrences.

An activity cost is the cost of all traceable expenses divided by planned activity volume. A standard (planned) activity cost is the sum of the standard (planned) expenses at a planned activity volume. Thus, an activity's standard cost depends on a forecast of both traceable costs and the number of activity occurrences. The cost behavior pattern has no impact on the ability to establish a cause-and-effect relationship.

The cost behavior pattern is related to the variability of cost with activity volume. In other words, traceability is related to cause-and-effect.

An activity's cost behavior depends on several attributes of the factors of service assigned to the activity. It is a function of the capacity of the factors of activity production and their flexibility to alternative uses. The primary attributes include:

- Used/Unused capacity rather than fixedness/variability
- Influenceability
- Flexibility

Used/Unused Capacity Rather Than Fixedness Versus Variability*

Traditional managerial accounting defines a **variable** cost as one that changes in proportion to service volume in the short term. (All costs are variable in the long run). A **fixed** cost does not vary with service volume in the short run. For example, a direct laborer's cost per hour is assumed to be constant, but total labor cost may vary with service volume (a variable cost). A point-of-sale scanner's cost per unit varies with service volume, but the total cost is the same regardless of service volume (a fixed cost).

To illustrate the traditional difference between fixed and variable cost, consider the process of issuing insurance policies. An underwriter and clerical support staff are the primary factors of service operations. The technology is a computer which has a direct link to TRW, Trans Union, or Equifax for a credit review of the applicant. In this environment, there is a relatively direct relation between the number/cost of credit reports and the cost of issuing the insurance policy itself. There may or may not be a direct relationship between the clerical support staff and the number of underwriters as the number of insurance applications increases or decreases. This relationship of insurance policy application volume to clerical staff and underwriters depends on the current and expected trend in volume, other tasks that these personnel could perform, and the company's policy toward layoffs. So these personnel could be fixed costs, variable costs, or mixed (semivariable) costs.

Variable costs tend to rise or fall directly in proportion to service volume. They are controllable in the short term. Traceable variable costs might include:

- People-related costs
- Supplies costs

---

*Acknowledgment: Much of this section is based on input from William Sullivan of the Virginia Polytechnic Institute.

- Credit service fees
- Overtime premiums

For people-related costs, an hourly rate is computed by dividing the employee wage by the available hours. A service would absorb the laborers' cost based on the number of hours consumed by the service, multiplied by their hourly rate. Unused hours are treated as an efficiency or volume variance.

Technology costs are treated differently. The cost of equipment includes depreciation, which is included in overhead and is allocated to services. For example, a computer terminal connected with the credit companies described above would be a primary factor of service operations for that department. Computer support personnel, computer maintenance personnel, programmers, and others would be important, but secondary, factors of service operations that support the credit review process. There is a stepped relationship between the technology costs and service volume. Additional service volume, where underutilized capacity exists, can be absorbed without the need to incur additional cost until full capacity is reached. Also, technology is sometimes inflexible, and the terminals may not easily be changed for alternative uses.

A better way to analyze cost is to divide fixed cost into two components—actual capacity used and unused capacity. Whereas the total costs of a machine are relative to actual volume usage, the treatment of unused capacity has a dramatic impact on cost. An activity rate based on actual or forecasted capacity charges unused capacity to current period services. An activity rate based on practical capacity, however, charges current service costs only with the cost of actual capacity used. The cost of unused capacity is transferred to a management account and classified as a **non-value-added** cost. To illustrate the difference between the two approaches, consider a computer workstation that annually costs $100,000 with an actual annual usage of 5,000 computer hours and a practical capacity of 8,000 computer hours.

Method 1—Traditional fixed cost allocation based on actual usage:

$$\frac{\text{Cost}}{\text{Actual usage}} = \frac{\$100,000}{5,000 \text{ hours}} = \$20/\text{computer hour}$$

5,000 actual hours multiplied by $20.00/hour = $100,000 to service

Method 2—Modern cost based on practical capacity:

$$\frac{\text{Cost}}{\text{Practical capacity}} = \frac{\$100,000}{8,000 \text{ hours}} = \$12.50/\text{computer hour}$$

5,000 actual hours multiplied by \$12.50/hour = \$62,500 to service

$$\frac{\text{Unused capacity}}{\text{cost}} = \frac{\text{Practical capacity less actual usage}}{\text{Practical capacity}} \times \text{cost}$$

$$= \frac{(8,000 - 5,000)}{8,000 \text{ hours}} \times \$100,000$$

$$= \$37,500 \text{ to unused capacity}$$

The accounting treatment of fixed cost is a direct consequence of the accountant's view of depreciation. Organizations purchase assets with the expectation of using them to generate revenue or at least to provide a service, in the case of the government. An expense is associated with generating this revenue (or providing this service), since using the asset causes it to deteriorate. For a proper statement of net income (or revenues in excess of expenses as in the case of nonprofits), revenue generated by an asset must be matched with the corresponding expense of using it. Depreciation is the accounting mechanism used to provide this match. Depreciation takes the historical cost of an asset and systematically allocates it in proportion to the contribution it is expected to make in the generation of profit (or service) each period. It is important to note that the accountant's motivation for depreciation is the proper determination of net income. Depreciation—an expense—appears on the balance sheet as accumulated depreciation, and acts as a contra-asset against the equipment asset account.

To properly assign a computer, car, truck, scanner, office, or other fixed cost requires a reasonable forecast of future service volume. Whether the service organization produces one unit or one million units, the cost of the equipment must be absorbed.

In addition to depreciable assets, other resources are often considered fixed. They are largely related to the support of the ongoing enterprise, the so-called overhead of management, market development, accounting, finance, advertising, sales, and research. All tend to build up as volume grows, and are controllable in the long term. The primary fixed costs might include:

- Property taxes
- Rent
- Cleaning

- Maintenance of building
- Insurance
- Executive salaries
- Auditing expenses

Other **shared (nontraceable)** costs are franchise fees and business registration taxes. These include all the other costs incurred to support the organization that are not readily traceable to any activity. They are included in overhead of the organization, division, or facility as well as SG&A (selling, general, and administrative) expense.

The distinction between fixed and variable cost has been considered very important since it determines whether a cost changes in steps or in a linear fashion in relationship to volume. However, looking at used and unused capacity is more actionable and helps improve decision making.

Influenceability

Managers have significant influence over the efficiency and effectiveness of the activities in their area of responsibility. Managers control how activities are accomplished and select or influence the factors required to perform an activity. An **influenceable activity** is one that can be changed by the organization in the short term. The degree of influenceability varies according to timing and organization policy.

Not all activities can be changed in the short term. Factors of service operations, such as equipment and information systems, are normally changed only in the medium to long term. However, they are traceable to the activity and therefore are controllable.

Certain activities are influenced by external factors such as regulations and weather. However, even those factors are somewhat influenceable in the long run. For example, regulations require approval for a new mutual fund. Even though an organization can't influence the regulations in the short run, it can control the speed, cost, and quality of the activity/business process "obtain regulatory approval."

Flexibility

The **flexibility** of an activity is the degree to which its factors of service operations are adaptable to alternative uses. The greater the degree of flexibility, the more linear the relationship between cost and service volume. Conversely, the lesser the degree of flexibility, the more steplike the relationship between cost and service volume.

ACTIVITY COST IN DECISION MAKING

An activity's cost behavior has traditionally been an important factor in decision making. Proponents of classical contribution analysis hold that separating fixed cost from variable cost is important, because an organizational decision that leads to the recovery of all the variable costs, and at least a portion of the fixed costs, improves the organization's financial position.

Fixed costs are considered **sunk costs**. The argument is that nothing can be done to influence sunk costs, so they are irrelevant to future decisions. The debate over whether to exclude sunk cost, long-term influenceable costs, from short-term decisions has been the subject of great controversy over the years. One problem associated with sunk cost is that there is no single, consistently used definition for the term. Often, the struggle over the concept of sunk cost arises because two very different ideas are being discussed under the same title.

In the context of management decision making, sunk cost has two distinct meanings. First, it corresponds to the accounting definition of book value minus salvage value. In this context, a sunk cost is the unallocated portion of the equipment's historical cost. Depreciation is an estimated value that seeks to allocate the expense of using the equipment over its useful life. This goal is not always attainable due to factors such as obsolescence, service changes, and capacity shifts. The result is that equipment is retired before the end of its initially estimated life. Because the equipment did not generate revenue over the period estimated, some of the retired equipment's historical cost remains unmatched to a revenue-generating period. This unallocated amount is called **book value**. The book value minus any proceeds from the sale of the retired asset is called **loss on disposal** or sunk cost. In the accountant's mind it is a sunk cost because it is lost. Part of the asset's cost was never recovered by revenue generation, so this lost cost must be recovered from other sources like a capital accumulation account. For example, suppose telephone switching equipment was purchased for $500,000 and depreciated over five years using straight-line depreciation. After three years, the switching equipment is scrapped (zero salvage value) and a new one is bought. The balance sheet would appear as follows:

Switching equipment	$500,000
Less accumulated depreciation	$300,000
Book value	$200,000

The accountant views the asset as an unallocated historical cost of $200,000. The unallocated cost must be recovered from somewhere—it can't be ignored. The account must be reconciled. The reconciliation is accomplished by claiming a loss on disposal or sunk cost. So to the accountant, a sunk cost is an accounting balance equal to book value minus salvage value.

Some accountants are reluctant to trace fixed costs or allocate them to specific services because of the mistaken view that they are not controllable in the short term, and should not affect short-term decisions. Also, it is impossible to allocate nontraceable costs with the perceived degree of precision that accounting professionals normally use to develop traditional financial statements. There is a natural aversion to allocating in an imprecise manner. There is simply no way, however, to know how well or how badly a service is doing without tracing these costs.

Second, sunk cost is viewed as any cost made in the past or any cost that will not affect the decision at hand. The central theme is relevance. Since past costs are viewed as nonrecoverable and unalterable, they are sunk. They are irrelevant to the current decision. So while the accountant views sunk cost as an accounting balance that must always be recovered, decision makers generally view it as an unalterable past expenditure.

An important issue in activity accounting is whether sunk costs are relevant for future decisions. Charles Horngren, in *Cost Accounting: A Management Approach*, speaks strongly against using sunk cost. He states, "The term sunk cost should not be used at all. It muddles the task of collecting proper costs for decision making. Because all past costs are irrelevant, it is fruitless to introduce unnecessary terms to describe past costs."* From an engineering economy point of view, John Canada and William Sullivan express a similar view when they state, "sunk costs are costs resulting from past decisions or commitments and ... are therefore

---

*Charles T. Horngren and George Foster. *Cost Accounting, A Management Approach*, 6th ed. (1987), Prentice-Hall, Englewood Cliffs, N.J., p. 326.

irrelevant to the consideration of alternative courses of action.'' The common theme is that because sunk costs will remain constant for all decisions, they must not be considered relevant.

Proponents of direct traceability, however, hold that the prime factor in routine decisions is whether the cost is traceable. A routine decision is one for which the current planning assumptions are valid. Managers must, therefore, treat all assets as an investment and obtain a fair return on the investment.

Under the concept of direct traceability, the primary factor in a routine decision is whether a cause-and-effect relationship can be established between an activity and the service. Where direct traceability is established, the cost is relevant to the organizational decision. The concept is based on the observation that for routine decisions all resources represent investments, and management should recover all costs associated with the investment.

Consider the insurance company obtaining credit reports through a computer terminal. If the process is performed by a human typing up a request for a credit report, putting it into an envelope, and recording it as an outstanding credit request, this person's salary cost would be considered a variable cost and included in the decisions based on the amount of labor. If the human were replaced with a computer terminal, the service would remain identical. However, from a contribution analysis decision perspective, the cost of the computer terminal would be considered a fixed sunk cost and excluded from the decision process.

A key difference between contribution analysis and direct traceability is the treatment of future alternatives. Advocates of direct traceability maintain that the assumptions made during the planning phase are valid, and that management has a responsibility to sell services that return at least the cost of the investment or, as is the case of the government, provide services within some cost guidelines. Advocates of contribution analysis assume that all future alternatives are known and an organization would choose a mix of services that contributes the most to covering the fixed cost.

There are several fallacies involved in the use of contribution analysis for routine decisions. First, a consequence of contribution analysis is that the organization's portfolio of services is a mixture of profitable services that subsidizes the fixed costs of other services. The same is true for government entities. The amount a citizen pays for garbage disposal is often either under or over the actual cost to dispose of garbage. The resulting cross-subsidization increases the vulnerability of an organization to competitive pressures from other organizations, nonprofits, or governments. Other organizations are most likely to compete for the most profitable services, since their services are not burdened by subsidizing the fixed cost of other services. For example, many schools want to offer an MBA or engineering program because it is usually very profitable for the school. Philosophy and social services courses may be more interesting, but they are usually cross-subsidized by the business and engineering classes.

As organizations lose market share, students, or citizens, the impact on profit margins for the most profitable services is devastating because the profit margins decrease at a faster rate than the loss of sales for services being subsidized.

A second impact of selling a service that does not cover all traceable costs is that it sets a market expectation. Once a customer or citizen becomes accustomed to a certain price level, it is more difficult to raise than to lower prices (e.g., U.S. air fares or income tax rates in the early 1990s).

A well-managed organization will strive to offer a mix of self-sufficient services and manage all internal investments to ensure that financial returns forecasted during the planning stage are realized. It may be easy to forgo managerial excellence and make decisions that appear to help the short-term performance (e.g., cutting research, maintenance, or schoolteachers), but increase the long-term vulnerability of an organization.

Costs in the traceable category are controllable in either the long or short term. Generally, as an organization expands, costs tend to be far more variable than they should be, and when it contracts, they are far more fixed than they should be. This is true for most organizations, not just the government and nonprofits.

A bill of activities does not require a distinction between volume-related or non-volume-related costs. Both are traced according to actual usage rather than allocated.

ESTABLISHING A CAUSAL RELATIONSHIP

When a cause-and-effect relationship can be established between a factor of service and a specific activity, the cost is said to be **traceable**. In many cases, tracing an activity is reasonably simple because the resource is dedicated to a single activity. An accounts payable clerk, for example, can be easily traced to the activity "pay vendors." When a resource supports several activities, the resource usage must he split among them. For example, in a small organization a single person may pay vendors, collect receivables, prepare financial statements, and issue payroll.

A causal relationship exists when a factor of service can be shown to be directly consumed by an activity. Assume a clerk spends fifteen minutes processing a work order. A causal relationship between the cost of the clerk and the activity of processing work orders has been established. It is an indisputable fact that the clerk spent fifteen minutes processing the work order. Therefore, the cost of the clerk is traceable to the activity process work order.

Typical causal bases include:

Factor of Service Production	Measure
People	Time
Technology	Equipment/technology hours
Facilities	Square footage
Energy	Kilowatt hours, gallons, mcf

ACTIVITY COST CONSIDERATIONS

The cost of an activity includes all the factors of operations employed to perform an activity. The factors of service operations consist of people, equipment, travel, supplies, computer systems, occupancy, and other resources that are customarily expressed as cost elements within a chart of accounts. Each significant factor of service operations is included in cost. For instance, the activity of scheduling a service requires a person to make the scheduling decisions and a computer system to perform the necessary calculations and data manipulation. Other resources, such as office space, supplies, and a desk, are required. The cost of the activity is determined by tracing the labor, technology, office rent, computer depreciation, and office supplies to the scheduling activity.

A causal relationship has been established between the factors of service operations and the scheduling activity. An interorganizational activity supports activities in other departments. It is a resource (cost) that is consumed along with the natural factors of service operations. Important characteristics of interorganizational activities are (1) their support for other organizational activities, (2) their importance to the using activity, and (3) their ability to be located there. Support activities are often centralized to achieve economies of scale.

When costs are not traceable to activities, they are allocated on a basis such as percentage of time, head count units of service operations, total cost input, or historical data. The assumptions on which allocations are based should be documented and tested for reasonableness. The activity management system must be able to support the choice of assumptions by making clear exactly what is being costed, where the factors came from (e.g., general ledger and statistical data derived from regression analysis), and how the results were calculated.

ACTIVITY MEASURES

An **activity measure** is an output, or a physical attribute of an activity. For example, the output to the purchasing activity is a purchase order. The cost of the purchasing activity can be expressed as a cost per purchase order line or purchase order. Other activity measures include:

Activity	Activity Measure
Pay vendors	Invoices
	Checks
Collect receivables	Customer orders
	Number of collection calls
Control inventory	Number of supply items
Plan for supplies	Number of plans
Issue purchase orders	Number of purchase orders/lines
Receive orders	Number of purchase orders/lines
Store supplies	Number of supply items
Inspect incoming supplies	Number of inspections/items
Train on quality	Number of people/classes
Evaluate vendors	Number of vendors
Certify vendors	Number of certifications

Activity Measure Characteristics

Selecting the right activity measure is critical. Since an activity measure makes the output visible and changes behavior, careful thought must go into selecting an output measure.

1. The ideal activity measure is simple to understand, easy to measure, easy to extract from existing data sources, and directly related to the activity's factors of service operations. It is critical that an activity measure be economically and practically available.

2. There must be a direct relationship between changes in the volume of an activity measure and the factors of service operations. The fixed/variable distinction has less important implications than used/ unused capacity measures. Used/unused capacity helps answer the following questions: Is the used/unused capacity for future growth? When can the growth be expected? How can the unused capacity be utilized? Are there other areas of the organization that can employ this capacity? Is cross-training needed? Should we eliminate this capacity? As activity volume varies with changes in organization, operations, technology, and sales, the service factors of operations will change accordingly. Can changes in resources occur as activity volume changes? What is the short- or long-term influenceability and capacity of this activity? When changes fundamentally affect how activities are performed, the activity measure must be revalued for its relevance.

3. Activity measures extend beyond direct service operation measures. Occasionally, the number of direct labor hours will continue to be an appropriate activity measure. But there are many activity measures other than labor hours/cost within a department. For instance, number of computer reports may be relevant for a computer department, number of orders received or processed for the receiving department, number of customer calls, number of physical measures (such as pounds) of orders shipped for the shipping department, and the number of sales presentations made.

4. By determining the output and users of activity information, the manager can determine whether specific activities are within short- and/or long-term priorities. An accurate definition of current activities and desired outcomes is fundamental to achieving those outcomes.

5. Knowing the cost per activity assists in planning and budgeting for activities/business processes. Each organizational unit is analyzed to determine the current activities and cost per activity. This information represents the current level of service. Activity costs are then combined to calculate business process costs. The impact on the budget of changes in service level is easily identified for both activities and business processes.

Activity Measure or Cost Drivers

Whereas the **activity measure** represents the factor by which th given process (activity) vary most directly, the activity measure is not the cost driver. The **cost driver** is the factor that creates cost. An activity measure is a dependent variable in the sense of a regression analysis.

To illustrate the difference, consider the activity of making sales calls. As the number of sales calls increases/decreases the factors of activity production (e.g., labor, travel) must be simultaneously adjusted. The activity measure is, therefore, the number of sales calls. However, the number of sales calls is caused by factors such as customer volume, customer size, competitive environment, the distance to customer; mode of transportation; number of customer requests for sales calls or organization policy. These factors represent the cost drivers. The cost drivers are therefore the upstream causes of cost and are removed from the analyzed activity. Using quality terminology, cost drivers are the same as **root causes.**

In the previous example, the number of sales calls is a physical attribute of the sales call activity and thus meets the definition of an activity measure. It is a good activity measure because a direct correlation can be drawn between the number of sales calls and the resources required to support the activity. However, an activity measure such as the time required per sales call is related to a cost driver (root cause) such as the service design. The measure is not directly correlated to the sales call activity and hence not a good activity measure. The service design is an excellent factor to manage the time spent on sales calls, but it is a very inaccurate mathematical basis for tracing cost.

SUMMARY

An activity cost is determined by examining each organizational unit to identify its business objectives, the individual work processes (activities), and the resources allocated to achieve its objectives. Activity costing therefore identifies the way an organization uses its resources to accomplish its objectives.

The traditional distinctions between fixed and variable and direct and indirect are secondary to the distinction between traceable and nontraceable costs. Classifying costs as relating to used and unused capacity is more actionable for many decisions and for continuous improvement.

8

CALCULATING AN ACTIVITY COST

The purpose of this chapter is to:

- Describe a five-step approach to calculating an activity cost
- Describe and contrast the use of different cost types
- Describe typical cost categories and their relation to **natural expense categories**.
- Explain how to determine an activity measure

An activity cost is calculated by tracing all elements of cost (e.g., salaries, supplies, utilities, rent) needed to perform an activity. The activity cost is derived after defining the enterprise activities. It is expressed in terms of the cost put unit of activity measure. The activity measure is what causes the cost of a given process to vary most directly. Examples of activity measures include number of claims processed, number of garbage containers emptied, number of customer requests handled, number of sales calls made, and number of payroll checks issued. Finally, activity costs are traced to cost objectives such as services, business processes, customers, channels of distribution, projects, and orders, based on the usage of the activity.

The key steps in this process are:

1. Select cost basis
2. Trace resources
3. Determine activity performance measurement
4. Select activity measure
5. Calculate cost per unit of activity output

STEP 1: SELECT COST BASIS

Selecting a cost basis involves the following steps:

- Determine cost type
- Determine cost time horizon
- Classify life-cycle activities

1a: Determine Cost Type

The first step in determining an activity cost is to select the type of cost. An activity management system can use a variety of cost types such as actual, standard, budgeted, planned, or engineered. The choice of cost types is influenced by the type of cost in the existing accounting system, but this should not be the only factor influencing the choice.

The typical cost bases include the following:

- Actual cost
- Budgeted cost
- Standard cost
- Planned cost
- Engineered cost

Actual cost. An actual cost is the exact cost paid for an expense element (e.g., supplies) based on a financial transaction. The advantage of using an actual cost is that costs are always current and reflect changes in the organization environment. The disadvantages are that actual costs are very sensitive to short-term fluctuations in the operating environment and represent costs that have already been incurred. Activity managment will exacerbate this situation. In activity management, an activity cost varies based on changes to both the cost elements and the volume of the activity measure. Cost reported under today's cost element-based cost systems varies primarily with changes in the cost of the cost elements, because activity measures are not incorporated.

Budgeted cost. A budgeted cost reflects management's opinion, generally a most likely or hoped-for scenario, regarding future financial circumstances. A budget is the outcome of a periodic, structured planning process. It is used as a yardstick against which actual performance is measured. A budget encourages adherence to a plan and motivates different units in an organization toward the same goal. However, budgeted costs should be used with discretion as a basis for an activity management system because they represent what management wants to happen rather than what does happen. When major changes have occurred in an organization or for new services, budgeted costs may be very useful.

Standard cost. A standard cost is a predetermined cost based on normal conditions of efficiency and volume of service. The cost is predetermined by either an analytical study or a management fiat. The advantage of a standard cost is that management control is directed only to costs that vary significantly between actual and standard (variance analysis).

Standard cost and its associated variance analysis often incite inappropriate behavior. For example, to achieve a favorable supplies price variance, a purchasing officer might buy in large quantities. However, the storage and obsolescence costs associated with the stored supplies often exceed the cost savings attributable to the favorable price variance. This results in greater cost to the organization. A source of this problem is that variance analysis assumes, often incorrectly, that cost control should be focused on the point of cost occurrence. In the purchase price variance example, the differences in purchase price at different quantity levels may be the only cost-related considerations directly visible to the purchasing department. The cost of supply movement, storage, and counting are buried in other departments' budgets.

Standard cost systems control cost at the cost element level, resulting in an intermingling of different cost behavior patterns. The cost of each cost element, such as labor, technology, or travel is aggregated for the department regardless of the number of activities supported. Also, standards do not portray life-cycle or organization process-related decisions. Finally, standards are set relative to current operating conditions, not competition or the philosophy of continual improvement. Thus, the standards often incorporate current operating inefficiencies and non-value-added activities into the standards.

Planned cost. A planned cost is derived from the strategic and operational planning systems. The output from the planning systems is a set of planning assumptions, including such factors as sales forecasts in dollars and units of service, number of purchase orders to be processed, and number of shipments. The planning assumptions provide a superior basis for computing activity cost because the resulting planned cost provides the feedback necessary to ensure planning assumptions are achieved or corrective action is initiated. What differentiates a planned (forecasted) cost from budgeted or standard costs is that it is continually derived from the operational systems. Budgeted and standard costs are typically derived on a yearly or semiannual basis.

Engineered cost. An engineered cost is derived from an industrial engineering study that provides insight into how an activity is performed, and whether method improvements can increase performance. The advantage of such engineered data is that they are more reliable than subjective estimates. The disadvantage is that they are initially costly to develop. The procedure for developing engineering data is an event rather than a repetitive process, and it is difficult to reconcile with financial systems.

Most activity management systems use a predetermined cost such as standard, budgeted, or planned. Actual cost is not recommended because it is too sensitive to short-term fluctuations in activity volume. Engineered cost is an excellent source for estimating the initial activity cost of a new technology for which historical data are not available. Engineered cost is also outstanding for validating, on an ongoing basis, the reasonableness of activity cost when there is evidence that it might no longer mirror the service process.

Once a cost basis for an activity management system has been chosen, several changes must occur in the way most organizations treat costs today. Primary among the changes are the following:

1. Costs must be set at the activity or business process level
2. Costs must separate the non-value-added component of cost
3. Costs must be summarized at the organization process level to identify overall, organization-wide costs and to isolate cost drivers

Whatever the cost basis used for an activity management system, it must be reconcilable with historical cost to ensure a consistent basis for comparing actual with planned performance.

However, the use of historical data in an activity management system is subtly but critically different from its use in a traditional management system. By custom, historical cost data have been used to project the future by extrapolating from past cost. In activity management, the cost behavior pattern of activities as they exist today is understood by tracing the elements of cost to the activities that use the resources. Projecting a future cost is primarily a function of estimating the usage of the activity (as reflected in the activity measure) and changes to the cost elements. Unless the method of performing the activity is changed, the cost behavior pattern will remain constant.

1b: Determine Cost Time Horizon

After the cost basis has been chosen, the next step is to select a time period for the cost data. Stability of data is an important consideration. Monthly data are very sensitive to short-term fluctuations. Anything less than yearly data is subject to seasonal fluctuations. For example, if one were to analyze the activities of a finance department in January, one might incorrectly assume that the department spends most of its time preparing W-2s and 1099s, and closing the annual accounting records. Although yearly data is stable, it does not incorporate the dynamic changes to the business environment.

It is advisable to use quarterly or yearly data but continually adjust them for changes in the operating environment—reorganizations, modifications to activities/business processes, and the like. The monitoring of quarterly variances between actual cost and planned cost at an aggregate department/cost center level, not at the activity level except in certain cases, facilitates a continual review of the dynamic business environment. Capturing actual cost on a monthly basis at the activity level is both expensive and cumbersome, and may lead to chasing ghosts. These ghosts are created because of the sensitivity of activity cost to changing activity volumes. Quarterly variances that are consistently skewed would indicate that planned costs are incorrect and should be reviewed. In certain cases, more precise data are required, and an organization may choose to capture actual activity usage more frequently.

1c: Classify Life-Cycle Activities

Appropriate classification of activities and their costs into life-cycle segments is critical to activity management. Traditional accounting systems expense many costs associated with startup, installation, field operations, maintenance, service retirement, and disposal that should be capitalized and matched to the services they benefit. The rationale is that because the future is uncertain, predictions of future benefits are imprecise and a cost based conservatively on known events is superior to one based on forecasts.

Costs have historically been reported in small segments of time that provide a periodic "score card" of financial results typically on a monthly/yearly basis. Periodic cost reporting results in a fragmented view of costs for services and business processes whose value exceeds the reporting horizon. Service profitability, for example, is rarely computed for more than a year except when an initial discounted cash flow analysis is performed. Seldom (less than 10%) do organizations post audits of their discount cash flow analysis.

The conventional practice distorts service cost and leads to disjointed cost control. Life-cycle accounting provides a framework for the development and reporting of cost and performance over the useful life of significant assets. The life cycle commences with the initial identification of consumer/citizen needs and extends through planning, research, design, development, service operations, evaluation, use, logistics support, retirement, and disposal. The cost of these life-cycle activities, in total, represents the service life-cycle cost. Assets for which life-cycle costs are normally computed include services, business processes, projects, and systems. Examples of life cycle costs include:

Years of Asset's Life	Rearrange Office	Develop Procedures	Program Computer	Design Service	Total
1	40,000	25,000	15,000	40,000	120,000
2			20,000	50,000	70,000
3			25,000	40,000	65,000
4			10,000	20,000	30,000
5			5,000		5,000
Totals	40,000	25,000	75,000	150,000	290,000

Life-cycle classification relates activities to the period when the benefits accrue, and depicts the interdependencies of activities in different periods. For example, the output of the design service activity benefits the service over its entire life cycle. It also has a major impact on subsequent activities since, to a large extent, it limits the type of personnel, supplies, and business processes that can be used. Therefore, the design service activity represents a life-cycle cost and should be apportioned to all units of a service sold over its life.

Life-cycle activities are classified as follows:

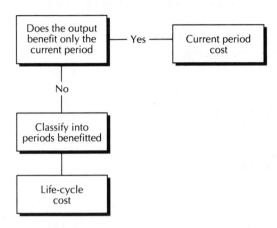

The benefits of on-going service-related activities are realized in the current period and traced to the corresponding services. The benefits of support activities may benefit either the current or future period. Consider an organization that, for example, offers a service for a special, one-time customer order. The cost of the associated activities are traced directly to the specific customer order and are not capitalized. Other activities, such as process improvements, benefit future periods. For example, when an organization develops a new service to be marketed over several years, the cost of these activities should be charged over the entire service life cycle.

Still other activities may involve the development of a new flexible service cell. These costs are traceable to the service operations process life cycle and charged to services that use the new cell during its life.

Life-cycle accounting requires that initial cost estimates be time phased and expressed in constant monetary units (dollars, sterling, yen, and so on) of the same base year. The constant monetary units should be adjusted periodically to reflect current (inflated) cost.

Activities provide an excellent foundation for a life-cycle management system because it is easy to determine whether an activity benefits current or future periods. Activities that benefit the current period are treated as a current period expense and activities that benefit future periods should be capitalized and spread over the life of the cost objective they benefit.

STEP 2: TRACE RESOURCES

Cost is traced to activities by causal relationship. The key steps in tracing resources to activities include the following:

- Determining source of data
- Grouping related general ledger costs
- Establishing causal relationship
- Tracing people-related costs
- Tracing all other costs to activities

2a: Determining Source of Data

The primary source of cost data is a general ledger. Alternatively, cost data can be derived from a detailed industrial engineering analysis or estimated relationships between similar activities and the physical and performance characteristics of a system (parametric approach).

The structure of an activity management system permits costs to be derived by any of the three methods. In most cases the general ledger is the recommended source of cost information because the costs imported under the activity management system would reconcile to the financial reporting system. This is important since it ensures consistency between financial accounting data and the activity management system. Typically, engineering studies and parametric cost estimates are used to supplement the general ledger information, particularly when historical information is not available or is not representative of normal operations.

The cost source selected for the activity management system depends on the significance of the cost and availability of information. Where high cost or significant uncertainty exists, cost estimates may be derived by more than one of these techniques. Using multiple methods allows cross-checking and validation, in which differently derived estimates are compared, analyzed, and judged.

The level of detail in the existing general ledger system rarely limits the cost analysis but rather affects the level of effort required to translate department costs into activity costs. For example, the accounts payable function may be performed by a separate department in a large organization. Translating this cost into an accounts payable activity is straightforward. However, if accounts payable is the responsibility of a large finance department with a single cost center report, a higher level of effort would be required to extract these costs in an activity analysis. Each general ledger account would have to be analyzed to determine which finance department activity it supports. This would require significant effort, but eventually the accounts payable activity costs would be isolated.

2b: Grouping Related General Ledger Costs

A general ledger classifies expenses according to types of expenditures. The tracing process is simplified by classifying cost in a department's general ledger with similar cost behavior patterns separated into **cost pools**. The entire cost pool can be input into the activity management system rather than requiring each cost element to be entered individually.

For example, consider technology costs. The cost of equipment capitalized on the balance sheet is normally limited to all the expenditures relating to its acquisition and preparation cost. This practice ignores factors such as the interest expense to finance the acquisition; nonrecurring costs such as software development, industrial engineering, and service design; legal costs; programs; accounting; consultant fees; and the cost of developing the procedures associated with the service process. These costs are carried in numerous overhead accounts. When one considers the recurring costs of utilities, supplies, maintenance, and other support services, the total cost of technology is often ten times as large as the initial investment. To hide these costs in numerous general ledger accounts is to mask their importance.

Because the decision to produce a service involves a long-term commitment to dedicate resources, it is important that the service cost system assign costs that reflect the actual amount of resources required to produce a unit of service. For a cost management system to provide meaningful information, it must mirror the service environment. In traditional service costing, a key to accuracy is the breakdown of the service process and support departments into discrete cost pools to determine an appropriate basis for allocation.

Expenditures such as salary and wages, office supplies, depreciation, insurance, and similar items are accumulated by department or cost center. The number of accounts depends on the extent and detail of the information desired by management.

For activity management systems, when the general ledger is chosen as the source of cost data, it is recommended that general ledger amounts with similar cost behavior patterns be summarized by natural expense category—labor cost, for example. Salary, employer taxes, and benefits accounts should be summarized into the natural expense category.

Natural expense categories include:

- Supplies
- Technology (e.g., electronic data interchange, scanners)
- Facilities (e.g., utilities, office rent, property taxes, property insurance)
- Information systems
- Shipping
- Travel

This section will discuss supplies, labor, and technology, and then turn to interorganizational activities.

Supplies

The cost of purchased supplies consists of the supplies purchase price and the expense of all other activities necessary to bring the supplies to the service process. This includes the cost of all activities related to the establishment, planning, acquisition, receiving, and control of supplies and purchased services. Typical supply-related expense categories include:

- *Supply purchase price*: Planned purchase costs are developed by the purchasing department for each supply and purchased service. These costs might include expected price increases, depending on organization policy.
- *Supply price variance:* this is the difference between the actual and planned/standard purchase price.
- *Scrap:* When certain supplies, rather than the operational activities, create scrap, these costs should be traced to that supply item (e.g., fuel evaporation in a transportation organization).
- *Off-fall:* When the amount of supplies of the finished service is less than the original supplies, these off-fall costs should be traced to the

supply. Supply off-fall results from the waste involved in such operations as wasted computer paper at the start and end of a ream of paper or at the start and end of a report.

Typical supply-related activities include:

- *Issue purchase order:* The cost is associated with the paperwork of placing a purchase order and following up on its progress.
- *Receive supplies:* This is the cost of receiving and storing supplies.
- *Inspect incoming supplies:* The cost of inspecting incoming supplies, including labor, cost of inspection equipment, facilities, and other traceable costs is part of this activity.
- *Move supplies:* All supply movement costs, including freight and in-process supply handling is included here. A standard organization-wide incoming freight cost percentage is used when freight cost does not vary significantly by individual order. When significant freight cost variations exist, however, they should be traced directly to the supplies ordered.
- *Support supplies procurement:* This includes costs generated by vendor evaluation, vendor certification, vendor coordination, and the supply review board. The costs associated with these activities are assigned to supply cost as vendor-related activities. It is often difficult to trace vendor-related activities directly to specific supplies. These costs are normally treated as secondary activities to the purchasing department and allocated to the primary activities.
- *Pay vendors:* This accounts payable activity is part of the procurement process and should be traced to purchased supplies. It is recommended that the accounts payable activity be charged to services, using the number of purchase orders or purchase order lines as the activity measure.

Other supply-related activities include:

- Control quality
- Store supplies
- Control supply inventory
- Plan and control supplies
- Supervise employees
- Manage supplies

Labor

Labor cost is the cost of all activities related to the acquisition, training, and support of people. These would include fringe benefits, salaries, training, physicals, and similar activities. Labor—both direct and support—is traceable to activities/business processes. Labor costs are assigned to the activities using information from the general ledger, payroll records, and staffing tables. Typical labor-related expense categories include:

1. *Salaries:* Salaries are the most significant component of an activity labor rate. Salary costs are traced at actual or standard rate by job classification.
2. *Fringe benefits:* Fringe benefits for salaried and hourly employees are normally computed separately because of significant cost behavior pattern differences between the two groups.

Typical labor-related activities include:

1. *Pay payroll:* It is recommended that the costs of this activity be traced to each department or work center according to head count or payroll check.
2. *Perform human resources activities:* Human resources activities typically include recruiting and administering benefits. It is recommended that they be charged to each department and work center according to head count or use.

Technology

Technology cost is the cost of all activities necessary to acquire and operate the technology, including the cost of capital employed to finance the acquisition, startup activities, operating activities, and directly affected support activities. Technology costs include hardware, software, and related information system support activities and service factors. Examples of technology costs include labor, depreciation, and energy. Technology-related support activities include programming and maintenance. Technology costs include both recurring and nonrecurring costs. The technology rate includes all traceable cost and uses an appropriate output measure that reflects actual usage, such as number of reports, number of orders, or number of scans.

It is recommended that a technology bill of activities be prepared. The bill of activities defines all traceable technology-related activities and identifies the amount of each activity consumed by the technology. The amount of activity usage is based on the estimated volume of output for each activity. Technology costs represent the total operating cost at normal service operations volumes.

Typical technology-related expense categories include:

- *Acquisition cost:* This is the historical cost of the equipment, based on fixed asset records and rental agreements.
- *Taxes:* These are equipment-related personal property taxes.
- *Interest expense:* This is the cost of financing the nonrecurring activities. The cost of capital is incurred regardless of whether the money is borrowed from an external source or from the shareholders.
- *Utilities/energy:* This is a direct charge only if it is significant, as in the case of fuel costs in transportation organizations. Otherwise, utility cost is included as part of facilities cost.
- *Facilities:* This cost is directly traced to technologies based on square footage. Detailed square footage is derived from office data. Total facilities-related costs and total office square footage are used to calculate a cost per square foot.
- *Small supply items:* This cost is based on estimated yearly consumption, or direct charges recorded in accounts payable as the small supply items (e.g., calculators, modems) are acquired.
- *Supplies:* This cost is based on estimated yearly consumption or direct charge recorded in accounts payable as supplies are acquired.

Typical technology-related activities include the following:

- *Facilities cost:* This is the cost of the facilities required to house the technology.
- *Industrial engineering:* This is the cost of industrial engineering support to design the service process for the new technology.
- *Programming:* This is the cost of initial programming and maintenance of programs used to control technology equipment, such as bar code and point-of-sale scanners and electronic data interchange.
- *Repair/debug equipment:* This is the cost of engineers or managers who program, debug, and repair equipment used in the service process.

- *Operate equipment:* This is the cost of the operator who tends the equipment, such as a crane operator on a loading dock, an X-ray technician, a bridge gate operator, a police dispatcher, or an attendant at an amusement park ride.

- *Supervise employees:* When significant time is dedicated to specific processes (technologies), supervision time is directly assigned. Otherwise, supervision time is allocated to all activities within the department. Typical methods of allocations are the percentage of total labor cost for each activity; percentage of time spent in each department or with each associate; and head count.

- *Maintain equipment:* It is advisable to use estimated maintenance costs for preventive maintenance and to directly charge unplanned maintenance costs. Maintenance costs can be extracted from the preventive maintenance records and accounts payable for spare parts (e.g., hard disks, spare tires, roller coaster wheels, cash registers, fire engine pumps, water department pipes) and outside services.

- *Lease equipment:* The cost of leased equipment should be traced to a service activity in the same manner as purchased equipment. Leased equipment differs from purchased equipment primarily in that its interest cost is reflected in the lease cost and not directly assigned to the activity.

Interorganizational Activities

Some important interorganizational activities include the following:

- *Provide management information:* Total computer room operating costs, including hardware and software costs are included here. Common methods of tracing MIS to the user departments include the number of reports, program changes, special reports, print lines, or transactions. The costs of programming and system development are charged to activities based on actual usage of these resources.

- *Support administration:* Administrative support costs are directly traced to the activity requesting the service.

Other interorganizational activities include:

- Provide financial statements
- Maintain facilities

- Provide industrial engineering
- Program computers
- Develop procedures
- Maintain benefits program
- Hire associates

2c: Establishing Causal Relationship

A causal relationship exists when a factor of service operations can be shown to be directly consumed by an activity. The key to establishing a causal relationship is defining an activity measure that is common to both the element of cost and the activity. Because people are paid on the basis of time, it is an excellent basis for costing people. Similarly, the amount of human resources consumed in an activity is normally stated in terms of time. Thus, time is common to the factor of service operations and the activity.

Typical causal bases include:

Factors of Service Production	Measure
People	Time
Technology	Equipment/technology hours
Facilities	Square footage
Energy	Kilowatt hours, gallons, mcf

Reproducibility and completeness are important in establishing a causal relationship. Reproducibility refers to the analyst's responsibility to record what was done so that others may understand the ground rules and assumptions made, the analysis performed, and the results obtained. In this manner, each estimate becomes both a self-contained, documented record of a complete cost estimate and a building block for future cost estimates.

Nontraceable costs could be allocated to the primary activities to ensure completeness or just labeled as nontraceable. Completeness refers to the communication of results in a format that encompasses the entire system, without the need for footnotes describing costs that were left out or that are considered nontraceable.

2d: Tracing People-Related Costs

Tracing people-related costs to activities requires information on:

- The activities performed by the employee
- The people-related cost for the department
- A causal tracing basis

Techniques for defining activities were described in Chapter 6, "Activities of an Enterprise." The source of labor costs is either the general ledger or special engineering studies, as described earlier in this chapter. This section explains how labor is traced to specific activities.

Employee costs are traced to activities on the basis of either time or the physical output of the activity. The use of physical output as a basis for tracing employee cost is valid only if the effort to complete each individual output is homogeneous. When employees work on several activities or outputs requiring different amounts of effort, the time expended by employees on activities is the preferred basis for tracing employee labor costs to activities.

The primary method of determining how a department spends its time is to interview the supervisors responsible for managing an organizational unit and the associates who perform the various activities. The number of employees supervised, the division of labor within the organizational unit, and activities performed are the key data to be extracted. In an activity management system, it is unimportant whether the employee directly worked on the service or indirectly supported the service. What's important is to trace workers' time to the activities they perform.

The organizational chart and its corresponding job descriptions provide an excellent starting point for tracing employee costs to activities. Through interviews, diaries/logs, engineering studies, or other appropriate techniques, each job classification is studied to determine which of the unit's activities the employee supports. The work activities of each group, or individual employee, are defined as shown in the following figure.

Activities	Manager	Secretary	Recruiter	Trainers
Number of personnel	1	1	5	3
Train workers			15%	10%
Hire workers			30%	5%
Administer department	7%	1%	2%	
Administer salaries	1%		3%	11%
Prepare annual budget	1%			2%
Administer benefits		4%		
Organize worker parties		3%		1%
Plan meetings	.5%			.5%
Miscellaneous	.5%	2%		.5%
	10%	10%	50%	30%

Employee cost is traced to activities by multiplying the people-related cost by the time percentages determined during the activity analysis process. There are three primary methods for charging labor to activities:

1. **Tracing total department employee cost** to activities by using the percentage of time spent on each activity department-wide
2. Tracing employee cost to activities by using the percentage of time spent on each activity **by a specific class of employee**
3. Tracing employee labor cost by using the percentage of time spent on each activity **by each individual employee**

The choice of method depends on the degree of accuracy and confidentiality required. In a department where wages are relatively standard, the first approach is preferable because it is the simplest. Some organizations use this approach because of salary confidentiality issues even though this approach may distort activity cost. When wages vary significantly within a department, the second and third methods are preferable.

To illustrate the difference in methods, assume a human resources department has the following staffing:

Job Type	Number of Employees	Total Salary $	Available Hours
Manager	1	60,000	2,000
Secretary	1	15,000	2,000
Recruiter	5	200,000	10,000
Trainers	3	60,000	6,000
Total	10	335,000	20,000

For the sake of this example, assume the activity analysis identified the following activities of the human resource department:

- Train workers
- Hire workers
- Administer department
- Administer salaries
- Other

Total labor method

Under the total labor method, employee-related cost is distributed to activities by multiplying the total department salaries and employee-related cost by the percentage of time spent on each activity. The total department salary is $335,000. Assume the activity analysis determined the following department-wide breakdown of time:

Activity	Time %
Train workers	25
Hire workers	35
Administer department	10
Administer salaries	15
Other	15
Total	100%

The $335,000 department labor cost is distributed to the activities according to the total department activity time percentages. Alternatively, the employee hours spent on each activity could be used, which would result in the same **cost tracing assignment**. The distribution results in the following tracing of labor costs to activities:

Activity	Cost	
Train workers	83,750	($335,000 × .25)
Hire workers	117,250	($335,000 × .35)
Administer department	33,500	($335,000 × .10)
Administer salaries	50,250	($335,000 × .15)
Other	50,250	($335,000 × .15)
Total	335,000	

Occupational code method

Under the occupational code method, salary and employee-related costs are distributed to the department's activities by multiplying the total employee-related cost in each occupational code by the corresponding percentage of time spent on the activity.

The first step in the occupational code method is to determine the labor grades within a department. The labor grades provide insight into the types of activities the workers perform. The departmental manager or a special study identifies, for each occupational code, the key activities and percentage of total time spent on each activity. A rate per hour for each occupational code is computed by dividing the average annual salary by the average number of hours available (e.g., 2,000 hours). For example, consider the human resource department:

Job Type	Number of Employees	Occupational Code	Average Salary $	Hourly Rate $
Manager	1	001	60,000	30.00
Secretary	1	002	15,000	7.50
Recruiter	5	003	40,000	20.00
Trainer	3	004	20,000	10.00

An analysis of time spent by each class of employee in the design department results in the following breakdown of time:

Activity	Occupational Code	Hours	Manager	Secretary	Recruiter	Trainer
Train workers	003	3,000			3,000	
	004	2,000				2,000
Hire workers	003	6,000			6,000	
	004	1,000				1,000
Administer department	001	1,400	1,400			
	003	400			400	
	002	200		200		
Administer salaries	001	200	200			
	003	600			600	
	004	2,200				2,200
Other	001	400	400			
	002	1,800		1,800		
	004	800				800
Total		20,000	2,000	2,000	10,000	6,000

The next step is to multiply the hours for each activity/occupational code by the occupational code rate as follows:

Activity	Occupational Code	Hours	Cost $	Hours × Rate
Train workers	003	3,000	60,000	(3,000 × 20)
	004	2,000	20,000	(2,000 × 10)
Hire workers	003	6,000	120,000	(6,000 × 20)
	004	1,000	10,000	(1,000 × 10)
Administer department	001	1,400	42,000	(1,400 × 30)
	003	400	8,000	(400 × 20)
	002	200	1,500	(200 × 7.50)
Administer salaries	001	200	6,000	(200 × 30)
	003	600	12,000	(600 × 20)
	004	2,200	22,000	(2,200 × 10)
Other	001	400	12,000	(400 × 30)
	002	1,800	13,500	(1800 × 7.50)
	004	800	8,000	(800 × 10)
Total		20,000	335,000	

The tracing of costs results in the following assignment of labor costs to activities:

Activity	Cost $
Train workers	80,000
Hire workers	130,000
Administer department	51,500
Administer salaries	40,000
Other	33,500
Total	335,000

Specific employee method

Under the specific employee method, all supervisors and employees are interviewed or a special study is conducted to understand their activities and responsibilities and to determine the time spent on key activities. Assume the analysis revealed the following breakdown:

	Salary $	TWK %	HWK %	ADP %	ASA %	OTH %	Total
		Activity					
Manager	60,000			.70	.10	.20	1.0
Secretary	15,000			.10		.90	1.0
Senior recruiter	60,000		.50	.20	.30		1.0
Recruiter 1	40,000		1.00				1.0
Recruiter 2	40,000		1.00				1.0
Jr. recruiter 1	30,000	.50	.50				1.0
Jr. recruiter 2	30,000	1.00					1.0
Sr. trainer	22,500		.50		.10	.40	1.0
Sr. trainer	22,500				1.00		1.0
Jr. trainer	15,000	1.00					1.0
					Total		10.0

TWK = Train workers
HWK = Hire workers
ADP = Administer department
ASA = Administer salaries
OTH = Other

% = % of workers time where 1.0 = full time to that activity and .40 = 40% of that workers time

A total activity cost is determined by multiplying the activity percentages by the employee's salary and summing by activity.

	TWK $	HWK $	ADP $	ASA $	OTH $	Total $
	Activity					
Manager			42,000	6,000	12,000	60,000
Secretary			1,500		13,500	15,000
Senior recruiter		30,000	12,000	18,000		60,000
Recruiter 1		40,000				40,000
Recruiter 2		40,000				40,000
Jr. recruiter 1	15,000	15,000				30,000
Jr. recruiter 2	30,000					30,000
Sr. trainer		11,250		2,250	9,000	22,500
Sr. trainer				22,500		22,500
Jr. trainer	15,000					15,000
Total	60,000	136,250	55,500	48,750	34,500	335,000

Comparing the three methods yields the results that follow. Using the total labor approach, we can conclude that activities requiring more senior people are undercosted because an average wage rate is used.

Tracing Method Activity	Total Labor $	Occupational Code $	Specific Employee $
Train workers	83,750	80,000	60,000
Hire workers	117,250	130,000	136,250
Administer department	33,500	51,500	55,500
Administer salaries	50,250	40,000	48,750
Other	50,250	33,500	34,500
Total	335,000	335,000	335,000

Although the highest accuracy is obtained by tracing specific employees to activities, this approach is not recommended for widespread use because it is too cumbersome and expensive. It would require that a time-reporting system be installed. Also, specific employee data are subject to short-term fluctuations in skill levels applied to activities, and this distorts activity costs. Problems can arise with disclosing specific salaries, especially those of managers. Some organizations use the specific employee method and just use a ghost number for manager salaries. Each organization must decide for itself what approach will help them achieve their objectives.

The cost per activity is based on the planned level of employee experience necessary to perform an activity. Use of more-experienced people (at a higher rate) should require less time, whereas use of less-experienced people (at a lower rate) should require more time. The actual cost (actual time multiplied by actual rate) can be compared to a plan and shown as a variance.

Cost information by employee occupation code normalizes the data. Thus, it is advisable to use occupation codes. It is important that the salary range of each occupation code be carefully constructed so as not to allow significant variations.

2e: Tracing All Other Costs to Activities

After employee-related cost is traced to activities, all other cost categories are investigated through interviews and a review of records to identify the activity that caused the cost to be incurred. In the example of the human resources department, costs are traced to activities as illustrated in the figure following this discussion.

Not all costs are cost-effectively traced to activities. These **nontraceable** costs represent general department/cost center support costs. To directly charge 100 percent of a department's costs to activities is seldom possible or cost effective. As a rule of thumb, an organization should strive to directly trace between 80 to 90 percent of its costs to activities.

The remaining nontraceable costs are general departmental costs. Being related to a specific department, they should not be allocated on the basis of an organization-wide cost pool. Therefore, it is recommended that a department's nontraceable costs be allocated to the organization's primary activities on the basis of:

- The department's largest expense category (e.g., usually labor)
- Head count
- Total expenses for that activity as a percentage of total expenses for the work center
- Some other rational system.

See figure on page 187.

For example, the nontraceable costs for the human resource department ($50,000) might be allocated to activities using labor costs—the department's largest expense category. The costs would be allocated as follows:

Activities	Time %	Allocated Costs $
Train workers	25	12,500
Hire workers	35	17,500
Administer department	10	5,000
Administer salaries	15	7,500
Other	15	7,500
Total	100%	$50,000

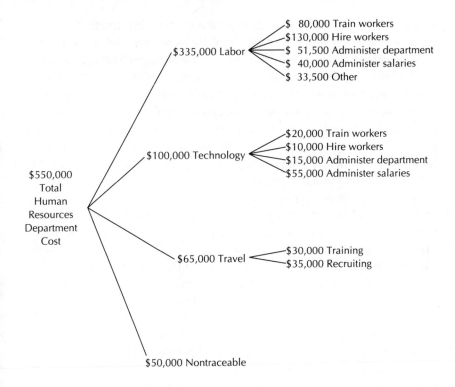

$335,000 Labor
- $ 80,000 Train workers
- $130,000 Hire workers
- $ 51,500 Administer department
- $ 40,000 Administer salaries
- $ 33,500 Other

$100,000 Technology
- $20,000 Train workers
- $10,000 Hire workers
- $15,000 Administer department
- $55,000 Administer salaries

$550,000
Total
Human
Resources
Department
Cost

$65,000 Travel
- $30,000 Training
- $35,000 Recruiting

$50,000 Nontraceable

STEP 3: DETERMINE ACTIVITY PERFORMANCE MEASUREMENT

Activities are described in both financial and nonfinancial performance measures. Activity accounting considers cost and nonfinancial performance information as attributes of an activity. Performance measures address questions about an activity such as:

- What does it cost?
- How much time does it take (lead and cycle)?
- How well is the activity performed?
- How flexible is the activity in response to changes in the service operations environment?

Each view provides a different insight into the activity. A commonly used analogy is several windows through which activities are viewed. One window shows an activity in terms of the cost of performing it. Another window shows an activity in terms of the time required to perform it. Other common views include flexibility, quality, and schedule attainment.

The relationship among performance measures is tightly bonded, so that a change to an activity simultaneously affects all aspects of performance measures. A reduction in time, for example, will affect cost, quality, and flexibility because it changes the way in which the activity is performed. As a consequence of the interrelationships of performance measures, it is misleading to judge activity performance by a single measure in isolation from the others.

Optimizing the performance of the enterprise as a whole requires considering the impact of relationships among performance measures. Consider cost. One method of improving productivity is to increase output using the same amount of resources. If this goal is accomplished at the expense of quality, the cost reduction achieved in one department is offset by additional activities to correct the problem in other departments. The organization's performance as a whole is diminished.

A key to effective management is to implement changes that improve multiple dimensions of performance simultaneously. This is only possible when the activity management system tightly couples nonfinancial and financial measures.

STEP 4: SELECT ACTIVITY MEASURE

Selecting an activity measure involves the following steps:

- Determine activity measure
- Gather statistics on output/transactions
- Validate activity measure for reasonableness

4a: Determine Activity Measure

As discussed earlier, activity measures are outputs or physical attributes of an activity. Surrogate activity measures are used when it is unfeasible to use the best activity measure.

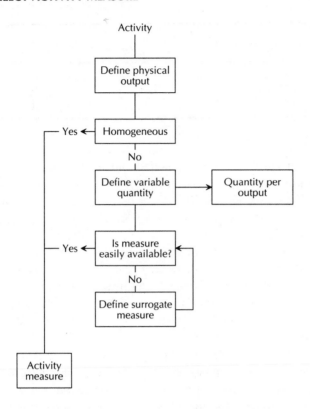

It is a common phenomenon that the greater the desired accuracy, the more difficult it is to obtain activity data to achieve it. Determining the total number of purchase orders, for example, may be simpler than determining the number of purchase order line items. In many cases, the activity management system must trade off the advantages of greater accuracy against the increased data collection costs.

Several activities might be aggregated into a surrogate activity measure in which no activities are significant enough on their own to warrant separate management. In this case, the concept of equivalent units might be employed. For example, the activity "maintain grounds" comprises "clearing the snow" and "cutting the grass." It takes twice as much time on average to cut the grass as it does to clear the snow. Therefore, if the organization cuts the grass 20 times and clears snow 10 times, the organization would have 50 units of output volume:

Activity	Equivalent Units	Times/Year	Total Units
Cut grass	2	20	40
Clear snow	1	10	10
		Total	50

Later, when an activity cost is calculated, the organization would find that cutting the grass costs twice as much as clearing snow. For example, if this activity costs $2,500 for 50 units of output, the cost per unit is $50. Therefore, clear snow costs 1 times $50 or $50 while cut grass costs 2 times $50 or $100.

Similarly, an activity measure might be chosen that is not the most accurate mathematical basis for tracing costs, because it is unfeasible to collect volume statistics for the most appropriate measure. The disadvantage of using surrogate activity measures is that they represent an imperfect compromise between the simplicity of the system and the resulting cost distortion.

It is important to choose a surrogate activity measure that will closely approximate the cost behavior of the activity or motivate a specified behavior. An example of a surrogate activity measure that will approximate a cost behavior is the use of purchase orders when the number of purchase order lines might be more appropriate. A behavior activity measure is used only when a surrogate measure cannot be found that closely approximates the cost behavior.

4b: Gather Statistics on Output/Transactions

After an activity measure has been selected, the frequency of its occurrence is determined. The following are common sources of activity volume information:

- Information systems transaction statistics.
- Department records: If service orders are numbered sequentially, for example, an approximation of the number of service orders is determined by subtracting the beginning number from the ending number.
- Sampling.

It is important that the period of time used for the activity volume statistics corresponds to the same time period used in determining the cost basis.

Activity	Activity Measure	Volume
Pay invoices	Invoices	13,000
	Checks	10,000
Process receivables	Customer invoices	20,000
	Number of checks	18,000

Activity measure considerations

The identification of an appropriate activity measure is critical to the successful implementation of an activity management system. Two key factors to be considered when selecting activity measures include:

- Activity measure homogeneity
- Relative costs of the aggregate activity

Activity measure homogeneity. An activity measure is said to be homogeneous when each output is of the same kind as the others. This means that the output must have consistent cost behavior patterns and require similar amounts of the cost elements. One test for homogeneity is the variability of the cost per unit. For example, a purchase order is a good activity measure for the purchase order activity only if the cost of each individual purchase order does not vary dramatically from others. This condition is not valid if an organization generates both complex and simple purchase orders depending on the service. Clearly, the issuing of a complex service purchase order is more resource-intensive than the issuing of a simple purchase order. In this case, a purchase order is not a homogeneous activity measure. Instead, the number of purchase order lines may be a more appropriate activity measure.

The homogeneity of an activity measure can be determined by calculating the cost per activity for a random sample of the occurrences of an activity. If the cost per measure does not vary more than 20 percent, the activity measure can be considered homogeneous.

The importance of activity measure homogeneity can be seen by the impact it has on service cost. For example, assume a purchasing department is incurring $150,000 to process 10,000 purchase orders. It might be concluded that the cost per purchase order is $15 ($150,000/10,000). However, a purchase order may vary in complexity from 1 line item to 200 line items. The amount of resources required for a 1-line-item purchase order is much less than for the 200-line purchase order.

To continue the example, suppose the average purchase order contains 20 line items. The cost per line item is, therefore, $0.75 [$150,000/(20 lines × 10,000 purchase orders)]. This means that the cost for a 1-line-item purchase order would be closer to $0.75 than $15. Similarly, the cost for a 200-line-item purchase order would be closer to $150 (200 lines × $.75) than $15. Unless most purchase orders contain approximately 20 line items, the resulting service cost distortion is significant.

The greater the heterogeneity of activities, the greater the distortion that is introduced. Services that are high consumers of purchase order line items are undercosted, whereas services that are low consumers of line items are overcosted.

Relative cost of the activity. The relative cost of the activity is a very important factor in selecting an activity measure. If the impact of an activity on total cost is insignificant, the resulting service cost distortion is minimal, and a surrogate activity measure is appropriate. The relative impact of an activity on total cost depends on how large the activity cost is as a percentage of the total cost of the service, business process, or other reporting objective.

To illustrate this point, assume an activity accounts for 20 percent of the total cost of a particular service. An inappropriate activity measure that traces twice as much cost to the service than would a valid output measure would therefore cause reported service costs to be 20 percent too high [(2 × 20%) − 20%]. However, if the activity accounts for only 0.2 percent of total cost, then the distortion introduced is only 0.2 percent [(2 × .2%) − .2%].

The purchase order example can be modified to demonstrate the effect of a relatively large cost impact of an activity on reported service costs for several services. Assume that the cost for the simple service was $120 and $1,500 for the complex service. The service costs were computed using the average $15 purchase order cost. The revised service cost using the cost per purchase order line is $105.75 ($120 − $15 average + $0.75) for the simple service and $1,635 (1,500 − 15 + 150) for the complex service. The simple service is overcosted by 12 percent [(120−105.75)/120] whereas the complex service is undercosted by 9 percent [(1,500 −1,635)/ 1,500]. It can be concluded that the purchase order cost is a significant percentage of total cost and the selection of an appropriate activity measure is critical.

4c: Validate Activity Measure for Reasonableness

The activity measure must be validated to ensure that relationships between the activity cost and activity levels, as represented by the activity measure, are valid. Alternative activity measures should be selected in cases where lack of homogeneity is detected. It is important to separate changes in the cost of resources due to technology changes, improved labor skills, or price level changes.

A number of techniques are available to validate activity measures for reasonableness. The primary ones include the following:

- High-low approach, which examines cost behavior at the highest and lowest levels of activity
- Curve fitting, which determines the line that best explains the relationship between changes in cost and the activity level by graphing historical relationships or using statistical regression analysis
- Multiple regression analysis, which is similar to curve fitting but is used when changes in costs are a function of multiple independent variables

Before a regression analysis of costs (the dependent variable) against volume (the independent variable) can properly be made, the costs should be adjusted to consider (among other possible considerations) inflation, seasonality, strikes, vacations, shutdowns, annual salary and wage increases, and accounting period anomalies. These adjustments are complex (consider seasonality, for instance), and most financial accounting systems do not easily adapt to such corrections. In fact, some expenses are often prorated over accounting periods (such as months or quarters) with the specific purpose of eliminating observable seasonal variations.

A simple regression rarely produces a completely desirable coefficient of regression because of the influence of cost drivers other than the single independent variable (activity volume) assumed in linear regression. Although a multiple correlation may eventually identify a relationship between the studied cost and some number of independent variables, the complexities introduced by such a calculation often make the process impractical for regular use by management. Therefore, sometimes a special study may be required to assure the organization they have the proper output measure.

STEP 5: CALCULATE COST PER ACTIVITY

Once an organization has traced cost to an activity, selected an output measure, and determined the quantity of the activity measure, it can complete the activity costing process. To illustrate this, consider a purchasing department that spends $120,000 processing 6,000 purchase orders. The average cost per purchase order is $20. A complex service requires $400 (20 purchase orders at $20) of the purchase order activity, whereas the simple service requires $20 (1 purchase order at $20). This is a dramatic difference.

The final step is to sum the extended unit cost of each traceable activity and allocated portion of nontraceable costs.

1. Obtain the total cost for the activity from the general ledger.
2. Obtain the total volume of activity measures.
3. Divide Step 1 results by Step 2 results to obtain the cost per activity measure.

$$\text{Activity cost} = \frac{\text{Traceable resources}}{\text{Activity measure quantity}}$$

In the following accounting department example, the activity costs would be calculated as follows:

Activity	Activity Measure	Activity Cost	Volume	Cost per Activity
Pay invoices	Invoices	$130,000	13,000	$10.00/invoice
	Checks	$130,000	10,000	$13.00/check
Process receivables	Customer invoices	$140,000	20,000	$7.00/customer invoice
	Number of checks	$140,000	18,000	$7.78/customer check

It is important to note that an activity cost is a productivity measure—inputs divided by outputs. As such, all the activities of the entire enterprise are measured in terms of productivity measures.

ACTIVITY COST EXAMPLE

Step 1: Extract accounting department cost from the general ledger:

Accounting Department	$
Labor	500,000
Travel	100,000
Mgmt. information systems (MIS)	100,000
Others	100,000
Total	800,000

Step 2: Determine the activities of the accounting department:

Pay invoices
Collect receivables
Prepare financial reports
Pay employees
Provide managerial reports
Manage employees
Train employees
Other

Step 3: Define percentage of time expended on each activity:

Accounting Department	%
Pay invoices	20
Collect receivables	20
Prepare financial reports	15
Pay employees	15
Provide managerial reports	10
Manage employees	5
Train employees	5
Other	10
Total	100%

Step 4: Trace cost to the specific activities using the total department method for the labor:

Accounting Department	Labor $	Travel $	MIS $	Other	Total
Pay invoices	100,000		30,000		130,000
Collect receivables	100,000	10,000	30,000		140,000
Prepare financial reports	75,000	20,000	10,000		105,000
Pay employees	75,000		20,000		95,000
Provide managerial reports	50,000		10,000		60,000
Manage employees	25,000	40,000			65,000
Train employees	25,000	30,000			55,000
Other	50,000			100,000	150,000
Total	500,000	100,000	100,000	100,000	800,000

Step 5: Determine activity cost per unit:

Accounting Department	Total $	Activity Volume	Cost per Unit of Activity Volume
Pay invoices	130,000	13,000	$10.00/invoice
Process receivable	140,000	20,000	$7.00/invoice
Prepare financial reports	105,000	12	$8,750/financial report
Pay employees	95,000	5,000	$19.00/check
Provide managerial reports	60,000	60	$1,000/management report
Manage employees	65,000	65	$1,000/employee
Train employees	55,000	20	$2,750/day
Other	150,000	1	$150,000
Total	800,000		

SUMMARY

Activities provide the building blocks for tracing costs to reporting objectives. Specifying all the activities necessary to accomplish an organizational objective provides the basis for understanding cost. To offer a service one might, for example, require activities such as perform market research, design service, modify facilities, and provide field support, in addition to the activities associated with the service operations process. The sequence of activities and the sum of activity costs is known as the bill of activities (BOA).

9

TRACING ACTIVITY COST

The purpose of this chapter is to:

- Describe the weaknesses of the conventional reporting methods
- Identify business decisions using an activity management system
- Identify reporting objectives
- Describe how to trace costs
- Describe how to construct a bill of activities
- Discuss the importance of cost precision and cost significance in the decision-making process

Cost is meaningful only when it is related to an enterprise mission. Knowing the cost of creating a service, placing an order, managing a department, or satisfying internal reporting requirements facilitates the decision-making process. The objective for which cost information is needed (e.g., new service cost, business processes, order cost, customer profitability, department cost, external reporting requirements, and special service) is known as the final cost objective.

Costs are linked to a final cost objective by a causal relationship. To do something such as provide a service or process an order involves activities. For example, creating a new service involves designing the service, defining the service process, procuring supplies and possibly hiring people, transforming supplies through various service processes, and providing customer service.

Activities provide the basis for costing. An activity is the most basic unit for costing and can be summarized in numerous formats to support various reporting requirements.

The process of identifying specific activities and determining how much of each activity is consumed in the final cost objective is known as

tracing. Tracing cost to the end user has two primary objectives:

1. To understand the current cost structure
2. To determine whether alternative activities might be superior

The number of possible reporting objectives is immense. Different management decisions require different levels of cost detail and therefore different cost roll-ups. Consider the "do-it-yourself" versus "buy-from-outside" decision. Knowing the cost of creating a service enables an organization to compare the do-it-yourself cost with the cost of buying from an outside source.

An organization must continually evaluate the cost effectiveness of each activity/business process to determine whether to restructure the activity/business process or to purchase it externally. In the long run, an organization will liquidate and reallocate resources from an activity center that fails to satisfy customers effectively, whether they be inside or outside the organization. To do otherwise would diminish the organization's long-term viability.

In a management system, the role of cost management is to ensure that the information necessary to support the decision process is collected as completely and efficiently as possible, and made available in the right form at precisely the right time. This requires that the cost management system be derived from and integrated with the organization's decision support system.

TRADITIONAL REPORTING OBJECTIVES

Traditionally, a primary use of cost accounting information has been to support external financial reporting. Thus, accounting methods are chosen on criteria such as consistency, simplicity, and conservatism. Accounting was used primarily as a "report card" to depict what happened after the costs were incurred. The new emphasis of cost management is to control cost by predicting cost behavior patterns during the planning stage, and **tracking actual results against the plan during the execution stage to more quickly initiate corrective action where required**.

In the conventional cost accounting system, the process of attaching costs to cost objectives requires an extensive number of allocations. The reason for these allocations is that costs are aggregated in large cost pools by cost element. To assign cost from aggregate cost pools to cost objectives necessitates numerous allocations that are often selected on criteria such as regulatory requirements and ease of calculation.

The accounting treatments of cost are often dissimilar for different decisions. Traditional cost accounting requires the development of a separate cost accounting system for each different view of cost. For example, an asset may use double-declining depreciation for tax purposes and straight-line depreciation for financial reporting. The choice of depreciation methods will affect cost throughout the life of the asset, resulting in separate-period reporting. Separate fixed asset accounting systems are thus required for tax and financial reporting purposes.

Dissimilar accounting methods promote the inherently non-value-added cost of maintaining separate systems. The compromise that most organizations choose is to operate a single system to support the multiple reporting objectives. Such a system requires the choice of one dominant accounting method on which to base cost.

For example, charging the cost of software development to the current period is conservative, and would be most appropriate in reporting external financial results. Alternatively, capitalizing software development better matches cost to future services and better mirrors the operations—an important requirement for internal decision making. However, with a single system, the organization must choose between external reporting requirements (conservative bias) and management control (better matching bias).

USES OF ACTIVITY MANAGEMENT

Activity management accommodates diverse reporting and cost control objectives. Having identified activities and their output, traced costs to activities, and computed a cost per activity, an organization is positioned to identify the users of activities business processes. Activity information can be summarized in numerous ways by tracing the activities to the reporting objectives. The viewpoints chosen depend on the scope and objectives of the cost control or reporting objective. Consider the decisions shown in the following table:

Decisions	Focus
Control cost	Predictive cost and performance
Do-it-yourself/buy-from-outside	Predictive cost and performance
	Vendor price and performance
	Risk
Estimating	Predictive cost and performance
Pricing	Competition
	Target cost
Investment analysis	Cost/benefit of new process
	Risk
Service planning and control	Resource allocation/constraints
Design to cost	Predictive cost and performance
Location analysis	Differences in factors of service
	operations cost
Service line analysis	Predictive cost and performance
	Service line cost
Marketing mix	Advertising, promotion, selling
Salesperson	Performance, evaluation, compensation
	plan
Channels of distribution	Type of activities
Abandonment analysis	Predictive cost and performance
	Service line cost
Customer	Volume or orders
Budgeting/forecasting	Organizational goals
	Predictive cost and performance with
	varying levels of support
Acquisitions/divestitures	Strong/weak activities
	Forecast demand for activities

Reporting Objectives

Typical reporting objectives include services, service lines, orders, administrative, organizational units, cost control units, marketing, channels of distribution, functions, and projects. The following is an explanation of each of these reporting objectives.

Service. This is the cost of all activities/business processes involved in designing, producing, and distributing a service.

Service line. This represents the cost of activities/business processes unique to each service line. A service line consists of a family of related services. Marketing and management normally forecast in terms of service lines, and operations thinks in terms of individual services.

Order. This includes the cost of all activities involved in acquiring and processing a customer or service order. Order costs represent a one-time cost per order and are often relatively fixed irrespective of the order quantity. When the cost of an order is large relative to the cost per unit, the profitability of the order is highly dependent on the order size. For example, if the order cost is $100 per order and the customer is buying one $300 service, then the total cost to the organization is $400 for the unit of service. However, if the customer orders 50 of the same service, the cost to the organization would be $302 ($100 of ordering cost/50 orders = $2/ order plus $300/unit) per unit of service.

Decisions on order quantity are made by consumers and the marketing department. The conventional practice of including the order cost in overhead and allocating it to all services obscures a key determinant of profitability.

Two important activities that should be traced to orders are processing invoices, and checking credit and collecting receivables:

- Processing accounts receivable: The cost of processing accounts receivable is directly related to a customer order.
- Checking credit and collecting receivables: The cost of credit checking and collecting the outstanding receivables represents a cost directly attributable to specific customers or a customer order. However, when the activity is directly related to tracking down problems related to poor service quality or mis-priced orders, the cost of the activity should be included as part of the organization cost of poor quality.

Administrative. This is the cost of all activities necessary to manage an enterprise including external compliance and reporting requirements. Administrative costs should be separated into department-related and corporate administration costs. These costs should be assigned to services based on the activities that cause the need for administration. For example, the cost of administration of quality activities in various operating departments would be assigned to the quality activities in those various departments.

It is common practice to allocate corporate administration—including human resources, senior management, accounting, legal, information systems, and customer service required for managing a organization—to services. The resulting administrative allocation is often equated to a franchise fee.

Organizational unit. An enterprise functions through its organizational structure. Managers have significant influence over the efficiency and effectiveness of the activities in their area of responsibility. They control how activities are accomplished, and often influence how money is spent. The degree of influenceability varies according to timing and organization policy. Operating costs such as depreciation on scanners, equipment, and information systems are normally changed only in the long run. However, they are traceable to the activity and are therefore controllable.

Cost control unit. The cost control unit represents the source of a cost. It includes all activities resulting from decisions made by an organization, even though the costs were incurred in other organizational units. It represents the cost driver. Managing cost requires understanding the underlying cause-and-effect relationship between the cause of cost and its occurrence.

Cost management systems that report costs only at the point of cost occurrence misdirect organizational resources by treating symptoms rather than solving problems. They also depend on the managers' ability to understand associated cost drivers. In other words, effective cost management requires a focus on the source of costs. Only by addressing the source can costs be minimized.

Marketing. Activity-based marketing analysis traces the costs of activities required to support the sales territory, salesperson, and different size orders. Conventional practices equate selling efficiency with increased sales volume as an indication of increased profitability. The idea is that more is better. However, too frequently increased sales volume does not equal increased profit, or increased gross fund-raising dollars does not increase the funds available for the charities' mission.

Activity-based marketing cost analysis stresses profits rather than the traditional sales volume as a basis for decisions and evaluation of marketing. It aids in controlling costs by first associating the cost of all specific marketing activities to the benefiting cost objective (e.g., sales territory, customer, distribution channel, and so on).

Traceable marketing costs are those incurred for and benefiting a single segment of sales and easily associated with specific commodities or sales segments. Accordingly, the cost to operate a district sales office is a direct cost of the sales territory in which the office is located. Nontraceable costs are those incurred for and benefitting sales generally but not traceable to specific services or sales units.

Customer. The cost of supporting specific customers is determined by tracing all activities required to support the customer. Some customers (citizens) are more expensive to serve than others (e.g., distributors versus individual retail customers; delivering to rural postal patrons versus delivering to city postal patrons). Consider the following:

Type of Customer	Characteristics
Distributor	Many units per order One shipping destination
Retail	Few units per order Many shipping destinations Many returns Consumer packaging Promotional programs

It is important to be able to answer the following questions:

- What does each channel of distribution really cost?
- Which channel provides the best service to the customers?
- What can be done to lower costs and improve service?
- Are certain specific customers (citizens, patients) more or less expensive?

The first step in a customer analysis is to classify customers—or service recipients in the case of governments and nonprofits—into groups based on sales or other volume measure, service mix, and buying (service usage) characteristics. Typical classifications include:

- Distributors
- National accounts
- Buying groups
- Independent dealers
- Individuals
- States, counties, universities

When analyzing customer-specific activities/business processes and costs, consider whether specific customers/channels require more or less support for the following activities or costs:

- Sales department time and sales commissions
- Accounts receivable (Do specific customers/channels take longer to pay their accounts and thus require more capital to finance?)
- Special handling
- Technical support
- Senior management time
- Freight
- Finished services inventory
- Order entry
- Insurance
- Returns
- Discounts
- Advertising
- Trade
- Promotions
- Literature
- Special invoicing
- Service liability and legal representation
- Credits

Business function. A business function is an aggregation of activities/business processes that are related by common purpose. Quality and operations are examples of business functions.

Most organizations are organized by the major functions of finance, customer service, marketing, management, administration, and service operations. However, the total spectrum of activities for a business function is much broader than the organizational unit responsible for the function.

Business functional analysis aggregates related activities that would otherwise be hidden in numerous departments. This is accomplished by classifying each activity by the function of which it is a subset. For example, the activities of the quality department are part of the quality function, but there are many other quality-related activities, such as quality planning, in-process inspection, and customer feedback, that occur in other departments. Determining the total cost of quality would necessitate knowing the cost of all these activities/business processes regardless of the department in which they are performed. Knowing the total cost for significant functions focuses management's attention on identifying solutions that transcend organizational boundaries.

A functional cost analysis is also a valuable budgeting tool because it identifies requirements for activities that are not part of the department's normal activities. Consider the impact of a change in policies relating to in-process inspection during service operations (e.g., checking that rent receipts or real estate brokerage checks are posted correctly). A service department would have to perform additional in-process inspection activities that would take away time from normal service activities. If the source of the requirements is unknown, the department's productivity would appear to have decreased.

A sample functional roll-up of quality-related activities into a cost of quality report might include:

- Incoming supplies inspection (e.g., checking incoming restaurant food)
- Vendor problem solving (e.g., insuring correctness of printed forms)
- Training (by quality department)
- Producibility analysis (e.g., can we perform heart transplants)
- Administer quality department
- Survey source (e.g., checking vendor's operations)
- Inspect in-process (e.g., reviewing audit work papers)
- Survey service operations (e.g., watching maids in hotel)
- Troubleshoot service operations (e.g., checking why french fries aren't crisp)
- Modify service operations (e.g., making sure nonfunctioning planes are replaced)
- Rework service (e.g., redoing a tax return)
- Handle scrap/spoilage (e.g., throwing away a burnt dinner)
- Replace obsolescence (e.g., replacing an obsolete form)
- Monitor total quality management program (e.g., ISO 9000 audit)
- Perform final inspection (e.g., reviewing final report before giving to client)

- Plan for quality (e.g., developing cost of quality reporting)
- Audit quality (e.g., inspecting trucks, store, rooms, forms, hospitals)
- Supplies analysis (e.g., combining forms into single form)

Project. A project is a chain of activities interconnected by time to accomplish a specific objective, such as the installation of a new service process or a computer system. The cost of a project can be thought of as a collection of the activity/business process costs necessary to complete the project.

WHICH REPORTING OBJECTIVES?

The cost objective depends on the decision to be made. A matrix of decisions and cost objectives portrays this relationship in the following table:

Decision	\multicolumn{8}{c}{Cost Objective}
	AA	Ser	Ord	Adm	BP	Org	Mar	Proj
Do-it-yourself/buy outside	x	x		x				
Estimating	x	x	x		x		x	x
Investment analysis	x	x			x	x	x	x
Plan/control service	x	x	x		x			
Design to cost	x	x					x	x
Location analysis	x					x	x	x
Service line analysis	x	x						
Expansion/abandonment	x	x				x	x	x
Budgeting	x	x			x	x	x	x
Acquisitions/divestiture	x					x	x	
Cost reduction	x	x	x	x	x	x	x	x
Order profitability	x	x	x					

y   x

  AA = Activity analysis
 Ser = Service
 Ord = Order
Adm = Administration
  BP = Business process
 Org = Organization
Mar = Market
Proj = Project

TRACEABILITY CRITERIA

Traceable activities should be distinctly identified in the final reporting objective. Traceable activities have an established cause-and-effect relationship with a reporting objective. Therefore, the cost of all traceable activities that support the final cost objective is relevant to the final decision involving the cost objective.

Consider a painting activity for a painting contractor. The primary cost for a human to paint a wall, ceiling, or building would consist of the time expended multiplied by the laborer's rate. Conversely, the primary cost for a robot to paint would consist of the time expended multiplied by the robot's rate. In either case, the component that was painted is unaffected by whether the painting was done by a human or a robot. An indisputable cause-and-effect relationship is established between the amount of painting and the service. The traceability criterion has been established. The secondary costs associated with painting include supplies, travel, and support equipment.

In an activity management system, it is important that all costs be traced where practical and economically feasible. A rule of thumb is that 80 to 90 percent of a department's costs should be traceable to the activities of that department. Tracing less than 80 to 90 percent does not provide the breakdown necessary to manage costs; tracing more is uneconomical. The remaining 10 to 20 percent of cost is considered nontraceable. Nontraceable costs should be clearly separated. Nontraceable cost can be allocated if a fully absorbed cost is important to the final decision.

A critical factor in decision making is relevance. Traceability and relevance are synonymous. Decisions involve alternatives—relevance determines which costs and activities are considered and which are excluded. Traceable costs are controllable because a cause-and-effect relationship is established. Each alternative is evaluated in terms of its impact on traceable costs, because traceable activities will differ among each activity.

Traceability helps bring management pressures to bear on service overhead or shared costs (e.g., selling, MIS, accounting, human resources, service support, and corporate overhead) that are otherwise difficult to evaluate and control. When organizations allocate these costs to specific services or cost centers, they represent a charge against earnings, and managers responsible for profits carefully scrutinize and challenge them. Because they are traceable, they are controllable. They are a powerful force for reducing overhead costs that would otherwise never be scrutinized by someone with direct profit responsibility.

Advantages of Tracing

Unlike the cross-subsidization of allocations based on organization-wide overhead rates, the tracing of activities/business processes to users on the basis of usage will distinguish between intensive users and light users of activities/business processes. Compare the impact of tracing the invoicing activity. In traditional accounting, the costs associated with issuing an invoice are grouped with accounting expenses and accounting expenses are grouped with other overhead and then allocated to services on a volume-related basis such as direct labor, total cost input, or total division gross revenues. In activity management, the costs would be traced by usage of the various activities/business processes.

By the traditional method, a division selling to thousands of small-volume retail customers is charged too little for invoicing costs. This division probably causes the need to allocate significant resources to the invoicing center. Meanwhile, a division with a small number of high-volume customers is overcharged for the invoicing activity.

For example, division A has 10,000 customers with an average invoice of $50 each. Division B has 5 customers who have an average invoice size of $100,000 each. Both divisions have total sales of $500,000. Therefore, if this organization allocates their invoicing costs on sales revenue, each division would be allocated the same amount of invoicing overhead. In reality, division A required 10,000 invoices and division B only 5 invoices. Therefore, the cost of running the invoice department should be traced mainly to division A.

Activity management works against the misuse of resources that is usually associated with such cross-subsidized allocation. This gives activity managers incentive to keep their operations competitive by continually identifying and cost-effectively eliminating generators of waste.

How to Trace Costs

Costs are traced to the final cost objective through a bill of activities. A **bill of activities (BOA)** specifies the sequence of activities and the quantity of each activity consumed in achieving enterprise missions such as creating a service, service operations, or servicing a customer or citizen.

The BOA includes all activities traceable to the final cost objective, such as service development-related activities, operational activities, and support-related activities. In other words, the bill of activities manages all activities/business processes over the entire life cycle. Activities that are independent of a service order are charged on a per unit basis over the planned volume of the service. A cost is computed by multiplying the activity quantity (as specified in the BOA) by the activity unit cost previously computed by the activity management system.

A typical bill of activities includes:

Activity	Life-Cycle Cost	Cost per Unit
Development		
Design service	x	x
Design service process	x	x
Plan quality into service	x	x
Service Operations		
Store supplies		x
Move supplies		x
Set up service		x
Perform procedure 1		x
Perform procedure 2		x
Logistics and Support		
Deliver completed service		x
Invoice customer		x
Process payments		x
Support in field	x	x

A BOA includes two primary functions:

1. A bill of activities separates the quantity of an activity from the cost of the activity. A bill of activities specifies the sequence and quantity of activities. The cost of an activity is separately computed by the activity management system. This approach simplifies the standard-setting process, because the BOA need only be modified if there is a change to the activity/business process. Changes to the cost of the factors of service operations don't require a modification to the BOA.

2. A bill of activities facilitates a mix of different cost behavior patterns without the need to choose a single allocation basis. Each activity in a BOA is separate and distinct. Therefore, each activity

with a unique cost behavior pattern will have a different activity measure. (See the table that follows.)

	Insurance Example			
Activities	Cost $	Measure	Volume	Cost Objective
Design insurance policy	80,000	designs	20	Design service
Develop BOA	20,000	BOAs	10	Design service
Design insurance forms	15,000	designs	10	Design service
Design procedures	20,000	procedures	50	Design service
Design quality program	10,000	program	10	Design service
Obtain regulatory approval	10,000	approvals	10	Design service
Develop sales literature	25,000	programs	30	Produce service
Train sales people	50,000	programs	30	Produce service
Program computers	90,000	products	10	Produce service
Maintain state approval	3,000	approval	10	Keep in force
Handle special order	50,000	specials	2,000	Special orders
Underwrite customer	400,000	customers	20,000	Customer
Invoice customer	60,000	invoices	20,000	Customer
Pay commission	200,000	policy	20,000	Policies
Process claims	90,000	claims	8,500	Claims
Manage organization	60,000	employees	40	Employees

A hospital might have the following activities:

Develop BOA. Bill of activities development occurs when a hospital decides to provide a new service, such as liver transplants, and must develop procedures for this service. The BOA provides the total cost of all the activities connected with providing this service. This is the cost of developing the BOA for the liver transplant procedures.

Maintain BOA. Bill of activities maintenance occurs when the hospital updates its liver transplant procedures and must change the original bill of activities.

Develop process. This phase is when hospital and medical personnel actually decide how this service will be produced. Once the actual procedures are developed, a BOA can be created.

Maintain process. This is the cost for the hospital and medical personnel to modify the procedure. Once the procedure is modified, then the maintenance to the BOA described above can be performed.

Handle special customer orders. Special orders provide for a nontraditional operation, for instance if a rock star were staying in the hospital and required special accommodations and/or privacy.

Monitor work center capacity. This is the cost of monitoring facilities and equipment that will be needed to perform a specific procedure (e.g., liver transplant).

Improve process. Process improvement provides for instances in which a better or more economical way is found to provide a service (e.g., performing plastic surgery on an outpatient basis).

Create special design. This involves special considerations that may be needed for a specific procedure. For example, some operating rooms require laminar air flow rooms—rooms with highly purified air. This is a special design that may have to be added to the operating room, and needs to be broken out separately.

COST PRECISION

The precision of a service cost depends on accurate knowledge of future business conditions, including the volume of each service or the number of years a service, technology, or other asset will be used. Such precise knowledge of the future is impossible. As a result, an activity cost must be based on estimates, and is necessarily imprecise. However, it is erroneous to assume that because activity costs are based on imprecise estimates, the information is not useful to managers. Estimates derived from realistic cost behavior patterns provide an excellent basis for making routine decisions and controlling service operations. These cost behavior patterns and estimated costs form the foundation for calculating service cost.

The issue of cost precision rests on three primary criteria:

- Consistency of cost and planning system
- Error tolerance
- Cost versus benefit of accurate information

Consistency of Cost and Planning System

For information to be of value to a decision maker, the information and the decision criteria must be consistent. For example, consider the investment decision to purchase a waste dump site. The investment decision requires forecasts from the service manager, service engineers, city planners, and others regarding the type and volume of waste to be processed at the new waste dump site during its anticipated useful life. The return on investment for the new dump site was predicated on these assumptions and expectations. If the cost accounting department decides to use time-basis depreciation, the reported cost may not bear any relationship to the assumptions used to justify the investment.

Skeptics might ask, "so what?" The investment and cost systems are separate and distinct. They would be correct if the goal of cost accounting is to report a service cost in accordance with external requirements. However, if the goal of the cost management system is to provide information that can be used to manage cost, then the analysis of deviations between actual operations and the investment plan provides a basis for implementing corrective action. If the actual level of waste, for example, was significantly below the forecasted level used in the investment analysis, then the dump site cost per ton of waste will exceed target. Knowledge of this situation early in the life cycle of the garbage site will enable management to take corrective action, such as redesigning services to use the garbage site or creating the site in steps.

Viewed from the myopic perspective of cost precision, time-based depreciation is superior. Viewed from the perspective of value to the decision maker, volume-based depreciation is superior.

Error Tolerance

Decision support systems are far less tolerant of certain types of errors than others. For example, being low on anchovies in a pizza-making operation is less critical than being out of cheese or flour. A customer might accept a pizza without anchovies by replacing it with another ingredient, but you can't make pizza without cheese or flour. A bill of materials error is usually significant in that it either calls out the wrong supply (e.g., mustard on a pizza) or omits a supply item (e.g., tomato sauce on a pizza).

The error tolerance of an activity management system is normally not an inhibitor to the achievement of value from the system. Consider an activity analysis that specifies fifteen hours of labor. When the labor processing is completed, fifteen hours will be credited against the plan (e.g., for building a highway, bombing the enemy, creating a contract, drawing a building). Even if the standard is off and the activity really took eighteen hours, fifteen hours were planned and fifteen hours were credited. The three-hour difference is most likely due to an efficiency variance at the activity level.

If an activity standard is wrong, then the earned hours when compared with actual hours show a significant variance that would be investigated. Thus there is considerable tolerance in the accuracy of the standards required in an activity management system. Obviously, if the standards are biased in any given direction, output will tend to be higher or lower than planned over a period of time. Nevertheless, the activity management system itself doesn't require absolute precision in the activity standards.

Cost versus Benefit of Accurate Information

Another important criterion to consider is the cost versus the benefit of the accuracy of the information. Although the only theoretically correct procedure is that which is based on the most accurate information, the cost associated with obtaining this precision often exceeds the value to the decision maker. Thus, the use of surrogate bases often provides an acceptable level of precision with a significant reduction in accounting for costs. Once a planned activity cost is determined, it should be used throughout the year. The planned cost will remain unchanged until the planning assumptions change.

COST SIGNIFICANCE

The significance of a cost is important in determining the precision required. The use of Pareto's Law (80/20 rule) is critical in determining significance. Typically, 80 percent of an enterprise's activities are consumed in producing 20 percent of the enterprise's outputs. The idea behind the 80/20 rule of thumb is to focus the planning and control resources on the significant activities/business processes. Surrogates are used for other activities that have much less demonstrable effect on cost and performance.

The flexibility of the bill of activities approach permits the activity management system to determine a service cost for a single service or a group of services. It is a common practice initially to determine a service cost for only "A" items (top 80 percent of revenue generators or top cost/time consumers) and not for all services/service lines. This approach is a practical method of starting and operating an activity management system without having to wait for all the services/service lines to be properly costed.

The use of surrogates early in the activity management development stage does not imply that an organization should not strive for accurate information. What is proposed is that as more accurate information becomes available as a by-product of computerization and continuous improvement, surrogates can be replaced with more accurate causal factors.

SUMMARY

Traditional methods of cost accounting are based on a service focus in the belief that all resources are acquired to support the service. As a consequence, costs are considered to be direct or indirect to services.

Activity management focuses on the cost of activities/business processes. Service cost becomes a secondary objective. In other words, once the cost of an activity is known, it can be related to any cost objective—a customer, business process, office, store, channel of distribution, project, or service. The process of identifying and quantifying the specific activities in the final cost objective is known as tracing. Because traceable costs are controllable, traceability facilitates management control.

Costs are traced to a final cost objective through a bill of activities, which specifies the sequence of activities and the amount of each activity consumed.

10

ACTIVITY SERVICE COST

The purpose of this chapter is to:

- Contrast the differences between traditional and activity-based service cost
- Describe the conventional approach to service cost, including its limitations
- Describe an activity management approach to service cost, including an in-depth discussion of the cost elements that are traceable
- Discuss special considerations such as:
  Service cost calculation frequency
  Setup costs
  Bottleneck costs
  Work orders

In activity management, resources are consumed in the execution of activities. Services consume activities and supplies. An activity service cost system assigns supplies and all traceable activities to services based on the usage of each activity. Activity management represents a major change from traditional cost management. The primary differences include:

- Emphasis is on improving the cost of the service and support activities. The cost of providing the service is a secondary cost objective.
- Direct labor is charged to the activity/business process rather than the service. This approach eliminates the need to voucher the labor to services except in cases where the accuracy is suspect because of the variability and magnitude of the estimated labor content.
- A cost pool is synonymous with an activity. The practice of using a single or limited number of cost pools is eliminated.

- Activity usage is based on the amount of activity/business process volume consumed by the service. Activity/business process volume is the number of activity/business process output units the service requires.
- The direct tracing of activities/business processes to services reduces the amount of overhead to be allocated.
- The direct tracing of activities to services does not distinguish between direct or indirect costs. The cost is directly assigned where a cause-and-effect relationship can be established between the activity and the service. Traceable costs such as marketing, accounting, administration, and other support costs are directly charged to services. This approach results in a focus on total organization cost, not just service operations costs.
- **Service cost** includes the total cost to design, produce, and distribute a service. Many life-cycle costs, which have traditionally been expensed, will be traced to the service and distributed over its life. Life-cycle cost provides management with an understanding of long-term profitability and makes possible the quantification of the cost impact of alternative business processes and levels of service.
- The impact of changes in the volume of activities on service cost is determined.
- Nonfinancial performance measures are incorporated to judge service and business process performance.

Two primary benefits of activity management are that it provides an organization with:

1. An accurate service cost
2. Visibility of cost reduction and performance improvement opportunities

Competition increases the need for an accurate service cost because an organization can't pass on inefficiencies through higher prices or higher taxes. Accurate and detailed information on the actual cost of activities that make up a service is vital in vendor selection, "do-it-yourself" versus "buy-from-outside" decisions, design to cost, and similar decisions. Perhaps even more important than knowing service cost is having visibility of waste and cost reduction and performance improvement opportunities to enable management to increase competitiveness.

USES OF SERVICE COST

An accurate determination of service cost is important, because a large number of organizational decisions use service cost data. To be relevant, the reported service cost must mirror the service operations process.

Service cost information is required in various forms and at different levels of detail to meet various objectives:

- Estimating cost for new services and special one-time services
- Determining profitability for expansion or abandonment of different service segments, such as service lines, market segments, distribution channels, or customers to be served
- Calculating the **margins** associated with individual services
- Facilitating do-it-yourself versus buy-from-outside decisions
- Assisting in the investment analysis process
- Valuing inventory and calculating cost of goods sold for external financial reporting purposes (e.g., retail store)
- Assisting in off-shore sourcing decisions (e.g., Massachusetts Mutual Life Insurance processes U.S. claims; Wright Investors Service organizes databases; Quarterdeck's, a computer software company, offers technical support staff; Cigna processes U.S. medical claims; and McGraw-Hill maintains worldwide circulation files all in Ireland).

TRADITIONAL APPROACH TO SERVICE COST

The service cost model implemented in most organizations identifies three major elements in the cost of a service:

- Direct supplies: This is the acquisition cost of all supplies that are identified as a part of the service and can be traced to the service in an economically feasible manner.
- Direct labor: This includes the wages of all labor that can be associated directly with a service in an economically feasible manner.
- Service and/or administrative overhead: These are all costs other than direct labor and direct supplies that are associated with the activities of a service. Service overhead is traditionally considered an indirect cost and cannot be traced directly to specific services. An

overhead application rate is used to assign a reasonable portion of overhead costs to services. The essence of overhead allocation is the top-down application of costs from a cost center to all services produced during the period.

The following figure illustrates the basic flow of costs in a traditional cost accounting system. To illustrate this approach, consider providing two services with equal volume.

Step 1

Labor and supplies are assigned directly to each service where feasible. Direct labor and supplies costs are easily attached to services. Supplies charges are posted from supplies requisitions and direct labor charges from time tickets.

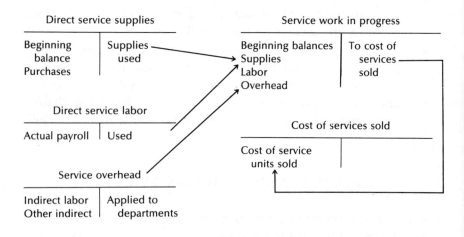

	Services		
	A	B	Total
Annual cost (in $1,000s)	$	$	$
Direct labor			
Direct labor wages	3,000	1,000	4,000
Direct supplies			
Direct supplies	3,000	3,000	6,000
Purchased items	500	500	1,000
Total supplies/purchased	3,500	3,500	7,000

Step 2

All remaining costs are considered overhead and applied to services on a predetermined basis. Overhead is typically applied to services according to an overhead rate computed by dividing overhead costs by a rate base such as direct labor hours, direct labor cost, supplies, total cost input, sales, or computer hours. An overhead application rate expresses a relationship of service overhead to a factor of service operations that can be traced directly to services. Service overhead is assigned to services in proportion to this factor.

The following procedures are used to apply overhead to services:

1. Determine costs to be included in overhead. Service overhead typically includes all costs other than direct labor, direct supplies and selling, general, and administrative (SG&A).
2. Determine the period of benefit. Two rules of thumb for determining whether a cost should be capitalized are:

● Costs that benefit current services should be expensed
● If the future benefit is uncertain, the costs should be expensed

The decision to capitalize or expense a cost centers depends upon whether the venture is expected to be successful and whether the future earnings are expected to be sufficient to match the known expenses. Expenditures that benefit multiple periods should be capitalized and charged to future periods as consumed, or based on estimates of the portion of the asset that is applicable to the current period.

An example of a service overhead budget follows:

Cost Category	$
Fringe benefits	4,000
Indirect labor wages	2,000
Indirect labor supplies	1,000
Supplies management	1,000
Utilities	750
Overtime premium of direct labor	500
Local administration and accounting	400
Depreciation—service operation equipment	300
Shift premium	300

Cost Category (Continued)	$
Local MIS	250
Quality assurance	100
Office management	275
Local personnel/human resources	200
Scrap supplies	200
Property taxes	150
Rework labor	150
Service equipment supplies	100
Special supplies/labor	200
Engineering	400
Research & development	1,000
Supervisory salary	225
Purchasing	50
Payroll department	200
Security	225
Depreciation building	100
Insurance property	25
Insurance liability	30
Invoicing	15
Miscellaneous	100
Total overhead	14,245

Determine level of overhead control. Cost centers represent the smallest area of responsibility for which costs are accumulated. Typically, cost centers correspond to departments.

Select an allocation base and calculate an overhead rate. An overhead rate expresses the relationship of service overhead to the selected base. Overhead charged to services according to sales, direct labor, or total direct costs, for example, assumes that the overhead cost component varies in proportion to sales, direct labor, or total direct costs. The procedure of calculating an overhead rate also assumes that budgeted overhead is a good approximation of actual overhead. As long as the actual total overhead cost and base rate approximate the forecasted volumes, the under/overabsorption of overhead cost is minimal.

Accounting practice does not dictate criteria for choosing a basis of allocation, thus allowing organizations significant latitude in their choice of allocation basis. The selection of direct labor as an allocation basis, for example, is based on the assumption that a strong relationship exists between the amount of direct labor used to create the service and overhead. Services that require more direct labor generally require more indirect labor (e.g., supervision and time keeping), more wear and tear on equipment (e.g., computer depreciation), greater use of utilities, accounting, MIS and human resource (personnel) departments.

An overhead rate is computed as follows:

$$\text{Service overhead: } \frac{\text{Service overhead}}{\text{Direct labor}} = \frac{\$14,245}{\$4,000} = 356\%$$

This results in the following overhead application:

	Service		
Annual Cost ($1000s)	A	B	Total
Service overhead	$10,680	$3,565	$14,245

Step 3

Selling, general, and administration (SG&A) costs are not part of service costs. SG&A represent a cost that benefits the entire enterprise and is not assigned to individual services. Selling costs are expenses incurred in marketing a service, including sales persons' salaries, commissions, and travel and entertainment expenses; advertising; sales department salaries and expenses; and samples. General and administrative costs include the cost of managing or directing an enterprise, including management, public relations, and legal services. Generally accepted accounting principles dictate that these costs be expensed in the same period in which they are incurred. They are usually shown as a separate and distinct division in a profit-and-loss statement. In a "funds balance statement" used by nonprofits and governments, they may also be broken out separately. Nonprofits have fund-raising expenses, which are the equivalent of sales and marketing expenses in for-profit organizations. The government does not have selling expenses except in cases such as the U.S. Postal Service marketing its overnight mail service, or the Bureau of Engraving marketing its postal stamp printing capabilities to the post office.

Examples of SG&A expenses include:

Expense Category	$ (in 1,000s)
Executives	750
Administration and accounting	400
Sales and marketing	300
Interest expense	100
Total selling, general & administrative	1,550

Applying the traditional cost accounting model results in the following cost breakdown:

	Services		
	A	B	Total
Annual Cost (in $1000s)	$	$	$
Direct labor wages	3,000	1,000	4,000
Direct supplies	3,500	3,500	7,000
Direct service overhead	10,680	3,565	14,245
Total direct service cost	17,180	8,065	25,245
SG&A			1,550
Total cost			26,795

SHORTCOMINGS OF THE TRADITIONAL SERVICE COST MODEL

The traditional service cost model distorts the cost of providing a service for several reasons:

1. Service overhead costs are allocated rather than traced to services.
2. The total overhead component of the service cost has historically grown faster than direct costs. As overhead becomes a larger per-

centage of service cost, the distortion inherent in the allocation process causes the total service cost to increase.

3. Generally accepted accounting principles often dictate or influence cost accounting practices. One of these principles—the conservatism principle—is inconsistent with accurate service cost determination in two important ways:

   a. The conservatism principle requires that reported cost be based on precise and easily verifiable data, whereas management often needs costs that are based on forecasts and plans.

   b. The conservatism principle encourages expensing many costs in the current period that should be capitalized. This practice distorts life-cycle costs.

4. Many activities included in SG&A are traceable to specific services.

Each of these issues is discussed in more depth in the remainder of this section.

1. Service Overhead Costs Are Allocated Rather Than Traced to Services

Service overhead includes all costs other than direct service labor and direct supplies that are associated with a specific service (e.g., direct labor would be police officers riding in their vehicles plus direct supplies of gasoline and oil; direct labor is also the phone installer, and wire/switches are direct supplies). Overhead is allocated from cost centers to services according to an overhead application rate. Whether a cost is allocated or traced depends on whether a cause-and-effect relationship is established.

For example, a common method of allocating purchasing costs to services is to include these costs in "supplies overhead" and charge them to services on the basis of supplies cost. These costs are allocated because a direct cause-and-effect relationship cannot be established between purchasing costs and individual services—so a surrogate, supplies cost, is used.

However, purchasing costs can be traced to services by identifying the cause-and-effect relationship between purchasing activities and services.

Consider the activity of ordering supplies. The number of purchase orders (the output of the activity of ordering supplies) can be traced to services based on the number of purchase orders consumed. The number of purchase orders necessary to acquire the supplies for any service can be precisely specified, that is, a cause-and-effect relationship can be established and the cost of ordering supplies can be directly traced to services rather than allocated. For example, if the purchasing department processed 6,000 purchase orders during the year and it costs $600,000 to issue purchase orders, then it costs the organization $100 ($600,000/6,000) to issue a purchase order. If a complex service required 25 purchase orders, then $2,500 (25 purchase orders at $100 per purchase order) is traceable to the service.

Under **responsibility accounting**, costs are assigned to managers of each organizational unit responsible for a set of related but unique activities. These costs are homogeneous with respect to function, but each activity has its own unique cost behavior pattern. The composite cost is therefore, a mixture of several cost behaviors. For example, consider a purchasing department:

Cost Center: Purchasing Department

Account	Description	Actual $	Budget $	Variance $
0009	Salaries	80,150	83,000	2,850
0010	Wages, hourly	124,360	110,000	(14,360)
0201	Benefits, salaried	21,812	22,600	788
0202	Benefits, hourly	37,688	32,600	(5,088)
0352	Travel	62,515	70,500	7,985
0366	Facilities	32,000	32,000	0
0380	Supplies	1,394	1,500	106
0463	Training	20,240	30,000	9,760
	Total	380,159	382,200	2,041

The purchasing department is responsible for plan procurement, selecting/evaluating vendors, negotiating contracts, ordering supplies, and coordinating vendors. The resources consumed in each activity, the cost behavior pattern, and cost drivers for each activity would be unique.

Consider first the resources consumed in each activity:

Activity Description	Actual $	Budget $	Variance $
Plan procurement	29,150	30,000	850
Select/evaluate vendors	43,360	45,200	1,840
Negotiate contracts	45,632	50,000	4,368
Order supplies	161,492	150,000	(11,492)
Coordinate vendors	100,525	107,000	6,475
Total	380,159	382,200	2,041

The department spends $161,492 or 42 percent (161,492/380,159) of the total department cost on the "order supplies" activity and $29,150 or 8 percent (29,150/380,159) of the total cost on planning procurement.

Next consider the cost behavior patterns and the activity measures of the activities. Select/evaluate vendors, for example, varies with the number of new vendors; order supplies, on the other hand, varies with the number of purchase orders or purchase order lines.

Finally, consider the cost drivers. The principal cost drivers for negotiating contracts include vendor policy (multiple vendors or sole source) and degree of service standardization. The principal cost drivers for order supplies include order size, purchasing policy, stocking policy (JIT or supplier stocking), and degree of service standardization.

Traditional cost systems muddle unique activities by capturing cost at the cost element level (e.g., supplies, travel) rather than by activities. This systematically distorts the cost of individual services by including a mixture of activities with different cost behavior patterns. For example, knowing the purchasing department spends $124,360 on hourly wages does not provide any insight into how the wages are being employed. Thus, costs must be allocated to services.

When costs are allocated, a service containing more direct labor hours (or total direct costs or sales) than another service is assumed to incur proportionately more indirect cost. Volume-related allocations reliably distribute overhead costs to services only if overhead varies directly with volume output.

By decomposing cost elements (e.g., supplies, travel) into unique activities, costs are traced through the activities that make up a service rather than being allocated. Costs are traceable if a cause-and-effect relationship is established between the activity and service operation process. Costs are allocated differently if no cause-and-effect relationship is established.

Consider the development of a process plan for a new service. The number of hours expended by service engineering to develop a plan on how the service will be delivered is directly attributable to that service. Failure to trace costs to services and business processes causes organizations to resort to allocating costs on an arbitrary basis with a resulting cost distortion.

2. The Total Overhead Component of the Service Cost Has Historically Grown Faster Than Direct Cost

Today, indirect cost has become a significant component of the cost of a service. In the past, when direct labor and direct supplies were the predominant cost factors and overhead costs were nominal, the service cost distortion caused by improper selection of an overhead allocation method was minimal. The concept of materiality dominated.

The rapid increase in overhead costs lies at the heart of this distortion created by using direct labor as the basis for allocating service overhead. Direct labor as a percentage of total service cost has decreased while service overhead costs have risen. As organizations have increasingly incorporated information systems and automation into the service enterprise, the overhead category, rather than labor or supplies, has grown at the fastest pace. Traditional systems consider service overhead as fixed in the short and medium run, yet instead it has been the most dynamic.

Because overhead is a significant component of service cost, the choice of allocation methods has a major impact on service cost. Consider a service organization that is evaluating labor hours and equipment hours as a basis to allocate overhead. Depending on which of the two methods is selected, a substantial difference in the amount of cost applied to the service would result.

Assume the first case, in which "other overhead" is split based on supplies.

	Service A $	Service B $	Total $
Labor (24 hours at $10)	40 (4 hours)	200 (20 hours)	240
Supplies	300	300	600
Technology (12 hours at $20)	200 (10 hours)	40 (2 hours)	240
Other overhead	385	385	770
Total	925	925	1,850

To illustrate the importance of choosing an appropriate basis of allocation, let us first compute a service cost by direct labor. An overhead rate is computed as follows:

$$\frac{\text{Direct labor}}{\text{overhead rate}} = \frac{\text{Total cost} - \text{Direct labor and supplies}}{\text{Total direct labor cost}}$$

$$= \frac{(\$925 + 925 - 40 - 200 - 300 - 300)}{(40 + 200)} = \frac{\$1,010}{\$240} = 421\%$$

The accounting system calculates a service cost by the direct labor based overhead rate as follows:

	Service A $	Service B $	Total $
Direct labor (24 hours at $10)	40	200	240
Supplies	300	300	600
Technology & other overhead (421% × 40, 200)	168	842	1,010
Total	508	1342	1,850

Next consider computing a service cost by the service equipment hour:

$$\frac{\text{Service equipment}}{\text{overhead rate}} = \frac{\text{Total cost} - \text{Direct labor and supplies}}{\text{Total equipment hours}}$$

$$= \frac{\$1,010}{12 \text{ hours}} = \$84.17 \text{ per hour}$$

The accounting system calculates a service cost by the service equipment-based overhead rate as follows:

	Service A $	Service B $	Total $
Direct labor (24 hours at $10)	40	200	240
Supplies	300	300	600
Technology & other overhead (@ $84.17/hour)	842 (10 hours)	168 (2 hours)	1,010
Total	1,182	668	1,850

This example illustrates how selection of an allocation basis dramatically affects cost when overhead becomes a significant proportion of total cost.

For illustrative purposes, assume the average difference between allocation methods is 40 percent. If the overhead component of total cost is 10 percent, then the 40 percent discrepancy in the choice of overhead methods results in only a 4 percent difference in total cost (40 percent × 10 percent). On the other hand, if the total overhead consists of 40 percent of total service cost, then a difference of 16 percent in total cost (40 percent × 40 percent) results. As overhead costs increase in magnitude, the importance of selecting allocation methods based on economic consequence increases.

3. Generally Accepted Accounting Principles Often Dictate or Influence Cost Accounting Practices

The conservatism principle requires that reported cost be based on precise and easily verifiable data

To accurately match overhead costs to services requires precise knowledge of future business conditions, including service volumes. Such precise knowledge of the future is impossible. As a result, the matching of overhead cost to services must be based on estimates, and is necessarily imprecise. An ingrained fear of making decisions on imprecise data causes organizations to resort to using allocation bases that are easily verifiable but irrelevant.

To illustrate this point, consider recent surveys demonstrating that the prevalent practice in U. S. industry is to use direct labor based allocation and straight line depreciation in spite of the fact that these practices increasingly are less reflective of reality. The reason that they are popular is that both direct labor-based allocation and straight-line depreciation use data that are easily verified and understandable. However, the reported cost is not relevant to decision making because the assumptions underlying the approaches are not valid.

It is important to base cost decisions on relevant information even if the data is based on imprecise estimates. Estimates derived from realistic cost behavior patterns provide an excellent basis for making routine decisions and controlling service operations. Consider equipment hour-based depreciation. The organization must estimate the number of hours of usage for the equipment per year and "in total" for the life of the equipment. Clearly, this type of estimating is much less precise than merely estimating the number of years the machine will be used and recovering the cost in equal increments during its period of usefulness.

However, consider the cost behavior patterns of equipment. First, rarely is the usage of the equipment steady throughout its life. As the service demands fluctuate, so will equipment usage. A depreciation method not based on equipment hours charges too much depreciation during periods of low demand and, conversely, too little cost during periods of high demand. Second, the only direct relationship between equipment cost and services is in equipment hours. This relationship is analogous to that of direct labor and services. The amount of time a piece of equipment takes to process specific services varies by service. An organization is forced to use surrogates such as labor hours or supply cost, which rarely reflect how much equipment cost is consumed in producing services.

The conservatism principle encourages expensing many costs in the current period that should be capitalized

The primary reasons that organizations expense costs of activities that benefit future periods are that this course of action is conservative, minimizes taxable income, and maximizes cash flow. If start-up costs are capitalized and the service, or investment is abandoned or unprofitable, then an organization must write off the asset. It is believed that an organization is financially healthier if it expenses costs that are potentially risky.

There are several problems with expensing, rather than capitalizing, the cost of activities that benefit future periods. First, any potentially traceable costs that are treated as an expense in the current period rather than matched to services result in service cost distortion.

Cost distortion occurs because of the following:

- The magnitude of cost is large. When one considers the many research, design, and marketing activities that are necessary to commercialize a service or implement an investment, a great number of costs are evident. They are needed if an enterprise is to remain in business in the long run. Governments and nonprofits also can have a variety of capital investments that allow it to provide a service (e.g., buildings, police cars, computers, firefighting equipment, garbage trucks, prisons, hospitals, therapy equipment, and classrooms)
- The expenditure pattern is uneven. The distribution of activities between those that benefit the current or future periods varies based on factors such as management policy and budgetary considerations.

Second, expensing confuses the issue of matching and risk. The goal of matching is to infer how costs attach to services. Risk is a function of the probability of achieving the desired results. Risk is directly related to anticipated variability of estimates.

The issues of risk and matching are separate and distinct. No matter what the degree of risk, the identification of how costs attach to services is unchanged. Risk should be managed through a rigorous review of all activities from start-up to retirement, as events unfold in relation to the original plan. Risk should not be managed by the choice of accounting methods.

Third, service life cycles are decreasing. Shorter service life cycles increase the need to understand the total service cost over its entire life cycle to determine profitability. Reduced life cycles mean organizations have less available time to respond to changes in market demand and to recover service development costs.

4. Many Activities Included in Selling, General and Administrative Are Traceable to Specific Services

Consider advertising as a cost that can be traced to specific services. General advertising benefits all services and is not traceable to individual services. Specific service advertising, however, is traceable to individual services. Although there is a spin-off effect to other services, the primary goal of specific service advertising is to increase the sales of the service being advertised. Failure to trace costs misrepresents the profitability of the services. Similarly, sales commissions are often service dependent and thus traceable to specific services. Again, failure to trace these costs distorts service cost.

IMPLICATIONS OF SERVICE COST DISTORTION

Service distortion leads to cross-subsidization of services. When used to guide marketing strategies, distorted cost information encourages managers to provide many low-volume services. The results, in many cases, are declining profit margins and perceived difficulty competing with focused competitors (e.g., Japanese banks).

Service variety and complexity increase cost distortion. Several factors have contributed to the growth of overhead in recent decades. The primary ones include customer demands; increased diversity, or scope, of output (not increased volume, or scale, of output); increased use of technology; and increased regulations. Thus, traditional cost accounting systems tend to overcost high-volume services—not the ones that cause most growth in overhead—and undercost the low-volume services that are chiefly responsible for the overhead growth.

Many overhead costs are driven by diversity of volume, services, business processes, and customers. This diversity increases the complexity of the service operations. Activities such as move supplies, scheduling, and setups tend to grow with the number of services in the service line and the support required in complex service environments. If an office produces only one service with no options, the scheduling function is a simple task; complexities (and the requirement for additional scheduling personnel and overhead) occur because of the variety of services, sizes, colors, customers, and options provided. Think of the overhead costs for the IRS. There are forms and laws for sole proprietors, partnerships, corporations, S corporations, limited liability corporations, foreign corporations, resident aliens, individuals, trusts, estates, and so forth. The vast multitude of forms and laws drives the number of employees and people in this organization.

The conventional methodology of allocating the cost of overhead activities related to service variety and complexity on a volume-related basis distorts service cost. Think of the complexity of running a hospital. There are infectious diseases, bone and heart problems, gun shot wounds, psychosomatic illnesses, and so forth. Some problems can be cured with a bandage, but some need sixteen hours of surgery and cost over $100,000.

ACTIVITY SERVICE COST

Activity management is based on the principle that activities/business processes consume resources, whereas services consume activities/business processes and supplies. Service costing is enhanced by more specific tracing of support costs that have traditionally been lumped in overhead and allocated to all services. Activity service cost is derived by identifying the supplies and activities/business processes necessary to produce a service and determining the quantity of activity/business process for each service. Service cost is determined by summing the costs of all traceable activities/business processes.

Consider the service of helping the birth of a child at a hospital. The procedures specify the following activities:

- Admit mother
- Prepare mother for labor room
- Check dilation/inform doctor/assist with labor
- Bring mother and father to delivery room
- Deliver child
- Check baby/tag and weigh baby
- Transport baby to nursery
- Transport mother to recovery room

When the cost of each activity required to help with the birth of a baby has been determined, the service cost can be computed. The cost of the deliver baby activity, for example, consists of the cost of direct labor (e.g., wages), depreciation on the delivery equipment, and the supplies consumed in the delivery process. Labor, supplies, and equipment are all specified by the procedure manual.

The factors of service operations are easily associated with each activity; the cost of the service process is directly computed from the amount of supplies and labor time the deliver child activity consumes. The service cost for the delivery is the sum of the cost of the various activities.

However, to concentrate exclusively on these prime service costs excludes the many activities that are required to support the production of a service. The service must be designed; the labor, equipment, facilities, and supplies must be procured; the service process must be scheduled and controlled (how many staff are needed on hand for deliveries today); performance must be reported to internal (mother and father, doctor's committee, patient accounting, candy stripers) and external parties (government, county, insurance company); and a myriad of other support activities must be accomplished (janitorial, supply room, maintenance, bookkeeping, grounds and facilities). Each of these activities consumes resources and is a prerequisite for service operations (e.g., delivering a child).

Support activities have traditionally been included in overhead and allocated to services on a direct basis such as direct labor, equipment usage (e.g., time spent in the delivery room) supplies, or sales. In activity accounting there is a need to trace support activities to services. Consider the design service activity (e.g., how to perform a hip transplant, how to sell cold beer on a hot day in August, how to remove snow from the highway, or how to conduct a jail and bail fund-raiser). A service cannot be produced without being designed. The design service activity is easily identifiable with a specific service; one need not lump design costs in overhead and allocate the costs to all services. Failure to trace support costs distorts service cost.

To further illustrate the importance of tracing activities to services, consider the major activities of a typical department that controls supplies. They include:

- Handle incoming supplies (e.g., bombs in military)
- Handle in-process supplies (e.g., blood brought to operating room)
- Handle outgoing supplies (e.g., food/drinks served on a plane/train)
- Store supplies (e.g., cleaning supplies for real estate management organization)
- Store work in process (e.g., operating room supply kits made up by hospital prior to surgery)
- Store finished services (e.g., donated gifts)
- Manage department
- Train department

The handle-supplies activity is controlled differently from the activity of store supplies. The costs of handling supplies attach to the services being moved. Services might or might not be stored, depending on the procedures (Red Adair might not store dynamite to extinguish oil well fires, but banks might store new account kits and fund-raisers might store information kits). Only services that require storage should be charged with the cost of storing supplies. To include store supplies costs in overhead and arbitrarily allocate them to all services penalizes services that don't use storage.

Activity cost is the sum of the factors of service operations (natural expense categories) and interorganizational activities. Determining activity service cost involves the following process:

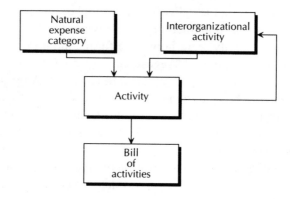

Activity management systems compute a service cost by tracing all service-related activities to services on the basis of the services' usage of each activity. For example, quality costs would be assigned where the quality effort is expended. Taxes and utilities would be assigned on occupied square footage. A service cost becomes a summation of the cost of all traceable activities to design, produce, and distribute a service. Activities represent the capabilities of a service enterprise. The production of a service uses varying amounts of those capabilities. A service consumes activities during its life cycle—research market, design service, plan marketing/sales, produce service, service, deliver service, and provide customer service. For example, one state-of-the-art service may require a significant amount of market research and design activities (e.g., architectural plans for a symphony hall). Another commodity-type service would require fewer of these activities (e.g., plans for a toll booth).

Many support functions, such as service supervision and quality control, involve service-related activities. From interviews with managers and service workers, the percentage of time spent on activities is determined and traced according to the number of transactions. When the interview has not identified specific measures for activities, a general measure such as the number of service hours per service is used.

Administrative support activities cannot be directly related to specific services or equipment. These activities relate to the people managed or supported. Activities of managers and secretaries have many administrative aspects that are nontraceable and must be allocated to services.

An activity management system better mirrors service operations and therefore distorts service cost less than the traditional model for the following reasons:

- Activities represent the lowest level of homogeneous cost.
- There are multiple bases of assignment inherent in the selection of activity measures.
- Activities facilitate the linking of related activities (business processes), which transcend organizational boundaries. This group of cost can then be assigned en masse to the originating cause.
- Most variances are caused by the activity rather than the service.
- Life-cycle costing permits better matching of time periods.
- Traditionally, there were two major classifications of service cost—direct service cost and SG&A (selling, general and administrative). In activity management there can be others, such as orders, customers, services, projects, contracts, or channels of distribution.
- It is possible to trace service-related costs, including SG&A.
- There is minimal dependence for accurate activity costs on an organization's existing organizational structure and level of detail captured within the accounting system.

ACTIVITY SERVICE COST APPROACH

Once activities are costed, they can be combined to form a bill of activities for the various services that an organization provides. This bill of activities will render a more accurate service cost than traditional systems.

Service Bill of Activities

The traceability of service cost can be improved by identifying all significant activities triggered by the decision to provide a service. The activities are subsets to service operations summarized in the statement, "Create service." One approach is to specify this process in terms of a bill of activity (BOA) based on the sequence of activities to provide this service. The BOA includes all organizational activities, both support and direct service, required to provide a service.

The BOA activity approach provides management with the capability of defining the quantity and cost of activities within a service, across service families, or within the entire enterprise.

A bill of activity is created in two steps:

- *Step 1:* Determine costed bill of activities for organizational processes. Key business processes that are consumed in a service are costed in total rather than listed individually.
- *Step 2:* Determine a costed bill of activities for each service.

The source for determining the service operation activities of a service cost is the service design process. The service design specifies how a service is provided. The typical information available on most designs includes:

- Procedures
- Department performing procedures
- Setup hours
- Labor grade for direct labor
- Direct labor hours per unit of service
- Equipment type
- Equipment hours (e.g., connect time on computer terminal)
- Service operations lead time for move, queue, setup, and run time for a typical service

It is essential that the design procedures represent the way the order actually moves through the office or facility and the service operation processes. If it doesn't, the wrong activities will be charged against the service. When an alternate procedure is used, the bill of activities for the order should reflect the alternate procedure.

Activity	Activity Measure	Activity Quantity	Activity Unit Cost $	Life Cycle Cost ($) for 5,000 Loans	Activity Cost	Subtotal
Life Cycle Costs						
Design loan	designs	1	5,000	5,000	1.00 ($5,000/5,000 loans)	
Design procedures	procedures	5	200	1,000	.20 ($1,000/5,000 loans)	
Acquire supplies	supplies	1	50	50	.01 (50/5,000 loans)	1.21
Subtotal of life cycle costs						
Take applications	application	1	150		150.00	
Order credit survey, appraisal	# reports	3	30		90.00	
Review documents	reviews	1	70		70.00	
Review by loan committee	applications	1	200		200.00	
Prepare loan documents	pages	30	5		150.00	
Disburse funds	disbursements	1	100		100.00	760.00
Total continuing operating cost						$761.21
Total cost of reports						$150.00
Total life cycle, operations, & report cost process						$911.21

A service cost bill of activities represents all the activities necessary to provide a service. The bill of activities represents all activities over the entire life cycle. Activities that are independent of a service order are charged on a per unit basis over the planned volume of the service.

A typical bill of activities includes:

Activity	Life-Cycle Cost	Cost per Unit
Design service	x	x
Design service procedures	x	x
Plan for quality	x	x
Store supplies		x
Move supplies		
Set up		x
Perform procedure 1		x
Perform procedure 2		x
Deliver		x
Provide customer service	x	x
Support in field	x	x

The primary costs that comprise a service cost include supplies, direct labor, technology (e.g., depreciation), quality, design, development, research and development, supplies handling, marketing and advertising, and service support, customer technical support, and finished services distribution. Those cost elements are described in greater detail below.

Supplies Cost

Supplies costs are derived from the budget or a **bill of supplies (BOS)**. A BOS is any document that defines the service from the design point of view by listing supplies for each portion of the service (e.g., supplies necessary to install a burglar alarm). The BOS structure pertains to the way the service is structured, and the supplies needed at the outset and in each state of completion. Thus, the BOS specifies not only the composition of a service but also the process stages in that service's production. It defines service structure in terms of levels of service, each of which represents a step in the production of the service. A graphic representation of a BOS is shown in the following figure:

The BOS is the key source of supplies cost used to compute a service cost. Several activity service cost systems incorporate the BOS into the service cost roll-up, while others interface with the BOS and extract supplies cost in total. In determining a service cost, several features of the BOS are important:

1. A given supply item can either be purchased or internally produced. The cost of purchased supplies consists of the purchase price and all traceable costs of bringing the supplies to the activity that consumes it. The cost of a service component consists of all traceable costs to provide the component (e.g., a portion of the insurance policy; the eye test, written test, and driving test for driver's license renewal; fuel for vehicles).

2. A given service can exist in its own right as a uniquely identified unit (supplies, component part, minimum coverage in an insurance policy, oil change) or as an item of another package (oil, air and oil filter change, grease job). In either case, the activities to provide the component are identical. However, if the service unit is stored, the component cost will be higher due to storage costs (e.g., cleaning and storing winter coats).

3. The BOS establishes the service item lead times (e.g., when promotional displays/bombs must arrive). This information is used for performance measurement.

Direct Labor Costs

In a pure activity management system, labor costs are charged to the service operation activities and not to the individual services. The approach is based on the observation that laborers perform activities and services consume activities. Labor cost is one component of activity cost.

Labor costs are assigned to services according to the amount of the activity consumed by the service specified in the bill of activities. For example, the cost of reports (credit, appraisal, surveys) is charged to the service according to the number of reports specified in the service bill of activities for a mortgage. Based on the rates and number of operators assigned to an activity, a cost per activity measure is derived. For example, the labor associated with workers obtaining credit reports is charged to the underwriting activity. Knowing the total number of credit reports allows an organization to compute a cost per credit report or cost per loan.

There are several reasons for charging costs directly to activities rather than services. First, labor variances are more often the result of process variances than any aspect of the service. Demand changes (up or down), operator experience, and training variations result in operator efficiencies and inefficiencies. These factors cause variances related to an activity rather than to the service. Second, labor reporting is greatly simplified because there is no need to voucher labor to services.

However, there are exceptions in which some labor-related costs require special time reporting. The primary situations include the following:

- Estimates of direct labor are very imprecise. It may be difficult to precisely estimate labor hours for one-time services.
- Labor may be transferred between activities. Determine if labor is being shifted between operations based on the complexity of the service (e.g., roofers helping carpenters in real estate construction, community service personnel assisting fund-raising personnel).
- Contractual requirements may apply to labor reporting. Defense department regulations, Federal Acquisition Regulations (FAR), and Cost Accounting Standards Board (CASB) requirements often require specific direct labor reports (e.g., Computer Science or EDS).
- Floating labor may complicate reporting. Determine if additional laborers are hired to fill in for absent workers. Proper service costing requires accountability for the use of these workers.

Process variances for an activity are computed by comparing the labor hours earned during a time period with the actual hours expended. The earned hours are derived by summing the total hours specified in the bill of activities for all services using the activity during the specified time period.

Continued significant variations between actual and earned hours might indicate that the service bills of activities must be reviewed. Those responsible for service profitability, such as the service/service line manager should identify instances of above-normal activity. Those responsible for the process, such as the service operation manager, should identify instances of below-normal activity. Earned hours can be periodically validated by industrial engineering studies and random checks of actual time spent on services as opposed to earned time.

Technology Costs

The costs of technology are traced to services on the basis of the usage of the activity, as reflected in the activity measure (e.g., computer time, transportation equipment hours, scanning time, typesetting time, filming time, and so on).

Quality Costs

Activities associated with quality are classified into four categories:

1. Prevention

   Plan quality (e.g., plan organization quality activities)

   Design and develop quality measurement and control equipment (e.g., check flow meters for a gas station)

   Calibrate equipment (e.g., set dispenser to control amount of liquor in a drink)

   Train associates (e.g., train for statistical process control)

   Administer quality assurance program

   Audit system (e.g., audit quality training system)

   Develop quality improvement projects

2. Appraisal

   Conduct laboratory acceptance testing (e.g., implement corporate testing of food in fast food restaurant chain)

   Inspect and test (e.g., test trained soldiers)

   Inspect and test setup (e.g., set up cash register test)

Inspect in-process (not by inspectors)
Audit service quality (e.g., hotels audit their properties)
Review inspection test results prior to acceptance
Evaluate at customers' sites (e.g., evaluate new software)
Process data of inspection and test reports

3. Internal failure (directly charged to department incurring cost but classified as a quality activity)

Handle scrap (e.g., discard burnt food)
Rework service (e.g., redo insurance policy with errors)
Troubleshoot service (e.g., troubleshoot new software)
Analyze defects and failures (e.g., errors in public law)
Reinspect and retest (e.g., review rejected audit report)
Provide for lost service production due to faulty vendor supplies (e.g., retail store receives merchandise that doesn't meet their needs)
Provide for lost service production due to own supplies (e.g., computer system crash causes defective contracts or will)

4. External failures (A suggested activity measure might be the number of returns from the field for poor quality. The source of information includes internal quality reports, vendor quality reports, and shipping reports.)

Administer complaints
Manage reliability: the engineering activity of tracking and analyzing customer returns to determine the causes of quality problems (e.g., analyze returned software)
Provide customer service
Handle liability (e.g., defend or settle lawsuits)
Process service returns (e.g., accept return of TV that still doesn't work)
Process service recalls (e.g., carry out recall of pacemakers)
Provide service replacement (e.g., replace service or cancel charge for meal or hotel)
Correct marketing errors (e.g., reprint promotion that has printing errors)

Additional service-related costs include:

Administer warranty/service contracts. The cost of warranty and service contract administration should be traced to the services according to the distribution of time and cost incurred in this activity. Additionally, warranty service costs should certainly be an element of the cost of quality report.

Provide customer service in field. Field customer service activities include installations and repairs performed by the field service personnel. These costs should be charged to the specific service being repaired. The regional supervisor's cost and the cost of maintaining the field service offices would be factored into the activity rates used for charging the cost of these activities to segments. Repair work represents a cost of quality (e.g., repairing the same street twice within a month or commissioning several studies for the same road expansion).

Perform in-house repair. In-house repair activities include installations and repairs performed by maintenance. These costs should be charged to the specific service being repaired. The supervisor's cost and the cost of maintaining the repair office would be factored into the activity rates used for charging the cost of these activities to services. Repair work represents a cost of quality.

Service Design Costs

The costs related to developing new or enhanced services are charged directly to specific service/service lines. Design costs are charged to specific projects/service lines by either the estimated number of designs, design hours or a project-tracking system. Project-tracking systems can be manual time collection systems or can automatically extract information from the computer project tacking system. The source of the information includes payroll records and design and quality control reports. The costs of outside services, testing, and supplies are directly charged to specific services through accounts payable.

Service design changes/documentation control activities originate from design enhancement of services. Normally they are triggered by a customer or by the marketing department through a design change order (DCO), and include control and administration of the following types of documentation:

- Marketing manuals
- Service manuals and specifications

- Installation manuals
- Bills of supplies
- Processes/service operation procedures

The cost of these design change activities should be traced to services according to the number of DCOs a service line generates. However, when these activities are performed for a new service under development, the costs should be directly assigned to the service on the basis of design hours.

Service Development Costs

Activities associated with service development include the following:

- Plan process and procedures
- Modify process and procedures
- Program service

Service development activities represent a life-cycle cost that should be associated with the service operation process.

Research and Development Costs

Activities associated with R & D include:

- Conduct basic research (e.g., new cancer insurance policy)
- Research service process (e.g., how to cook hamburgers with less cholesterol)
- Develop new service (e.g., McDonalds' Happy meal for children)
- Develop new service procedures (e.g., how to perform plastic surgery on an outpatient basis)

Basic research and service process research should be charged to an organization-wide nontraceable overhead, or applied to development projects as a secondary activity, depending on organization policy.

Customer Technical Support Costs

In-house technical support people handle a variety of questions from end users and sales representatives. They also deal with customer returns. Their costs are directly traceable to service lines on the basis of the number of return authorizations generated during the quarter for each service. Where the analysis is unable to trace costs to the specific service/service lines supported, these costs are considered a common organization cost. However, in service life-cycle costing all costs of this activity can be charged to specific services.

Finished Services and Distribution Costs

Activities associated with finished services and distribution include the following:

- Store finished services (e.g., store collected garbage or cars towed by the police)
- Ship service (e.g., deliver promotional items bought by customer)
- Package service (e.g., choose type of seminar notebook)
- Provide support in field (e.g., give computer technical support)
- Supply spares (e.g., provide spare computers, salt trucks)
- Maintain equipment (e.g., inspect and repair postal trucks, tanks, computers)
- Coordinate dealership/franchises (e.g., coordinate hotel, fast food chains)

These costs should be directly traceable to services/service lines through service bill of activities.

COST MANAGEMENT EXAMPLE

To illustrate the significance of tracing costs, consider the impact of tracing the following costs:

Traceable Labor	Annual Cost ($1,000s)
Direct labor and fringe benefits	4,500
Setup of service	600
Rework	300
Overtime premium	250
Training	150
Shift premium	125
Workman's compensation	75
Miscellaneous	50
Subtotal	6,050

Traceable Supplies	($1,000s)
Supplies	6,000
Purchased items	1,000
Incoming shipping charges	575
Subtotal	7,575

Other Traceable Costs	($1,000s)
Supplies labor	2,500
Supplies storage	800
Quality assurance	900
Service operation utilities	500
Depreciation on service equipment	1,150
Scrap	200
Service designers	600
Industrial engineering	225
Service-specific advertising	320
Operations control	400
Subtotal	7,595

Nontraceable Costs	($1,000s)
Office supervision and management	275
Building utilities	280
Office security	75
Information systems	925
Building taxes and insurance	175
Depreciation on lobby/parking lot	100
Miscellaneous supplies	600
Other purchasing	50
Other capital carrying costs	50
Miscellaneous	800
Subtotal	3,330

Selling, General & Administrative	($1,000s)
Basic research & development	550
Administration	350
Marketing	250
Corporate human resources	840
Corporate information systems	750
Accounting	425
Subtotal	3,165
Total cost	27,715

The new reported service cost would be calculated as follows:

	Services		
	A $	B $	Total $
Direct labor			
Direct labor wages	4,695	1,565	6,260
Direct supplies	3,909	3,909	7,818
Direct technology	464	2,000	2,464
Quality	600	360	960
Research & development	1,000	2,033	3,033
Service work in process	100	41	141
Marketing and advertising	70	71	141
Service operation support	626	400	1,026
Finished services and distribution	250	336	586
Nontraceable overhead	1,847	1,565	3,412
Total service costs	13,561	12,280	25,841
Selling, general & administrative			1,874
Total cost			27,715

SPECIAL CONSIDERATIONS

There are a number of special considerations including: the service cost frequency, service set-up costs, bottlenecks, profit velocity, and work-orders.

Service Cost Calculation Frequency

A bill of activities (BOA) separates the quantity of an activity from the cost of the activity. A BOA specifies the sequence and quantity of activities. The cost of an activity is separately computed by the activity management system. This approach simplifies the standard-setting process because the BOA need only be modified if there is a change to the activity/process. Changes to the cost elements of service operations do not require a modification to the BOA.

Service Setup Costs

The conventional practice of service operations in lots (e.g., operating room kits) in advance of current demand is intended to spread the setup and ordering costs over a larger number of service units and, as a consequence, to reduce the total annual cost of operation. For example, making food in large batches can be economical because it can then be ordered and prepared in quantity.

Setup involves preparing a service process for operation for the first time. Setup is dependent on the service operation schedule, the service complexity, and the service operation technology. If a process must be set up from scratch, a fixed amount of effort will be required. However, where the preceding process was set up for a service item within the same family of service items, a changeover rather than an entire setup is required. A **changeover** is a partial setup in which not all procedures are required.

For example, a changeover for a printing press might require changing all guides for different sizes and print stock thicknesses. To change the color is much more extensive and requires a full setup. Therefore, only a minor effort is required to change from one paper thickness to another paper thickness, as long as the color remains the same. This is a changeover. In the post office's system of sorting mail, there is frequently a major setup effort for different envelop thicknesses, but only a minor effort to change from one envelop size to another size within certain parameters.

The cost of a setup could be insignificant (e.g., serving one type of mixed drink versus another type of mixed drink) or significant (e.g., reconfiguring a plane for cargo at night and for passengers during the day). An obvious cost is the time that it takes an operator to set up the equipment to create the next service. Less obvious costs include the cost of paperwork associated with each setup, the cost of personnel sitting idle during the setup, and the scrap loss on the initial service run in some cases (e.g., changing from cola ice cones to lemon lime ice cones requires that the line be flushed with lemon lime to remove the cola taste in a convenience store). When operators are not experienced with a setup, a learning curve occurs before the process is working at standard efficiency. Finally, when the equipment is operating at full capacity, the service operating time lost during a setup increases cost.

Bottleneck Costs

Service operation bottlenecks are generally considered to be temporary blockages to increased output; they may occur anywhere in the service operation process. The stationary bottleneck is easy to identify because work in process accumulates behind it (e.g., mortgage applications waiting for credit reports, surveys, and appraisals; insurance policies waiting for underwriting to review them). Its cause is usually also clear—long waits for vendor services, equipment has broken down, key workers are absent, or demand has outstripped the capacity of the process.

More subtle are bottlenecks that shift from one part of the organization/business process to another or have no clear cause; work builds up in different places at different times. Perhaps they result from flaws in a service's quality caused inadvertently by one or more workers trying to keep pace with service operation demands that should not have been placed on them. They may also be caused by missing service items (e.g., different missing supplies during construction of a building), new service startup, or changes in the mix of services through the organization (e.g., less demand for building permits, but greater demand for bankruptcy filings). In such cases the remedies are less clear-cut.

A nebulous bottleneck situation is a chronic management dilemma of job shops (e.g., business loans each structured differently) and batch flow processes (e.g., airline processing tickets for the government). In a batch flow (job shop), process capacity usage is volatile because the process now is indeterminate. For example, a new order or service introduction changes the service mix and might place excessive demands on a single department (e.g., a new special education department at a school).

Coming to a decision on how to remedy a bottleneck calls for an analysis of the cost associates with each option—specifically, the analysis involves comparing the extra costs incurred by each alternative, because those were the only costs that differed between the options being considered.

The following example evaluates a service setup time reduction to highlight some of the problems with understanding the cost impact of bottlenecks. Suppose that two types of equipment (e.g., computers), A and B, support the same service operation activity. The time necessary for equipment A to change from producing one service to producing another averages about ten minutes, whereas the setup time for equipment B is one hour. An engineering study indicates that the setup time of equipment A could be reduced by half at a cost of $50,000; equipment B's setup time could also be cut in half at a cost of $5,000.

Superficially, equipment B seems to pay off better in terms of time reduction per investment cost. This approach focuses on the work center at which the setup reduction occurs by examining the cost savings in work center service inventory and direct labor costs. However, this myopic view ignores the impact of the setup reduction on subsequent operations and services.

When the effects of a setup time reduction are evaluated for the entire service operation system, the economics of the decision can alter dramatically. If, for example, equipment A is set up twenty-five times a day, it can produce 1,000 units per day with its current changeover times. If equipment B is set up four times a day, it can produce 1,500 units per day. As a consequence, the output of the service operation line is limited to the 1,000 units per day that equipment A can produce.

Few benefits would be gained by reducing the setup time on equipment B, because the output of the line would still be 1,000 units per day and no additional revenue would be generated. A small labor savings will result, but unless this savings reduces the number of employees or their time is redeployed to alternative activities, the cost savings is not realized. In most cases, there are minimal benefits to reducing setup time on equipment that is not creating a bottleneck.

Two substantial benefits can be realized by reducing the setup time on equipment A. First, the time saved increases organizational capacity, because equipment A essentially controls the output of the organization. Alternatively, the additional time can be used to reduce the service operation lot sizes, thus increasing flexibility. Or it can be used to expand the range of services to the line, both of which increase the effective variety of the organization output.

Benefits of a setup time reduction should be examined in terms of capacity. If the setup time of equipment A is reduced to five minutes, the output of the equipment activity will increase by 125 minutes [(10 − 5 minutes) × 25 setups] per day; the two extra hours of activity capacity are worth a substantial sum of money. More throughput also decreases the overhead costs per unit. Seen another way, gains in capacity can offset reduced batch sizes, which in turn reduce work-in-progress service inventory, increase response time, and improve customer service.

The cost management systems used in most organizations are practically useless for this type of bottleneck decision. Estimating the benefits of reduced changeover time requires information other than the cost of equipment and the hours saved. What is needed is an estimate of the value of increased capacity, variety, and flow times. Tracing the impact of the reduction to activities will better quantify the impact of the decision.

Thus, focusing on the work center may lead to an overestimation of the savings in setup time reduction for equipment B and an underestimation of the benefits of a setup time reduction for equipment A. System-wide information is required for appropriate analysis. Such information must assess the effect of setup time reduction at a specific work center on the entire service operation process, as well as the effect of such a reduction on service quality.

Profit Velocity

Profit velocity is the ratio of service profit to lead time.

$$\text{Profit velocity} = \text{Profit/lead time}$$

Profit velocity is based on the observation that organizational profitability is a function of both the absolute profitability of a service and the number of services that can be produced during any given period of time. To illustrate profit velocity, consider two services:

Service	Profit $	Lead Time (days)
A	50	5
B	35	2

Conventional cost accounting would proclaim service A more profitable than service B—which is correct in absolute terms. The profit velocity of the two services presents a different conclusion. The profit velocity for service A is $10 ($50/5 days) per service operations day, while for service B it is $17.50 ($35/2 days) per service operations day. Assuming sufficient demand for service B, the organization would be most profitable selling service B rather than service A. The organization may want to redirect its marketing effort to emphasize service B.

Work Orders

Work orders should not be used for standard services—or for nonstandard services when the estimate is deemed sufficient. Work orders should be used when estimates might be considered suspect.

AN ACTIVITY SERVICE COST EXAMPLE

The steps in calculating an activity service cost are very similar to those in chapter 8, "Calculating an Activity Cost." However, when calculating an activity service cost, allocate secondary activities to the primary activities before calculating the activity cost per unit of activity. Therefore, the key steps for calculating activity service cost are:

Step 1 Select cost base
Step 2 Determine activities
Step 3 Define percentage of time per activity
Step 4 Trace cost to activities
Step 5 **Allocate secondary activities**
Step 6 Determine total cost for each activity
Step 7 Calculate cost per unit of activity output
Step 8 Create bill of activities

Step 1: Extract accounting department cost from general ledger:

Accounting Department	$
Labor	500,000
Travel	100,000
Mgmt. information systems	100,000
Others	100,000
Total	800,000

Step 2: Determine the activities of the accounting department:

Pay invoices
Process receivables
Prepare financial reports
Pay employees
Provide managerial reports
Manage employees
Train employees
Other

Step 3: Define percentage of time expended on each activity:

Accounting Department	%	Primary/Secondary
Pay invoices	20	Primary
Process receivables	20	Primary
Prepare financial reports	15	Primary
Pay employees	15	Primary
Provide managerial reports	10	Primary
Primary subtotal	80	
Manage employees	5	Secondary
Train employees	5	Secondary
Other	10	Secondary
Total	100%	

Step 4: Trace cost to the specific activities using the total department method for the labor:

Accounting Department	Labor $	Travel $	MIS $	Other	Total
Pay invoices	100,000		30,000		130,000
Process receivables	100,000	10,000	30,000		140,000
Prepare financial reports	75,000	20,000	10,000		105,000
Pay employees	75,000		20,000		95,000
Provide managerial reports	50,000		10,000		60,000
Manage employees	25,000	40,000			65,000
Train employees	25,000	30,000			55,000
Other	50,000			100,000	150,000
Total	500,000	100,000	100,000	100,000	800,000

Step 5: Allocate secondary activity costs to primary activities using primary activity labor time as the basis of allocating secondary cost. The total cost of the secondary activities is $270,000 (65,000 + 55,000 + 150,000).

Accounting Department	Secondary Costs $		Primary Activity %/Total Primary %	Secondary Costs Allocated $
Pay invoices	270,000	×	(20%/80%)	67,500
Process receivables	270,000	×	(20%/80%)	67,500
Prepare financial reports	270,000	×	(15%/80%)	50,600
Pay employees	270,000	×	(15%/80%)	50,600
Provide managerial reports	270,000	×	(10%/80%)	33,800
Manage employees				
Train employees				
Other				
Total				270,000

Step 6: Determine total cost for each activity:

Accounting Department	Labor	Travel $	MIS $	Secondary Allocation	Total $
Pay invoices	100,000		30,000	67,500	197,500
Process receivables	100,000	10,000	30,000	67,500	207,500
Prepare financial reports	75,000	20,000	10,000	50,600	155,600
Pay employees	75,000		20,000	50,600	145,600
Provide managerial reports	50,000		10,000	33,800	93,800
Manage employees					
Train employees					
Other					
Total	400,000	30,000	100,000	270,000	800,000

Step 7: Calculate cost per unit of activity output:

Accounting Department	Total $	Measure (Units)	Measure	Cost/ Unit $
Pay invoices	197,500	13,000	invoices	15.192
Process receivables	207,500	20,000	collections	10.375
Prepare financial reports	155,600	12	reports	12,966.67
Pay employees	145,600	5,000	checks	29.12
Provide managerial reports	93,800	60	reports	1,563.33
Manage employees				
Train employees				
Other				
Total	800,000			

Assumptions for bill of activities below:

- Assumes one invoice per 100 loans; therefore, quantity is .01.
- Assumes each loan is collected monthly over ten years; therefore, quantity is 120 months.
- Assumes that external reports are not traceable to service.
- Already charged to other above activity costs.
- Assume each managerial report has approximately 2,000 loans. Average loan is for 120 months; therefore, the quantity is 120 months. The monthly cost per loan for managerial reports is $1,563.33/average of 2,000 loans per month equals $.78/loan.

Step 8: Create bill of activities:

Activity	Activity Measure	Activity Quantity	Activity Cost $	Life Cycle Cost ($) for 5,000 Loans	Current Unit Cost	Subtotal
Life Cycle Costs						
Design loan	designs	1	5,000	5,000	1.00 ($5000/5000 loans)	
Design procedures	procedures	5	200	1,000	.20 ($1000/5000 loans)	
Acquire supplies	supplies	1	50	50	.01 ($50/5000 loan)	
Subtotal life-cycle costs						1.21
Continuous Operating Costs						
Take applications	applications	1	150		150.00	
Order credit survey, appraisal	reports	3	30		90.00	
Review documents	reviews	1	70		70.00	
Review by loan committee	applications	1	200		200.00	
Prepare loan documents	pages	30	5		150.00	
Disburse funds	disbursements	1	100		100.00	760.00
Subtotal continuing operating costs						761.21
Total cost of reports						150.00
Subtotal life-cycle, operating, & report costs						$911.21
Accounting department						
Pay invoices (a)		.01	15.19		.15	
Process receivables (b)		120	10.38		1,245.60	
Prepare financial reports (c)						
Pay employees (d)						
Provide managerial reports (e)		120	.78		93.56	
Accounting department subtotal						1,339.31
Other departments						320.00
Total bill of activity cost for loans						2,570.52

SUMMARY

An activity-based service cost is derived by tracing the usage of all activities to build a service. An activity service cost becomes a summation of the cost of all traceable activities to design the service, procure supplies, and produce and distribute a service.

Activity management directly relates activities to the services that consume them. This is in contrast to the conventional cost accounting model, which spreads overhead costs among services on a basis that does not mirror their actual consumption. Activity service costing is enhanced by more specific tracing of support costs, which have traditionally been lumped into overhead and allocated to all services.

11

ACTIVITY-BASED BUDGETING

The purpose of this chapter is to:

- Discuss problems with traditional budgeting
- Define activity-based budgeting (ABB)
- Discuss the ABB process

A budget is a financial expression of a plan. Traditional budgeting focuses on planning resources for an organizational unit. Each year managers look at history and any significant changes, and create an annual budget. The budgeting process starts with the senior executive announcing budget goals. These may consist of revenue and profit goals, as well as goals for new services.

Many managers respond by looking at last year's numbers and increasing their budgets for the year based on inflation and/or the amounts of the increase in revenues. For example, if revenues increase 10 percent, then the various department managers might increase the budget for their department by 10 percent. The problem with this approach is that last year's inefficiencies are incorporated into this year's budget. Often, little attention is paid to improvements in each department. Finally, little incentive is incorporated into the budgeting process for continuous improvement. Changing workload for each department often isn't considered.

Senior managers during budgeting often make arbitrary cuts across the board. A potentially negative consequence is that the better-managed departments may have already cut the majority of waste and may have to cut into necessary resources. Instead, other, less efficient departments should make more radical reductions to bring them to the same level of efficiency as the better-managed departments.

Budgets, in this environment, often become wrestling matches in which those who are the best presenters are given larger budgets. The theory goes that the best at presenting the reasons for the larger budget, deserves the larger budget.

Once the budget is agreed on, it is often locked in concrete for the year.

TRADITIONAL BUDGETING DOES NOT SUPPORT EXCELLENCE

First, the budgeting process should highlight cost reduction and the elimination of wasteful activities and tasks. Yet traditional budgeting does not make visible what the organization does. Instead, managers look at their history of spending and simply increase last year's budget and/or actuals based on inflation and/or dollar sales growth.

Second, budgeting should be a formal mechanism for reducing workload to the minimal level to support enterprise objectives. Excess workload due to poor structuring of activities and business process drives up cost and does not improve customer satisfaction. The budgeting process itself should give insight into how to reduce workload and how to set workload reduction goals.

Third, budgeting should consider all costs as variable, yet budgeting often formalizes the laissez-faire attitude toward occupancy and equipment cost. Most are familiar with the concept of fixed and variable costs. The problem with this classification is a psychological one. The term "fixed" costs seems to imply that these costs cannot be eliminated because they are fixed. Yet we all know that buildings and equipment can be put to alternative use, sold, demolished, or leased. Many assets are often dedicated to specific activities. By making these assets more flexible, the total capital base of an enterprise can be lowered. Even property taxes and property insurance can be reduced. A budget based on variable and fixed costs often focuses attention on the variable costs and implies that the fixed costs are not controllable.

A better classification would be utilized and unutilized capacity. This classification simply shows that some assets are being used and some are not. It does not present the psychological barrier to change by using the term fixed costs. Unutilized capacity can be saved for future growth, eliminated, used for other purposes, or consolidated with another division.

An important goal of budgeting should be to improve each process on a continuous basis. Traditional budgeting, as it is commonly practiced, seems to focus on simply repeating history. Activity budgeting sets improvement targets by activity/business process. Thus, this approach is something everyone can understand and use to work toward improvement. However, traditional budgeting sets goals like "reduce costs" by a specific percentage, without giving employees insights on how to achieve those targets.

Activity budgeting works to synchronize activities and thus improve business processes. Traditional budgeting may take the approach of "every department for itself." Managers pay lip service to coordinating between departments. However, managers will almost certainly respond in a way that will maximize their own department's performance. The inevitable consequence is to lower the performance of the organization as a whole.

Activity budgeting sets business process improvement goals, which requires the joint efforts of employees from a variety of departments. Since the goal is to improve the business process, old barriers between departments begin to crumble.

Traditional budgeting does not formally consider external and internal suppliers and customers. However, activity budgeting requires asking the internal and external suppliers and customers to describe their needs and their respective workload requirements.

Too often, the focus on traditional budgeting is to control the result. For example, consider the organization that closes its financial books in four to fifteen days. Each month managers focus on information that is thirty-four to forty-five days old.

It makes more sense to control the process, rather than to try to control the result through financial statements. The Japanese have unsophisticated accounting systems compared to U.S. companies of a similar size. If the secret was a more sophisticated accounting system, then U.S. companies should be superior. Yet that isn't necessarily the case.

Activity budgeting and activity management focuses on controlling the process. Only by controlling the process can results improve.

In a similar vein, traditional budgeting tends to focus on the effects rather than causes. For example, it often requires a long time to hire new employees or introduce a new service. In reality, organizations should focus on the causes of these long lead times. In Japan, managers come to meetings asking their peers for suggestions to solve their problems. In the United States, our individualistic attitude often makes managers consider a request for help as a sign of weakness. So managers make up excuses to explain the reasons they were over budget, rather than concentrating their efforts on how to improve operations.

Since activity budgeting focuses on the root cause of problems, everyone can work to identify how to reduce or eliminate them. Only by eliminating the "root cause" of the problem can the cost be permanently eliminated.

Activity budgeting requires that the customer is asked for their requirements. Only by asking the customer can an organization understand whether it has properly applied resources to meet the customer's needs (e.g., Do the patrons of the U.S. Postal Service want two- to three-day delivery, or do they want consistent delivery within some stated time period?). By asking the customer, the workload connected with the activities necessary to please the customer can better be determined.

Activity budgeting focuses on output, not on input. It focuses on what work is done, how the work is performed, and how much work is done. The required resources are only a consequence of the activities. The problem with traditional budgeting is that it lacks ownership. Even if the department manager owns the budget, seldom do the individual employees in that department own the budget. Activity budgeting asks each person to look at the activities he or she performs and set performance targets for those activities in the context of customer requirements and organizational objectives.

Activity budgeting allows people to be empowered to manage their activities properly. If there is something wrong, if there is a better way to perform the activity/business process, or if a quality issue arises, the employee(s) who performs the activity/business process should make the necessary improvements or corrections without requiring management approval. This assumes that the employee isn't changing the service nor the quality provided to the customer, and is improving the service or business process at a lower cost.

Senior management needs to remember that people won't work themselves out of a job. People will only contribute ideas to improve operations if they understand that improvement in value-added activities allows the transfer of resources to growth-enabling activities.

Under activity budgeting, mistakes are acceptable, but repetition of mistakes is unacceptable. An executive told Sam Walton of a $10,000,000 mistake and submitted his resignation. Walton told the executive he couldn't resign because the company had just spent $10,000,000 training him. People need to know they can make mistakes, but they must learn from those mistakes and not repeat them.

Activities budgeting uses a common language, the language of the activities/business processes that everyone is performing. Traditional budgeting uses terms that the accountants are familiar with. This Tower of Babel makes communication more difficult and encourages specialization at the expense of cooperation.

Activity budgeting looks for consistency of the output. This means that the activity should be performed in a consistent way over time. Continuous improvement must be encouraged, but the activity should only be performed in accordance with current best practice. Success depends on finding the best possible way to perform an activity/business process and consistently looking for ways to improve it, while performing the activity/business process in a consistent manner.

Activity budgeting requires setting activity/business process targets as the minimum level of performance rather than the absolute level. These activity/business process targets should identify the minimum level of performance necessary to support organizational objectives. Managers should not try to exceed these minimum levels. Instead, they should look at ways to reduce waste and non-value-added portions of various activities.

ACTIVITY-BASED BUDGETING DEFINITIONS

Activity-based budgeting (ABB) is the process of planning and controlling the expected activities of the organization to derive a cost-effective budget that meets forecast workload and agreed strategic goals.

An ABB is a quantitative expression of the expected activities of the organization, reflecting management forecast of workload and financial and nonfinancial requirements to meet agreed strategic goals and planned changes to improve performance.

The three key elements of an ABB include:

- Type of work to be done
- Quantity of work to be done
- Cost of work to be done

Principles of ABB

ABB must reflect what is done, that is, the activities/business processes, and not cost elements. Resources required (cost elements) must be derived from the expected activities/business processes and workload.

Workload is simply the number of units of an activity that are required. For example, in the human resource department, the workload for the activity "hire employees" might be to hire twenty-five employees. The cost elements to perform that activity might be the wages and benefits of the recruiter, travel, advertising, testing, supplies and occupancy costs for the space occupied by the recruiter and for interviewing. If a hiring freeze occurs, then the workload for this activity would be zero.

Budgets must be based on the future workload in order to meet:

- Customer requirements
- Organizational/departmental goals and strategies
- New/changed services and service mix
- Changes in business processes
- Improvements in efficiency and effectiveness
- Quality, flexibility, and cycle time goals
- Changes in service levels

The final budget must reflect the changes in resource cost levels and foreign exchange fluctuations. However, it is better to initially budget using constant cost to facilitate comparisons, and then to add inflation at the conclusion of the budgeting process.

As part of the activity budgeting process, it is important to highlight continuous improvement. Each department should identify the activities/business processes to be improved, the amount of improvement, and how it plans to achieve its improvement targets.

Requirements for Successful ABB Budgeting

The organization must be committed to excellence. If the organization doesn't have this commitment, then resources will be wasted on data analysis activities that will never be implemented. Changing is not easy. It is easier to "study the problem" than to make the difficult decisions required to improve.

Process Management Approach

The organization must use a process management approach to improvement. This requires defining each activity as part of a repeatable, robust business process that can be continuously improved and the variability removed. Activities defined this way can use various techniques to decrease time, improve quality, and reduce the cost of those activities.

Process management is crucial to excellence, since high levels of performance are possible only when activities are done to best practices, the unused capacity is minimal, the best practices are continually made better, and the activities are executed perfectly. Activity definitions must support process management. Activities must be in the form of verb plus a noun. There must be a physical output. Two-stage definitions of drivers are usually not adequate. For example, the activity "pay employee" is compatible with process management. To define an activity as "supplies handling" and the output measure the "number of service production runs" would not be a compatible activity definition. Two-stage activity definitions might be used in assigning costs to a service, but it doesn't help in improving operations. A better way to define the above activity would be "move supplies," with the output measure defined as the "number of moves."

One of the first steps that an activity manager may have to take is to review activity definitions to make sure that they are compatible with a process approach.

Culture Encourages Sustaining Benefits

The organization culture should encourage sustaining benefits. These benefits should not be something that lasts for a short while followed by everyone going back to the old way. These benefits should change the way the people in the organization think and act. Often this means changing the way the employees are compensated, so that they share in the productivity improvement.

Organizations must overcome the following cultural barriers. Next to these barriers are actions the organization must take in order to overcome these cultural barriers.

Cultural Barriers	Actions
Departmental structure often interferes with departments interacting in order to minimize total enterprise cost.	Change information systems so the organization can see total cost of business processes rather than just the costs in a specific department.
Policies and procedures provide guidelines for employee behavior. These were often set up in order to ensure consistency and to make it easy for the employees to handle specific situations.	Empower employees to handle various situations to ensure customer satisfaction. Use policies to set general guidelines, and train, support, and empower the employee to satisfy the customer.
Suggestion programs usually require the approval of management in order to implement change. This slows the change process.	Suggestion programs are only for changes to the service or for capital requests. Changes to efficiency should be made by employees without management approval
Measurement systems tend to focus on the department level.	Abolish micro management. Give managers/employees the tools, authority, and responsibility to do their jobs. Make them responsible for outputs and a budget level of resources to do their work.
Specialization assumes that lowest cost is achievable through economies of scale.	Today flexibility is critical. People must be cross-trained for a variety of tasks. First, as slack or heavy periods occur, employees can help out in other departments. Second, they need to understand how what they do affects other departments and how what other departments do affects them.

Commitment To Excellence

Many organizations take a short-term approach to improving operations. Costs are easy to control—simply stop spending money. This approach is similar to a crash diet. The problem with crash diets is that the dieter usually regains what he or she lost, and often gains even more weight. If an organization is committed to excellence, then its goal is to change the way it does business. This is similar to changing eating habits. For example, organizations must start compensating people based on business process performance, rather than the traditional actual versus budget of cost elements that most organizations have historically used.

ACTIVITY-BASED BUDGETING PROCESS

The activity-based budgeting process begins with the customer. The organization must determine who their customer is and what the customer wants. It must look to its competitors. Competition consists of both direct competitors and alternate services that might compete with the organization's services.

Then, the organization must develop a strategy to meet customer needs. A restaurant must decide whether to be a five star restaurant with crystal and linen table cloths, or to provide good food in a clean environment with less sophisticated decor but with good value to the customer.

Next, the organization should forecast workload. Management/sales determines what sales levels will be, and managers need to estimate their workload as a result of these sales levels. Often, the sales forecast includes new services and new markets, as well as any change in strategy.

Planning guidelines must be articulated to each manager to establish their specific activity level targets within a business process context. Eventually, every activity manager should have targets for improving his or her respective value-added activities and eliminating their non-value-added activities.

Next, interdepartmental projects should be identified. Since these projects will affect the workload, as well as the activities in several departments, they must be coordinated and done prior to each manager improving his or her own activities.

At this point in the budgeting process, specific activity-level projects can be identified. These are projects to improve operations at the individual activity level. However, improvement should always be within organizational objectives, a business process context, and a customer satisfaction context.

Activity-based investment analysis consists of defining improvement projects, evaluating those projects, and then using committees to select projects that will meet the organization's goals and meet customers' needs.

The final step is to determine the activities and workload for the coming year.

LINKING STRATEGY AND BUDGETING

One of the problems with traditional budgeting is that a clear link between the enterprise's strategy and budgeting often does not exist. Therefore, operating managers do not know how to incorporate strategy into their budget.

Principles of Strategic Management

There are a variety of seminars and books available on the subject of strategic management. This book will not discuss those techniques, but simply assume that a strategic plan exists. The role of senior management is to set performance targets based on the strategic plans. The performance targets might be for sales, number of new services and/or markets, cycle time, cost, quality, or customer service levels. The role of the activity manager is to achieve or exceed those targets.

Strategic objectives and performance targets must be translated into activity level targets. Activity managers must ensure that service requirements are a direct derivative of customer needs.

The translation process starts with customer requirements and an analysis of competitive strategies. Then strategic objectives are set. The price for services allowable by the market are determined, and time, quality, and cost targets are determined. Then these targets are translated into activity level targets.

There are several important strategic management tools to assist with this process. The key ones include:

- Customer surveys
- Core competency analysis
- Benchmarking
- Quality function deployment
- Reverse engineering

Customer Surveys

One of the first steps in the strategic management process is to perform a customer survey. The customer survey can be done in person, by telephone, or by direct mail. The survey asks a variety of questions, but the focus is on the factors that are important to the customer, a ranking of those factors by the customer, and, finally, the customer's perception of the organization's performance regarding those factors.

Based on this survey, the organization needs to start with the factors most important to the customer and determine whether or not it is satisfying the customer on those factors of performance. Activity/business process and investment preference must be given to those activities/business processes that the customer feels are most important. Especially in cases where satisfaction levels are not satisfactory to the customer, the organization needs to change, improve, or increase resources and effectiveness of those activities/business processes.

For example, if an organization determines that it needs to allow the nurses to spend more time with patients and less time doing paperwork, then it could create an activity budget in the following way.

For the activity "complete medical charts":

Total Cost	Salaries	Depreciation	Supplies	Phone	Occupancy
$24,410	22,000	400	900	150	960

The assumptions are that a person would be hired to "complete medical charts." The employee's salary and benefits would be $22,000 per year. Depreciation on his or her desk and computer would be $400. Supplies connected with filling out the charts are estimated to be $900. Since this person would be communicating with other departments, a phone would be necessary for interhospital calls. The fully loaded cost of hospital space, including depreciation, heat, electricity, building maintenance, and janitorial cost based on the number of square feet occupied, equals $960.

Hiring this person will enable the ten nurses to spend 10 percent of their time comforting, informing, and answering questions for patients. A nurse earns $36,000 annually, including benefits.

For the activity "communicate with patients":

Total Cost	Salaries	Depreciation	Supplies	Phone	Occupancy
$46,320	36,000	1,000	2,000	320	7,000

The following assumptions were made. Annual salaries and benefits for ten nurses at $36,000 per nurse equals $360,000. Since they will spend 10 percent of their time on this activity, the salary portion of this activity cost equals $36,000. There would be some depreciation on the desk for the portion of time performing this activity. There would be some educational literature given to the patients, which would total approximately $2,000. Nurses would need a phone line for tracking down answers to patient questions, and a reasonable percentage of the total phone cost was estimated at $320. Since the nurses spent some time sitting at a desk for this activity, 10 percent of their total occupancy cost was apportioned, which amounted to $7,000.

Now senior management can look at their customer survey and their performance as it relates to nurses communicating and comforting patients—a high priority item in the eyes of the customer. Then they can determine if it is worth spending a total of $70,730 ($24,410 plus $46,320) in order to improve customer satisfaction in this area.

Core Competency Analysis

An organization starts by asking what activities/business processes are critical to its industry. These activities/business processes become the core competencies of that industry. Then the organization can ask itself which activities/business processes it performs well. It needs to compare itself with external benchmarks and determine where there is a core competency gap. Then the organization can set budget targets in terms of cost, quality, and time.

Industry	Core Competency
Banking	Accuracy, fast turnaround, full service
Insurance	Low rates, knowledgeable representatives, fast claims handling
Hospitals	Friendly nurses, full service, high success rate
Airlines	On-time, convenient departures
Fast food	Quality, service, cleanliness
IRS	Rules that are easy to comply with, fairness, easy access
Fund-raisers	Good cause, larger percentage of funds directly to cause

An auto dealer decided that a core competency of the repair shop was to provide quality repairs the first time. A further analysis revealed an opportunity to improve performance by conducting auto repair training seminars for the mechanics. Four seminars for twenty mechanics who earn $14 per hour were planned. Each seminar was to be five hours long with $500 in training supplies. The trainer charges $3,000 per training session.

For the activity "train mechanics":

Total Cost	Salaries	Supplies	Phone	Consultant
$18,100	5,600	500	0	12,000

Benchmarking

The benchmarking process compares performance to other organizations, either internally or externally. Benchmarks may measure:

- Activities
- Business processes
- Time
- New service introduction
- Customer service
- Quality
- Cost

Comparisons should be made where possible across divisions, with competitors, and with the best organizations in the world. For example, one telephone company can process a request for new phone service within forty-three seconds. This is a speed few other organizations can duplicate and would serve as a great benchmark for the activity "process new customers' credit requests."

One association felt it was important to answer the phone after only two rings. This would be a high-quality service to its members and would avoid lost sales on books and seminars, because people get tired of waiting for someone to answer the phone. The association's operators were currently answering the phone on the third or fourth ring. It decided to increase the number of telephone operators by three. Telephone operators could be hired for $18,000 per year. They would need desks, PCs, phones, and supplies for order taking. Fully loaded occupancy costs were running $10 per square foot. Each operator would need 64 square feet of space.

For the activity "answer phones":

Total Cost	Salaries	Depreciation	Supplies	Phone	Occupancy
$60,120	54,000	2,000	1,200	1,000	1,920

Quality Function Deployment

Quality function deployment (QFD) is a concept originating in the quality field and is applicable to activity budgeting. In QFD, the organization compares the customers' requirements with the activities/business processes necessary to meet those requirements. For each activity/business process, a comparison is also made with the competition to determine how the organization is doing against the competition. Also, a correlation is made between activities to show which activities have a strong positive or strong negative correlation with meeting customer requirements. Some activities will have no correlation with each other. Finally, a correlation is made between various activities and customer requirements. Thus, the organization can determine which activities are critical to the greatest customer satisfaction. Customer requirements are ranked as part of this analysis.

Although a complete explanation of this technique can be found in a number of quality books and seminars, a simple example will be discussed here. An airline is looking to increase market share by better satisfying its customers. Using QFD, the airline determines that quick turnaround time is important in order to have on-time departures. One way to improve in this area is to have two jetbridges to load passengers instead of only one. There are two activities—"move jetbridge" and "maintain jetbridge"— connected with this second jetbridge.

The airline determines that 10 percent of a ticketing agent's time is needed to handle this second jetbridge. A ticketing agent earns $32,000 per year. Two hundred ticketing agents will be affected. This means that salaries with benefits dedicated to the activity "move jetbridge" would be $640,000 (200 × 10% × $32,000). An additional 100 jetbridges would need to be purchased at the rate of $10,000 per jetbridge. Therefore, the depreciation on $1,000,000 (100 × $10,000) using a five-year life would be $200,000 per year. The annual cost of maintenance labor is $100,000 on these jetbridges and is $50,000 on maintenance parts. Occupancy costs are $20,000 for the maintenance space needed for these jetbridges.

For the activities "move jetbridge" and "maintain jetbridge":

Total Cost	Agent Salaries	Depreciation	Maintenance Salaries	Parts	Occupancy
$1,010,000	640,000	200,000	100,000	50,000	20,000

Reverse Engineering

Reverse engineering involves studying a competitor's services. At first glance, one would think that reverse engineering is a concept that only applies to products. However, applying reverse engineering to a service and seeing how competitors perform the service is a very useful tool.

For example, consider a company that has a regulatory affairs department that must file with the FDA in order to get regulatory approval. The company's managers studied the process of filing for regulatory approval. The objective was to determine how to perform the process more effectively.

Using reverse engineering principles, they started by asking the customer, in this case the FDA, the testing requirements in order to get this new product approved. Then, based on the FDA comments, they improved how they designed their products and their testing procedures in order to get approval more quickly.

For the activity, "improve the FDA approval process," the following activity costs are determined:

Regulatory personnel salary of $50,000 will spend 10 percent of their time on this project. They will have travel costs amounting to $3,000. A 10 percent share of their office occupancy cost is running $2,000 per year. A seminar on this topic will cost $1,700 per year. Supplies are expected to run $600.

For the activity "improve FDA approval process":

Total Cost	Salaries	Travel	Supplies	Seminar	Occupancy
$12,300	5,000	3,000	600	1,700	2,000

TRANSLATE STRATEGY TO ACTIVITIES

Strategy must be translated to an activity level to identify necessary changes. An example of a translating procedure follows:

Steps	Example
Define mission statement, with enterprise goals	Dominate the market & diversify where advantage can be applied
Establish critical success factors	Grow market share; increase new service sales as percentage of total sales
Establish service targets	Increase market share: Service 1 by 7%; Service 2 by 8%; discontinue Service 3
Establish service level targets	Service 1: increase sales 5%; decrease cost 8%; deliver in 2 hours

Identify Activity Targets by Bill of Activities

The next step is to identify activity targets for each service. For example, the mission might be to dominate the consumer loan business in Dallas; the critical success factor might be to grow market share; the service target might be to grow auto loan revenue by 7 percent; and the service level targets might be to increase auto loan sales by 5 percent and decrease costs by 8 percent.

Bill of Activities

Activity Description	Cost/ Output $	Units of Output	Service $	Target Activity Reduction %	Target Activity Reduction $	Target Cost/ Output $
Take application	100	1	100	⟨5%⟩	⟨5⟩	95
Order reports	50	3	150	⟨10%⟩	⟨15⟩	135
Review loans	200	1	200	⟨7%⟩	⟨14⟩	186
Complete paperwork	25	4	100	⟨30%⟩	⟨30⟩	70
Disburse funds	250	1	250			250
TOTALS			800	⟨8%⟩	⟨64⟩	736

The above table shows that the employees have established cost reduction targets for four of the five activities. The total reduction of $64 is an 8 percent reduction from last year's total bill of activities costs.

Strategic Management Tools and Targets Summary

Once these strategic management tools are employed, then cost, time, and quality targets can be set by the employees for each activity. The following is an example of cost, time, and quality targets.

Tool	Activity	Cost	Time	Quality
Customer survey	Communicate with patients	C: 46,320 T: 40,000	C: 10 minutes T: 30 minutes	C: 80% satisfaction T: 90%
Core competency	Train mechanics	C: 18,100 T: 22,000	C: 20 hours T: 24 hours	C: 9% redos T: 5% redos
Benchmarking	Answer phone	C: 60,120 T:	C: 4 rings T: 2 rings	C: T:
Quality function deployment	Operate jet bridge	C: 1,010,000 T: 900,000	C: 45 minutes T: 30 minutes	C: 85% T: 90% on time
Reverse engineering	Obtain FDA approval	C: 12,300 T: 10,000	C: 5 years T: 2 years	C: 75% approval T: 80%
		C = Current T = Target		

Match Resource to Goals

Next, match resources to goals. Goals should be set to be achievable. Resources should be oriented toward goals. Identify improvements to business processes as well as activities.

DETERMINE WORKLOAD

There are three major steps in determining activity/business process workload. These include the following:

1. Forecast service-determined activities/business processes
2. Forecast non-service-related activities/business processes.
3. Forecast special projects

Workload of Service-Determined Activities/Business Processes

The first step in forecasting total organization workload is to forecast workload for service-determined activities:

- Identify activities for new services
- Identify planned changes to services
- Create/update bill of activities for each service line
- Forecast services by service line rather than individual service in most cases
- Explode bill of activities to determine activity quantity for each service line

Explode bill of activities

To explode a bill of activities, simply list each service line and the forecasted quantity of that service line. Then list the units of each activity used by each service line, multiply units of service times units of each activity to calculate the activity quantity volume by service, and sum the total activity quantities.

Service	Service Quantity	Activity	Quantity	Activity Quantities
Mortgages	5,000	Order report	3	15,000
Auto loans	1,800	Order report	1	1,800
Personal loans	1,000	Order report	1	1,000
		Total Reports	17,800	

Workload for Non-Service-Related Activities

The second step is to forecast workload of non-service-related activities. Non-service-related activities are those performed by support departments, such as MIS, human resources, security, and accounting.

Activity Class	Activity Measure
General management	Number of employees
Financial reporting	Number of financial reports
Corporate advertising	Number of TV advertisements
	Number of promotions
Marketing	Number of trade shows
	Number of market surveys
Research	Number of new services
Facilities	Number of square feet

Workload for Special Projects

The third step is to forecast workload for special projects. Examples of special projects include:

- Install activity-based management
- Install activity-based budgeting
- Install new computer system
- Expand office

Then the organization needs to set up a calendar for each special project with the activities and tasks listed by time period.

ABB Calendar						
Brief senior management	*					
Select team	**					
Select departments/services	***					
Review activity definitions		**********				
Review strategic plan			****			
Explode bill of activities				******		
Start improvement projects					***	

Each * equals a day

Create Planning Guidelines

An organization should identify activity/business process-level projects with the goal of continuous improvement. Look at the budgeted workload and divide it into mandatory, discretionary, and optional units for each activity/business process. This split helps to decide what portion of value-added activities to eliminate. For example, an organization might determine that it only needs one quote to purchase supplies. The workload to obtain quotes is the minimum mandatory work. Discretionary work occurs when the purchasing agent believes a lower price is obtainable through two quotes. For optional work, the agent feels better by getting three or four quotes, some of which are from noncertified vendors.

IDENTIFY INTERDEPARTMENTAL PROJECTS

The organization should look at its business processes to eliminate duplicate activities and synchronize the remaining ones. Consider the following business process to "procure supplies."

Activity-Based Budget For Procuring Supplies

See the table below and on the following page.

After reviewing last year's total costs for each activity, the next step is to calculate lat year's unit cost for each activity. For example, the activity "prepare quotes" cost $103,445. Last year 2,000 quotes were prepared. By dividing annual quotes into total cost, the unit cost for this activity is $51.72 per quote.

Activities	Workload Measures	Volume	Total Cost	Unit Cost	Target Cost
Prepare quotes	Quotes	2,000	103,445	51.72	50.00
Issue P.O.	P.O.	5,679	117,265	20.65	19.65
Administer P.O.	P.O.	5,679	315,295	55.52	53.00
Source supplies	New suppliers	100	38,167	381.67	375.00
Manage area	Staff	28	72,243	2,580.11	2,200

ABB Example of Target Cost

The organization has set a target of $50 per quote. This is a reduction of $1.72 from last year's cost of $51.72 per quote. The improvement process for 2,000 quotes at $1.72 per quote results in a savings of $3,440. Managers feel that they can reduce supplies by $440 by keeping more information on the computer and less on paper. Travel could be reduced $1,000 by having more vendors come to the organization's offices. Since quotes will be kept on the computer, there will be a reduction in the filing activity, saving $2,000 for part-time employee wages and benefits.

Activity	LY/TY	Labor	Technology	Facility	Utilities	Supply	Travel	Other	Total
Prepare quotes	LY	89088		7827	1293	1075	4000	162	103445
	TY								
Issue P.O.	LY	101479		8915	1472	1225	4000	175	117266
	TY								
Administer PO	LY	108404	190299	9524	1573	1308	4000	187	315295
	TY								
Source supplies	LY	29211		2568	424	353	5562	50	38168
	TY								
Manage area	LY	65545		5871	938	578	200	111	73243
	TY								

LY = Last year　　　TY = This year

Creative Thinking Approaches

Continuous improvement requires innovative approaches to streamlining the way an activity is done. While creativity is a very personal trait, studies have shown that certain environments and methods are better suited to drawing out creative ideas. Some of the more effective methods are:

1. Challenging assumptions about:
   people
   supplies
   business processes
   location
   capital
   automation
   activities
2. Viewing activities/business processes based on new assumptions
3. Perceiving patterns from other:
   divisions
   offices
   services
   departments
4. Making connections with other organizations
5. Establishing networks between suppliers, supplier's suppliers, you, customers, and end users
6. Exploiting failures (e.g., the glue for Post It notes was too weak)
7. Performing activity backwards and from the middle
8. Using idea triggers (e.g., a new idea for each of Baskin and Robbins' 31 flavors)
9. Creating superheroes
10. Imagining you are the service, activity, or business process

Brainstorming

Brainstorming techniques are fairly common today. They consist of:

1. Suspending judgment until all ideas are on the table
2. Emphasizing quantity of ideas without worrying about quality

3. Stimulating a free-wheeling session with wild ideas encouraged
4. Involving people from throughout the organization
5. Reminding people that wild ideas often will fertilize their thinking process

Storyboarding

Storyboarding is a creativity tool that consists of using colored index cards to show business processes, activities, and tasks. The first step is to define the department mission statement. For a hotel, the department mission for the maids might be: "to keep rooms clean in order to delight customers at a minimum cost."

Value Management

Value management is an organized way of thinking. It is an objective appraisal of functions performed by services and procedures. The focus is on necessary functions for the lowest cost. It increases reliability and productivity. Costs are decreased. Value management challenges everything an organization does.

It starts by gathering information such as:

• The purpose and use of each service
• The operating and performance issues
• The physical and environmental requirements

For example, fresh fish must be kept cold. Jewelry must be kept in a secure environment. What types of support requirements are there? What problems exist? Which and how many liaison personnel are required? What are the economic issues?

These requirements are translated into required functionality of the service. Begin by determining the worth of each portion of the service. Then calculate the value improvement potential. What part of the service does the customer want? Which parts add cost? Which part is the customer willing to pay for?

Begin using creativity. Ask the customers to value different features.

Ask suppliers for ideas. Use cross-functional teams and brainstorming. Use reverse engineering techniques and look at the competitor's services. Benchmark in other industries. Find the best customer service, warehousing, and order fulfillment organization. Eliminate part of the service. How can the organization create more commonality of services and support services as well as common reports and forms?

Evaluate whether it would be better to buy a portion of the service from outside (e.g., catering/training/maintenance for airlines, check processing and MIS for banks, body work for car dealers, janitorial, engineering, waste collection for cities) or to perform those services and support services in-house. Analyze customer tradeoff of cost and features. Calculate value versus cost to produce various portions of the service. Eliminate functions, procedures, and reports. Simplify procedures, business processes, and functions. Use alternate supplies, specifications, and methods. Shorten the service operations cycle with cross-training of departments.

Task Level Analysis

Sometimes it is useful to analyze the tasks of an activity in order to determine the improvement potential. For example, the activity "pay vendor invoice" has the following tasks.

Task	Total	Non-value-added	Value-added	Best Practice
Receive P.O. (PO)	.50	.50		
Locate receiver (R)	.50	.50		
Get vendor invoice (I)	.50	.50		
Match PO,R,I	2.00	2.00		
Enter data	4.50		4.50	2.00
Determine errors	2.50	2.50		
Expedite payment	1.25	1.25		
Make payment: computer	3.00		3.00	2.75
Make payment: manual	1.00	1.00		
Document file	3.00	1.50	1.50	1.25
	18.75	9.75	9.00	6.00

IMPROVEMENT PROCESS

The improvement process starts with creative thinking to determine solutions. An investment proposal is then prepared. Management selects those projects that have the highest priority in meeting customer needs. The solution is implemented and incorporated into the activity budget.

Ranking Budget Requests

After all the budget requests have been made, they are ranked. One convenient way to rank them is through a rating system in which management looks at the budget requests in comparison with the customer needs. Another useful tool is to classify them according to whether they support the current level of service or whether they are at the minimum, intermediate, or expanded service levels. "Current" implies that this is the cost of activities as they are presently performed. "Minimum" implies that this is the minimum level of service for an activity. "Intermediate" implies that this is not a final solution. "Expanded" implies enlarging the level of service.

   Then the organization should look at the impact of these projects in terms of the change in workload, but also in terms of the changes in activity/business process cost.

FINALIZING THE BUDGET

Budget proposals are created for the most promising projects. They should be reviewed, and the highest priority projects selected. An implementation plan should be conceived. An activity impact report should be generated to include its cost impact. This should be done assuming no inflation or foreign currency issues. This allows for comparisons with previous activity/business process performance. Finally, inflation and foreign currency should be incorporated into the budget.

Budget Review Panels

Budget review panels should consist of cross-functional teams whose purpose is to question and review the budget. A review panel might consist of the directors, support departments such as human resources, administration, quality, finance, and operations.

Budgeting Options

An organization has two options for activity budgeting. First, budget and report by activities. Second, budget by activities and convert the activity budget into a traditional cost element budget. In this second approach, the organization plans on an activity/business process basis. Managers would use activity costs per unit to determine cost elements. Then they would summarize by cost elements.

Steps in Implementing ABB

	Months			
Activities/tasks	1	2	3	4
Train and educate	**			
Perform strategic analysis	****			
Forecast workload		******		
Establish planning guidelines		****		
Propose interdepartmental improvement			****	
Propose activity improvement			********	
Select improvement options			*******	
Finalize budget				***

Initial Project

A steering group of three to five members should be created. A series of panels with five to six members from different departments should be created to discuss cross-departmental issues. Each budgeting unit should have a budgeting manager, which could be someone other than the department manager. There would be ten to twenty budgeting units per in-house coordinator or per consultant.

Performance Reporting

Remember that the most effective reports are those that do not have to be made. Therefore, introduce proactive control rather than reactive cost monitoring wherever possible. Activity-based budgeting encourages this approach.

Emphasis should be made to control the process so that output is consistent. Also, make sure resources can be shifted when workload varies. Workload seldom stays the same throughout the year. Plan and budget for using those slack times to improve the organization.

Data Capture

There are three methods for data capture within an ongoing system. First, there is dedicated resources. Set up cost centers and define workload measures at the activity/business process level. Second, there is shared resources, in which an organization does time reporting by activity. Third, use a surrogate in which actual outputs are used at a standard activity cost. Actual costs would be compared to total department earned cost in this approach. Total actual cost could also be compared to best practices earned value.

Activity-Based Budget Report

	Department Total		Activity Analysis			
Expense	Budget $	Actual $	Issue P.O.	Certify Vendor	Expedite Order	Other
Wages	180,000	180,000				
Supplies	40,000	38,000				
Space	30,000	30,000				
Equipment	18,000	18,000				
Travel	22,000	20,000				
Other	10,000	8,000				
Total	200,000	194,000				
Output measure			Number of P.O.	Number of certification	Number of orders	
Charge rate			$50	$2,000	$10	$9,000
Budgeted volume			3,000	20	100	1
Budgeted value	200,000		$150,000	$40,000	$1,000	$9,000
Actual volume			2,700	18	90	1
Earned value		181,000	$135,000	$36,000	$900	$9,100
Earned value variance		13,000				

In the above example, the organization budgeted the activity "issue purchase orders" at $50.00 per purchase order. It budgeted 3,000 purchase orders. This yielded a budgeted value for the "issue purchase order" activity of $150,000. The same activity budgeting process was followed for the remaining activities including an "other" or miscellaneous category of activities. This yielded a total activity budget for this department of $200,000 which was backflushed back into expense categories.

The actual expenses for the period were $194,000. Compared to the original budget of $200,000, this looks very good. However, when the earned value is calculated, the department is shown to have an earned value variance of $13,000. Earned value is calculated for each activity by multiplying the actual volume for each activity by that activity's charge rate. For the "issue purchase order" activity, the actual volume of 2,700 purchase orders yields $135,000. The same calculation is made for all activities and the answers added for each department. This earned value total of $181,000 is compared to actual expenses of $194,000 to yield an earned value variance of a negative $13,000. This is a different picture than simply comparing actual with budget. Managers can now use this as a planning tool as well as a means to operate their organization more efficiently.

Business Process Reporting

In business process reporting, activity cost could be shown for each department, as well as for each business process that delivers a service. This is an exercise for organizations that are more advanced in ABM techniques.

SUMMARY

Activity-based budgeting gives managers the tools they need to make better decisions about running their organization. This budgeting technique spends most of the time on improvement rather than form filling out, which is often the case with traditional budgeting. This technique gives managers a method to improve activities as well as business processes.

12

ACTIVITY MANAGEMENT—A PROCESS APPROACH

Activity-based management supports excellence by providing a formal management system that compels people to understand their activities and how they contribute to achieving strategic objectives. ABM changes traditional management practices to guide managers to emulate best practices and establish process controls to ensure consistently good performance. ABM supports the quest for continuous improvement by providing managers with new insights into customers of activities/business processes and by permitting managers to adopt practices that add greater value to the organization.

The quest for excellence or, even more basic, survival in the 1990s has brought dramatic changes in most organizations. Global competition and increasing customer demands have forced organizations to simultaneously lower cost, improve quality, and reduce cycle time. Meanwhile, boards of directors, financial markets, and citizens expect top managers to continue meeting yearly financial objectives. Few organizations have met this challenge without a major overhaul in management practices.

In the name of progress, managers have employed management techniques that emulate practices by Attila the Hun. These methods compensate for poor revenue or high cost by slashing headcount and discretionary expenditures. Today we refer to Attila's methods as downsizing, restructuring, and flattening the organization structure. These efforts often result in major short-term savings. The savings come from wasteful areas where excess "fat" has built up. Often this is due to poor management practices.

Longer-term savings are envisioned to result from implementing major initiatives such as:

- Total quality management (TQM)
- Customer satisfaction
- Time-based management
- Business process re-engineering (BPR)
- Employee involvement/empowerment
- Activity-based costing (ABC)
- Concurrent engineering
- Target costing
- Organizational redesign
- Score boarding
- Benchmarking

However, the savings resulting from the short-term improvements are often transient. Savings from the long-term initiatives are too often on paper rather than on the bottom line.

Management must accept that world competition will continue to impose financial constraints. Customers will continue to be more sophisticated and demanding in the future. This will result in the need to improve operational capabilities. Since the **quantity** of resources will not increase, the effectiveness of the resources must improve. All organizations must find a way to improve.

Such a system is known as **Unified initiative management (UIM).** UIM gets an organization to a higher level of performance by using the formal management system to motivate all employees to continually improve the way they work to better meet customer requirements. This is done by removing wasteful and bureaucratic activities and observing best practices when doing work. The concept of process management is the foundation of UIM.

Why Conventional Management Systems Are Not Working

The conventional approach to managing is to create specialized units of similar skills to do work. A manager is assigned responsibility for the unit's performance. The manager develops financial plans by type of resources needed. The unit's performance is controlled by reporting actual performance against plan, after the fact.

Waste, bureaucracy, and unsatisfied customers are the likely outcome of this management system. The prime reason is that conventional management practices expect people to know the correct things to do and how best to do them, and expect that employees have the proper environment in which to do them. In reality, this model is almost the exact reverse of the business environment.

To understand why this is true, one needs merely to examine the underlying assumptions of the conventional approach. Specialization has many advantages. People become experts in their jobs and are more efficient than generalists. Specialization facilitates people with similar skills working together and sharing experiences so as to learn from one another. On the negative side, specialization creates boxes. The specialist spends more time talking to colleagues than to users of their services. The specialist becomes too familiar with the old way of doing work and doesn't challenge established practices. This leads to unhappy customers.

Planning by type of resource is ineffective because resources are the consequence of doing work. Costs are caused by work. Planning what resources are needed should start with planning the work to be done. Conventional planning often regresses to reviewing what resources were needed in the past and assuming a percentage change in the level of resources that will be needed in the future.

After-the-fact variance management is ineffective because the problem has already occurred. It is too late to take corrective action. The longer the time difference between the occurrence of the variance and the detection of the variance, the less the likelihood of correcting the problem. Long time lags result in explaining rather than correcting.

Finally, and most importantly, the concept of responsibility assignment assumes people have the authority, knowledge, and freedom to do their work. Rarely is this true. Many managers are promoted because they were very good in a technical specialty. These people are rarely given adequate training on how to manage. Organizations then fail to provide adequate management tools to help them manage. Often, a spreadsheet program and word processing program are the most powerful tools provided. Many conflicting demands are placed on the managers. Above all, they must complete their assigned work within their allowable cost. It is little wonder that people struggle to do their best.

Process Management—The Key to Excellence

Managing for excellence requires process thinking. A process is a repeatable way of doing work. Process thinking requires everyone to think of work as a recurring set of steps. Viewing work as a process is powerful since it facilitates establishing best practices and ensuring that these practices are rigorously adhered to for consistent output.

The alternative to process management is ad hoc management. Ad hoc means that each situation is new and unique, and implies that one cannot learn from past mistakes and improve.

A process can only lead to excellent results when it is managed as a series of flexible, repeatable tasks that are continuously improved and the variability removed. The key points of this definition are that the process is:

- **Repeatable**: Repeatability occurs when a process is done more than once. Repeatability facilitates establishing "best practices" and is the opposite of ad hoc.

- **Flexible**: Flexibility occurs when a process is adaptable to changes in the environment in which the activity operates. A flexible activity minimizes the adverse effects of unutilized capacity.

- **Continuous improvement**: Continuous improvement occurs when a process performance is better than its previous performance.

- **Consistent**: Consistency occurs when a process output is identical, because the process is continually repeated in the same way.

Process management requires managers to continually question the users of outputs about their needs. Process management scrutinizes all the work steps that transform inputs into outputs to identify opportunities to lower costs and reduce time. Finally, process management establishes controls to ensure that activities and business processes (i.e., a collection of related activities) are performed consistently.

Process management leads to great value, consistency, and superior results. Value is achieved by focusing on the needs of the users and the outputs they receive. Consistency is achieved by performing the process correctly and the same way repeatedly. Superior results are achieved by establishing the "best practice" way of doing the activity/business process and constantly searching for better ways of doing it.

Good management practices can be emulated by studying the best management practices and developing a systematic process to ensure these practices are adhered to. A manager who rigorously follows excellent practices is more likely to produce excellent results.

ABM in Practice

ABM is a process-based approach to planning the ongoing activities and business processes of an organization to ensure it meets strategic objectives. ABM is **neither** a cost-cutting tool nor a financial system. ABM is based on process management practices. It links diverse management initiatives into a cohesive formal management system. ABM is a technique that empowers all employees to be responsible for managing their work. The management process includes the following practices:

- Senior management sets market-driven targets.
- Targets (strategy) are linked with work to ensure activities are relevant to customer and strategic requirements.
- All employees are empowered to continuously improve the way they work and redirect their resources and capital to most relevant activities and formalizes the continuous improvement program in an activity based budget.
- Process controls are established to ensure work is done consistently.

Activity-Based Management

Implementing ABM involves five basic steps:

- Activity analysis
- Market targeting
- Business process improvement
- Activity improvement
- Activity planning
- Process controls

A warehouse for a retail store will be used to illustrate the principles and practices of ABM. The objectives of the warehouse are to receive incoming goods, ensure the goods meet quality standards, provide temporary storage, and deliver them to the various stores.

ACTIVITY ANALYSIS

Excellence begins with understanding the work done. Work is best identified by starting with the outputs of a department and identifying the processes that generate the output. Managers then develop an understanding of the resources currently assigned to the activity, the volume of work, and how well the work is performed. The receiving manager identified the repeatable work:

Output	Activity	Budget $	Current Workload	$/output
Received goods	Receive goods	185,000	150,000	1.23
Inspected goods	Inspect goods	128,645	60,000	2.14
Stored goods	Move to storage	104,235	100,000	1.04
Delivered goods	Move to stores	29,570	50,000	.59
Expedited goods	Expedite goods	78,230	15,000	5.21
Trained associates	Train associates	18,000		
Managed employees	Manage department	97,000		

Looking at work in this way enables a manager to describe the way the department employs its time and resources. It summarizes how the department converts resources (e.g., people, supplies, and equipment) into outputs (e.g., services).

After determining the work, the next question is: How effectively is the work being done? There are five prime criteria for judging effectiveness:

1. Is the work a consequence of a customer requirement?
2. Is the work wasteful?
3. Are the best practices followed in doing the work?
4. How much unused capacity exists?
5. How much time does it take to complete the activity?

Is the Work a Consequence of a Customer Requirement?

Work should only be undertaken to satisfy a customer need. The customer in this sense may be either an external customer or another department in the organization. The output of work must be of a quality that is of value to a customer, at a cost that the customer is willing to pay, and within the required time. Work done without a customer need in mind results in waste and a deterioration of competitive position.

Managers must ask the customer to specify in detail their definition of a good output. The work process is of little consequence to the customer as long as the output satisfies their needs. Thus the role of the manager is to structure the work to deliver the needed output with the least possible resources.

The customers of the warehouse stated two primary needs: the correct goods must be at the store at the exact time they are needed and the goods must be undamaged 100 percent of the time. The customer needs are mapped to the warehouse activities as follows:

Activity	Need
Receive goods	Goods in store at time needed
Inspect goods	N/A
Move goods to storage	N/A
Move goods to stores	Goods at store when needed
Expedite goods	N/A
Train associates	N/A
Manage employees	N/A

When the activities of the warehouse receiving department are looked at in light of customer requirements, it is evident that several of the department's activities are a consequence of management decisions on how the work should be done, rather than being a direct result of a customer need.

Is the Work Wasteful?

Several of the receiving department's activities are wasteful. Waste occurs where the activity can be eliminated with the organization continuing to meet customer requirements. An excellent manager will constantly eliminate wasteful activities. Waste results from errors (correction, detection, and interruption to operations), useless paperwork, ineffective policies and procedures, mismanaged capacity, and ineffectual physical/organizational structure. Waste does not help meet customer needs. It merely adds cost and lowers performance.

The wasteful work identified by the department manager were:

- Inspect goods
- Move goods to storage
- Expedite goods

The manager believed that inspecting goods was wasteful because it duplicated the inspection process done by the supplier. Organizations that work with the supplier to guarantee error-free goods would eliminate the need to inspect incoming goods.

The moving of goods to storage was considered wasteful because storage only exists because of problems in getting needed goods when required at an acceptable price. An excellent enterprise could synchronize the receipt of goods with its use, and eliminate most storage of goods.

Finally, the need to expedite goods was a primary result of the failure to meet the time expectations of the customer. Certifying vendors for quality and timeliness and then only using certified vendors would eliminate much of the need to expedite.

Are the Best Practices Followed in Doing the Work?

One important goal of ABM is to structure work by following the best possible work practices. The difficult task is to determine the best possible way of doing an activity. When determining the performance of an activity, it is critical to determine how well the activity could be performed.

Imagine the insights to be gained if best practices were identified across all units, and action programs were developed to bring all activities up to these standards. Imagine, furthermore, that a systematic analysis was undertaken to identify best practices of direct competitors and other organizations that do the activity. The knowledge gained by these competitive benchmarks serves as a basis for establishing competitive advantage.

How Much Unused Capacity Exists?

Excellent managers continuously convert unutilized capacity into utilized assets, and redeploy or sell the unused capacity. Profitability is highest when the minimum necessary capital is employed to do the work. Managing all the assets of an organization is becoming increasingly important.

The equipment used by the receiving department remained idle for significant amounts of time. Few organizations would allow their employees to remain idle for great periods of time, but these same organizations think very little about their equipment. The key to an excellent organization is to make the equipment and processes as flexible as necessary to cope with changing demands.

How Much Time Does It Take to Complete the Activity?

Excellent managers emphasize the speed of doing work. Doing work quickly without unnecessary delays is essential to producing good results. Many changes can occur during long delays. These changes can affect the work, resulting in additional cost and further delays as the work is redone. Long periods of time can also result in physical damage to the goods or obsolescence. The greater the amount of time, the more information is needed to keep track of the status of operations, the greater the possibility of expediting, and the longer the period before the customer pays for the goods and services.

The receiving department looked at how much time it took to do its activities. Particular attention was direct to those activities critical to the department's mission—receive and distribute goods. Reducing the time required to do these activities would increase flexibility and customer satisfaction, and lower cost.

The results of assessing the improvement potential of activities are summarized in the table on following page.

MARKET TARGETING

ABM requires senior management to continually assess what customers need and to set operational targets to meet those needs. The role of line management is to plan the resources needed to do its work, carry out the plan, and institute controls to ensure consistency in actual performance to plan. This process is known as strategy deployment. It requires a strong target cost system.

Future workload is of paramount importance to the manager in setting the targets. Workload is derived from numerous sources. Some workload

Activity	Workload measure	Customer Requirements	Value-Added	Best Practices	Unused Capacity	Time
Normal						
Receive goods	Number of goods received	Y	Y	Y	Y	.30
Inspect goods	Number of goods inspected	N	N	N/A	N/A	N/A
Move to storage	Number of goods stored	N	N	N/A	N/A	N/A
Move to stores	Number of goods delivered	Y	Y	Y	Y	N/A
Expedite goods	Number of goods expedited	N	N	N/A	N/A	N/A
Train associates	Number of training days	N	Y	Y	N/A	8.00
Manage employees		N	Y	Y	Y	N/A
Project						
Implement TQM	Number of days	N	Y			
Implement JIT	Number of days	N	Y			

is derived from providing services. Reports are often triggered by a specific time in the month or year. Project work is one-time.

The receiving department manager determines the anticipated workload by evaluating next year's sales forecast. A study showed that while total sales were forecasted to be lower by 7 percent, there would be a shift to specialty items rather than items sold in bulk. Typically, specialty items require much greater receiving activity because goods are bought in smaller quantities. The manager estimated that the total workload for the following year would be equivalent to this year's. The lower bulk item receipts would be offset by higher specialty item receipts.

The department manager was also expected to begin implementation of a Total quality management (TQM) program. This program would require additional time since all employees would be trained and initial data analysis conducted.

Finally, the department manager met with the store personnel to discuss their level of satisfaction. The store personnel stated that time from goods receipt to store delivery needed to be reduced from three days to one day.

Activities	Workload Measure	Current Workload	Future Workload
Normal			
Receive goods	Number of good received	150,000	150,000
Inspect goods	Number of goods inspected	60,000	60,000
Move to storage	Number of goods moved	100,000	**70,000**
Move to stores	Number of goods delivered	50,000	**80,000**
Expedite goods	Number of goods expedited	15,000	15,000
Train associates	Number of training days	20	**100**
Manage employees			
Project			
Implement TQM	Number of days		**120**
Implement JIT	Number of days		**90**

To meet these market-set targets, an organization must improve the way it works.

BUSINESS PROCESS IMPROVEMENT

Excellent managers synchronize the various business processes. An important activity of the receiving department is to unload and inspect incoming goods. Because the shipments arrive randomly during the day, the staffing level had to be set to handle multiple trucks. Much of the time, as a consequence of random deliveries, the workers waited for trucks to arrive or were assigned to unnecessary work.

The obvious solution to the problem was to require the vendors to deliver according to a set delivery schedule. It was determined that $120,000 per year could be saved by this change. A natural question is how did this significant level of non-value-added costs arise?

The management of the receiving department was aware of the problem, but could not take any direct action because the vendor delivery policy was the responsibility of the corporate purchasing department. On several occasions, the receiving department manager had discussed the issue with the purchasing department. No action was initiated because the vendor responded that they wanted higher prices to deliver on a set schedule. The problem was aggravated by the performance measures of the purchase department being lowest cost purchases.

The management system was a major part of the problem. The purchasing manager had a negative incentive to incur an unfavorable purchase price variance to help the performance of the receiving department. Even if the manager was willing to lower the purchasing department performance, the enterprise did not have a simple way to determine whether the cost savings to the receiving department offset the higher purchase cost.

The receiving activities are part of a longer process known as "procure goods." The activities of determining needed goods and selecting vendors precede the "receive goods" activity. Errors and inefficiencies in these preceding activities drastically affect the receiving activity. Similarly, activities that follow the receipt are dependent on successful receipt of goods.

When work is handed off from one department to another, delays and errors are inevitable. Accountability blurs, and critical issues fall between the cracks. Functional specialization emphasizes each organizational unit as if it were an independent self-contained discipline. The manager has limited incentive to take action that hinders his or her department's performance but is in the best overall interest of the organization. The managers substituted the narrow goals of their particular departments for the larger goals of the enterprise.

ACTIVITY/BUSINESS PROCESS IMPROVEMENT

All employees must have a constant focus to improve services, business processes, and activities.
The best way to improve activities/business processes is to:

1. Eliminate wasteful work
2. Eliminate root causes of problems
3. Reduce workload
4. Improve working methods
   a. Simplify tasks and methods
   b. Emulate best practices
   c. Employ alternative resources
5. Minimize unutilized capacity

Eliminate Wasteful Work

The logical first step is to pinpoint the wasteful work and reduce service levels for work that is not highly valued by users. Part of the freed resources can then be allocated to the new initiatives. This approach both meets short-term cost reduction needs and funds the needed long-term productivity improvements.

Eliminate Root Causes of Problems

An excellent manager will eliminate causes rather than treat symptoms. Management information systems detect problems when they occur. However, the cause of the problem has occurred before the problem is detected. If people don't understand the cause of the problem, they cannot find the solution.

A manager must always search behind a problem to determine the factors that cause cost to be incurred. For example, the receiving department manager realized the unit incurs significant waste when a product manager changes the selection of goods or changes a vendor. One impact of this is that current stock of an item will sit in storage until notification of disposition. While the receiving department has not caused the change of item or change of vendor, its activities are affected and costs are in-

curred in its cost center. A permanent improvement is not possible until
the root cause (cost driver) has been addressed.

Failure to address the root causes of waste results in a permanently
high level of cost in the receiving department. To address these costs
requires cooperation with other departments or changing detrimental organization policies that caused the problem. To eliminate or minimize the
need to expedite, for example, one must fix the root problems that cause
the need to expedite. If these causes are not eliminated, in the future a
similar problem will occur that necessitates expediting.

What are the root problems that cause expediting? The best way to find
out is to hold a brainstorming session with key department people. Most
people who perform the work know the source of their problems, although they may not have articulated those problems in the past.

The department manager held a brainstorming session and determined
six significant problems that led to expediting:

- Poor forecast/schedule
- Poor vendor quality (e.g., goods out of specification)
- Poor vendor delivery performance
- Absenteeism
- Poor packaging of goods
- Poor coordination between the advertising and purchasing depart-
  ments

With the root causes of the problems identified, it can be determined
what actions are necessary to address these problems. Three programs
were identified by the receiving department that, if implemented, would
decrease the need to expedite. These programs include:

1. Better coordination between the advertising and purchasing departments
2. Vendor certification
3. Employee incentives

Upon successful implementation of these programs, the receiving department would commit to less resources because they would have fewer
needs to expedite.

With action underway to minimize expediting, the department manager turned to the value-added activities. Starting with the "receive goods" activity, three potential improvement actions are possible:

- Reduce workload
- Improve the way the activity is done
- Improve the output consistency

Reduce Workload

Excellent managers continuously reduce workload. There is a strong correlation between the amount of work and the resources needed to do the work. The first activity analyzed was "receive goods." A brainstorming session found several alternative ways of reducing the workload:

- Order in large quantities
- Reduce the number of different items carried
- Decrease the number of suppliers

The first solution of ordering in large quantities was rejected because it increased the cost of storing the goods. While the cost of receiving goods decreases, the productivity gain is offset by higher storage costs. Marketing determined that reducing the number of different items carried would negatively impact sales and strategic objectives. The idea of reducing the number of suppliers was accepted.

Improve Working Methods

Improving working methods involves studying how the activity is done to identify more effective steps or alternative resources. A process can be performed in numerous ways with different factors of production. The resources involved in scheduling the goods receipt manually or with the aid of a computer system are quite dissimilar; yet they are alternative methods of ensuring that the needed resources are available.

The first step in improving methods is to identify the steps in performing the activity. The tasks in the "receive goods" activity included:

- Load/unload
- Unpack

- Prepare documentation
- Move to incoming inspection

The receiving department identified several improvement options. Vendor certification could lead to eliminating the need to inspect incoming goods. The vendor would be accountable for delivering goods that were within acceptable specifications. All inspection would be done at the vendor location, and packaging would be improved to ensure goods were not damaged during delivery.

Minimize Unutilized Capacity

Unused capacity represents potential revenue. Turning unused capacity into revenue requires an organization to bring in new work or to find alternative uses for the asset. To illustrate the used/unused concept, the receiving department streamlined its storage facility and created unused floor space. According to contribution thinking, they had not saved money because the cost of floor space still had to be paid.

Management believed, however, that working at greater efficiency must lead to greater competitiveness. Progressive management thinking prevailed. They lowered the facilities costs charged to receiving based on actual floor space used. This provided incentive to department managers to use facilities space as effectively as possible. The cost of the unused space was transferred to a management budget. The message conveyed by this approach was that facilities represented a revenue opportunity which was management's responsibility to achieve.

People always argue that the unused space did not go away; that the organization is still paying for it. These are true statements. However, now that this unused capacity is made visible and management can see how much this unused capacity costs, they can sell it off, lease it out, or save it for future expansion. Making unused capacity visible and costing it allows managers to make better decisions.

PROCESS CONTROLS

The way work is done will vary, even if only slightly, each time the process is done. A uniform and predictable process is required to produce good quality. Processes that produce excessively variable results will also produce defects and errors, and, consequently, waste.

Inconsistency in the work leads to unacceptable outputs and, consequently, a significantly amount of activity to rectify the problem. The objective of the receiving activity is to receive an item in a proper package, unpack it, deliver it on time to the user, and notify the system of the receipt. Consider the consequences of an inconsistent process. First, if the item is delivered to the incorrect location, the item would have to be found, the information system updated, and store efficiency lowered while awaiting the item. The resulting worker's time necessary to chase the item results in higher cost and no value to the customer.

An inconsistent process could also result in high cost of detecting errors that would not be necessary if process consistency were established.

An inconsistent process may not result in an unacceptable output but increases cost as a consequence of:

- Excessive goods
- Ineffective processes
- Potential customer dissatisfaction

An inconsistent process could also result in late delivery. The potential impact on advertising might be devastating as the promotional schedule is redone. Second, if the process of unpacking was done inconsistently, the time required to unpack would take longer than best practice. The greater the amount of time, the higher the activity cost. Also, if the tools needed to unpack the items were not in good condition—if blades were worn out, for example—the amount of time would again be longer.

The receiving department manager needed to understand how consistently the current processes are being performed. Consistency was measured in three different ways. First, errors were measured by approximately the amount of time spent correcting errors. Second, the time detecting internal errors was estimated. Third, the manager calculated the amount of time it would take to do the work if there were no errors. The error-free work time was compared to actual work time. The effect of output variability was approximated.

Using these approaches, the manager estimated the impact of inconsistent work on the department to be as follows:

Activities	Time Correcting %	Time Detecting %	Wasted Time %
Receive goods	5	1	25
Inspect goods	5	1	10
Move to storage	8		7
Move to stores	2		10
Expedite goods	3		15
Train associates			25
Manage employees	10		30

The only way of ensuring consistent output is to minimize the factors that cause inconsistent output and institute process controls. A process control monitors the process to ensure it is operating effectively to produce consistent output. The process must be studied to determine where a potential error might occur. A study of the "receive goods" activity reveals the following possible weaknesses:

Task	Potential Error
Unload goods	Goods damaged due to mishandling

The manager identified potential improvements to the activity to minimize the occurrence of the problem.

Task	Potential Solutions
Unload goods	Improve equipment used Improve working environment

Process controls monitor key factors that would cause the activity to function inconsistently. Some important factors include:

1. Weight received   Deviations in weight might cause problems with
                      the equipment used to receive goods

2. Storage space   As space devoted to receiving becomes full, the
                      manager would investigate to determine why
                      the process was not operating effectively

SUMMARY

ABM facilitates achieving the following benefits:

- Less resources consumed by disjointed management initiatives through elimination of duplicated effort, with synergistic benefits between project initiatives
- Cross-functional employee involvement resulting in long-term lasting improvements
- Faster implementation because multiple initiatives build momentum
- Formalization of the elimination of cost through the budgeting process to ensure financial results are achieved
- Reduced employee skepticism of the "Project of the month" by packaging common sense initiatives into one framework

Achieving and sustaining a competitive advantage via enterprise excellence requires continuous improvement by all employees in every aspect of performance. More importantly, it requires an organization to understand and improve the processes through which managers perform their daily activities. No matter how logical the management initiative, it will have minimal value to an enterprise if employees do not changes how they think and do their work.

APPENDIX: ACTIVITY-BASED MANAGEMENT EXAMPLES

BANKS/SAVINGS AND LOANS

Here is how one savings organization applied activity management to the teller department.

Activity Dictionary

Process deposits. Inputs are deposit slips, negotiable instruments, or cash. Tasks include verifying information on the deposit slip, adding checks and/or counting cash, and memo-posting the deposit to the customer's account. Output: a processed deposit. Activity measure: cost per deposit processed.

Process withdrawals. Inputs are a withdrawal slip or a check to cash. Tasks are memo-posting the debit and counting the cash. Output: a processed withdrawal. Activity measure: cost per withdrawal processed.

Answer customer inquiries. Inputs are customer requests for information about account balance, cleared checks, CD rates, overdraft policies, funds availability, bank policies. Tasks might include: obtaining customer account number, looking up balance, printing information, and giving information to customer. Output: an answered inquiry. Activity measure: cost per customer inquiry.

Sell negotiable instruments. Inputs are requests for cashiers' checks, money orders, travelers checks, and gift checks. Tasks include accepting payment, typing the check, and logging the transaction. Output: a typed check or money order. Activity measure: cost per negotiable instrument.

Balance drawer. Inputs are cash in drawer and cash transactions. Tasks include adding cash in drawer, cash receipts, and cash deposits, beginning cash, and any cash taken from drawer and put into vault or cash taken from vault and put into drawer. Output: balanced drawer. Activity measure: cost per balanced drawer.

Process batch transactions. Inputs are bundles of transactions to be sent to the operations center. Tasks include running a "zero tape" to make sure all debits and credits match up; preparing a batch header for each bundle of transactions; correcting any mistakes; notifying customers of errors and correction; and microfilming, logging, and preparing batches for courier to pick up. Output: batched transactions. Activity measure: cost per batch.

Although processing deposits and withdrawals, selling negotiable instruments, and answering customer inquiries are value-added, batching and balancing were thought to be non-value-added.

Activity Map

Activity	Alternatives
Process deposits	teller mail ATM direct deposit
Process withdrawals	teller mail ATM automatic debit
Answer customer inquiries	teller customer service automated phone line representative
Sell negotiable instruments	money order cashier's checks combination
Balance drawer	daily semi-daily weekly none
Process batches	batch at branch batch at operations center

Cost drivers for the activities processing deposits and withdrawals include: number of items per transaction, day of week and month, incomplete or incorrect forms, insufficient funds, holds, return items, computer system failure, weather, general economy, and interest rates.

By tracing the costs of running this department to these six activities, the savings and loan calculated a cost per activity for this branch. The company could then develop a bill of activities for one of its checking products.

Activity Cost per Unit

Activity	Total Cost $	Monthly Volume	Cost/Activity $
Process deposits	2963	3325 transactions	.89
Process withdrawals	2608	2275 transactions	1.15
Answer inquiries	2486	4500 inquiries	.55
Sell negotiable instruments	486	110 instruments	4.42
Balance drawer	429	130 balances	3.30
Process batches	528	92 batches	5.74

Bill of Activities

Activity	Monthly Volume	Cost/Activity	Total Cost
Process deposits	4	$ .89	$ 3.56
Process withdrawals	4	$1.15	$ 4.60
Answer customer inquiries	2	$ .55	$ 1.10
Balance drawer batch	1/6	$3.30	$ .55
Process balance batches	1/9	$5.74	$ .64
		Total	$10.45

Now the savings and loan can better compare the actual cost of this checking account product with the revenue it receives.

FEDERAL GOVERNMENT REIMBURSEMENT FOR PROCESSING DISABILITY CLAIMS

In 1992, the federal government started to reimburse the states for processing disability claims in a new way. Historically, the federal government simply shared the cost of processing these claims with the state. The government set up some comparison charts to show the various states how much the average state spent to process a social security disability claim. In addition, the low and high cost states were highlighted.

Now the government has decided to reimburse the states on an activity basis. The government will pay the states a given amount per social security disability claim processed (the activity of processing such a claim), regardless of how much or how little the state spends processing that claim.

A similar approach is being used for processing food stamps. There are several activities concerning a food stamp recipient. One activity is to initially approve a person to receive food stamps. A second activity is to reapprove a person. A third activity is to distribute food stamps. A fourth activity is to track the inventory of food stamps.

U.S. ARMY

Historically, the army sent its tanks to Anniston, Alabama, for repairs and replacement of damaged parts. Now the Department of Defense (DOD) has initiated a new procedure, which allows battalion commanders to get their tanks repaired anywhere within the DOD. This policy is causing quite a stir, as now these agencies must determine how they will price their various repair services. However, there is one advantage: they don't have to go from a bad cost accounting system to a more meaningful system. They can just start fresh with a good system.

Some of the activities in the business process "repair tank" include:

- Estimate cost
- Schedule repair
- Receive tank
- Store tank
- Move tank
- Inspect tank
- Order parts
- Repair tank
- Inspect tank
- Return tank
- Create invoice
- Record payment

Some cost drivers for the activity "estimate cost" are: experience of estimator, amount of damage, nature of damage, age of tank, sophistication of tank, prior repair experience for type of repair. The output would be an estimate. The logical activity measure would be cost per estimate.

Using a similar approach for the other activities, the location develops a bill of activities to determine the total cost to repair tanks.

TRANSPORTATION COMPANY BUDGETING DEPARTMENT

In a major transportation company, activity analysis of the budgeting department comes up with the following activities:

- Create operating budget
- Create capital budget
- Modify operating budget
- Analyze capital expenditure requests
- Analyze variances

Activity Map

Activities for Budgeting Department			
Create operating budget	No budget	Departments create	Management creates
Create capital budget	No budget	Budget by department	Budget company as a whole
Modify operating budget	No modifications	Departments modify	Management modifies
Analyze capital expenditure requests	Only in capital budget	Departments analyze	Budget department modifies
Analyze variances	No analysis	Self analysis	By management

Some cost drivers for the activity "create operating budget" are: budgeting method, number of cost centers, number of budgeted line items, cooperation of management, communication of executive management, cooperation of field personnel, quality of field personnel, number of unusual transactions, seasonality, quality of budget department personnel, availability and quality of current year information, degree of budget detail and documentation required, data compliance, and regulatory requirements.

The activity measure for "create operating budget" could be the number of cost centers or number of budgeted line items.

It was thought that each of these activities had value-added and non-value-added components.

Budgeting Department			
Activities	Value-Added	Non-Value-Added	Total
Create operating budget	$142,484	$29,424	$171,908
Create capital budget	$ 26,763		$ 26,763
Modify operating budget	$ 83,331	$ 6,254	$ 89,585
Analyze capital expenditure requests	$ 16,408	$ 5,064	$ 21,472
Analyze variances	$ 81,335	$ 6,305	$ 87,640

Assuming there were 200 cost centers, the cost to create the operating budget per work center would be $860 ($171,908/200 work centers). The cost to create a budgeted line item would be $2.15 ($860/400) assuming 400 budgeted line items per work center. Since each of the budget centers also has a capital budget, the cost of creating the capital budget would be $133.82 ($26,763/200 work centers). Even though the create capital budget activity measure was the same as that for create operating budget, some work centers had very small capital budgets. So the output measure for this activity might be changed as the ABM system is refined.

Since each work center might have on average 2.5 modifications, then the cost per modification of the operating budget was $179.17 ($89,585/ [200 work centers times 2.5]). The activity "analyze capital expenditures" might calculate cost per capital expenditure request: $71.57 ($21,472/300 requests) assuming 300 requests. And finally the activity analyze variances might calculate cost per work center analysis: $36.52 (87,640/200 work centers × 12 months).

Based on this information, management can make some decisions concerning the value and cost of the various activities in this department.

COMPUTER SYSTEMS INTEGRATION COMPANY

One computer systems integration company has traditionally allocated division overhead based on direct labor hours. It has allocated corporate and group overhead based on total cost input (e.g., direct labor cost, other direct charges, and division overhead). Organizations doing business with the Department of Defense (DOD), NASA, or the Department of Energy (DOE) are currently required to follow the cost accounting standards (CAS) as presented in the federal acquisition regulations (FAR). Current discussions suggest that these rules would be applicable to all government contracts rather than just to DOD, NASA, and DOE.

As the defense budgets shrink and the industry becomes more competitive, organizations and the government are looking for ways to reduce costs. One way to accomplish this is to use activity management.

For example, division overhead may consist of marketing, accounting, MIS, human resources, program control, contract administration, security, and facilities. The following figure shows the activities, cost drivers, and activity measures for the program control and the contract administration departments.

Program control department:

Activities	Cost Drivers	Activity Measures
Track contract costs	Contract size, number of direct labor personnel working on contract, contract life, staff experience, skills, education; training; time into contract; contract complexity; number of cost elements; location of sites	Number of contracts tracked

Table (Continued)

Activities	Cost Drivers	Activity Measures
Forecast to end of contract/Estimate to Completion	Contract size, number of direct labor personnel working on contract, contract life; staff experience, skills, education, training; time into contract; contract complexity; number of cost elements; location of sites.	Number of forecasts/estimates
Create annual budget	Contract size, number of direct labor personnel working on contract, contract life, staff experience, skills, education; training; time into contract; complexity; number of cost elements; location of sites	Number of contracts
Create contract reports	Number of direct labor personnel working on contract, staff experience, skills, education; training; number of reports, report complexity; number of cost elements; number of sites reported; time restrictions	Number of reports

Contract administration department:

Activities	Cost Drivers	Activity Measures
Negotiate contracts	Contract price, terms, competition, staff experience, administrative contracting officer's (ACO) experience, government regulations	Number of contracts
Select subcontractors	Skill, experience of staff; past experience with subcontractor; number and type of subcontractors required;	Number of subcontractors
Prepare contracts	Contract size, skills of staff; regulations; complexity of contract; number of subcontractors; number of other direct charges (ODCs); amount of travel, relocations	Per contract Per contract element
Facilitate client relations	Number of progress reports, number of clients, size of contracts; number of contracts; clients expectations; skills and experience of staff; number of meetings	Number of progress reports

The program control department and the contract administration department use a variety of activity measures. By using activity management, not only does the company better understand what drives division overhead, but the government understands which requests increase cost to the government.

INSURANCE UNDERWRITING

In 1976, hospitals were looking for an alternative source to purchase malpractice insurance. Although Marsh & McLennan insurance brokers didn't know about activity-based costing, they worked on a project using ABC when creating a standby malpractice facility for the American Hospital Association (AHA). At that time, the malpractice industry was at a crisis stage. Insurance underwriters were getting hit with multimillion dollar malpractice claims. Most malpractice insurers stopped issuing policies except for the St. Paul Insurance Company. The AHA asked Marsh & McLennan, insurance brokers, to create a standby malpractice insurance facility that would stay in business and still be able to underwrite hospitals.

At that time, malpractice insurance was underwritten based on patient days. So if a patient delivered a baby and stayed three days, then that hospital was charged a certain rate per day for malpractice insurance for three days. The obvious problem with that system was that not all patient days are equal in risk to the hospital for malpractice insurance.

For example, if a patient comes in for a tonsillectomy, the risk to both the patient, as well as to the hospital, for a malpractice claim is relatively low. However, if a woman comes in for an unscheduled Caesarean section, or someone has triple bypass heart surgery, or someone has an orthopedic or neurological operation, the risk of a malpractice claim is much higher. Likewise, a teaching hospital tends to attract more difficult cases. In addition, students may be involved with diagnosis and respond to critical situations. This situation tends to increase the risk of a malpractice suit. Also, an anesthesiologist who gives a spinal tap daily in a large urban hospital is probably more skilled than a country doctor who performs such a procedure only a few times a year, or even less. Thus, these considerations must be evaluated.

Based on analysis of the procedures (activities) involved, different hospitals were rated for malpractice insurance. Thus, a rate per activity (procedure) was developed and multiplied by the expected number of procedures performed each year. The total cost for each activity was then added up to derive a total cost for malpractice insurance for a specific hospital.

A similar approach was used when rating physicians for malpractice insurance in creating a standby malpractice facility for the American Medical Association (AMA). Based on some information obtained from the Insurance Services Organization (ISO), we were able to develop a set of rates per activity for physicians. For example, there is a variety of operations that a general surgeon can perform, from high risk (e.g., liver/ heart transplants, neural and infant surgery) to low risk (e.g., removing tonsils). A malpractice rate per type of surgery (activity) can then be multiplied by the number of that type of surgeries to develop a total malpractice insurance cost for those types of procedures. Then the cost of all the various types of surgeries can be added to derive a total cost for that surgeon for malpractice insurance.

DEFENSE CONTRACTOR'S AUDIT AGENCY

In applying ABM to the Department of Defense Contractor's Audit Agency (DCAA), the following list of activities was defined:

Receive and expedite audit request
Review submission for adequacy
Perform preliminary audit steps
Test and examine cost representation
Perform field work
Draft report
Review report
Issue final audit report

Activity Map

Activities	Alternatives			
Expedite audit request	Don't perform	Perform manually		
Review for adequacy	Don't perform	Use internal auditors		Use external auditors
Perform preliminary audit steps	Don't perform	Use internal auditors		Use external auditors
Test cost representation	Don't test	Teleconference		Fax
Perform field work	Use manual test	Use automated test	Use internal auditors	Use external auditors
Draft report	Don't perform	Wordprocesser		Handwrite
Review report	Don't review	Test		
Issue final audit report	Don't perform	Wordprocesser		Handwrite

Cost drivers for the activity "review for adequacy" include: FAR criteria, complexity of proposal, experience of DCAA staffer and defense contractor, number of proposals, number of audit requests, and training of DCAA staffer. The activity measure that was chosen was number of audit requests. The resources of labor, supplies, occupancy, travel, and so on were traced to these activities. Then an estimate was made of the volume of the various activity measures. Then a cost per activity was calculated. This helped the DCAA and senior government officials better understand what the cost was of these various audit activities. Now it could better be determined whether the benefits of these activities justified the cost. Also, these activities could be divided into value- and non-value-added to determine which activities should be improved for speed, cost, and quality, and which activities should be eliminated.

OVERNIGHT CARRIER BILLING DEPARTMENT

In applying ABM to the billing department of an overnight carrier, the following activities were defined:

- Sort pickup records
- Review nonregister rejects and recycles
- Prepare register
- Process register
- Review weekly error and memo corrections
- Create billing manifest
- Review missing pickup records
- Perform audits
- Other

Resources were assigned to these activities to derive the following activity costs for this one location. They included:

Activities	Monthly Activity Costs $
Sort pickup records	1,166
Review nonregister rejects and recycles	862
Prepare register	608
Process register	1,064
Review weekly error and memo corrections	2,180
Create billing manifest	2,840
Review missing pickup records	2,984
Perform audits	2,736
Other	760
Total	15,200

Preparing and processing the register, creating the billing manifest, and performing audits were value-added activities. Reviewing rejects and recycles, errors and memo corrections, and missing pickup records were non-value-added.

SELLING PHONE BOOK YELLOW PAGES

When a company that sells yellow pages applied ABC to their sales organization, they discovered some interesting results. Historically, sales people were sent to small and large towns to sell advertising. When activity analysis was applied, the sales organization found that the revenue generated in small towns did not justify the expense of sending sales peoples to those small towns. The organization then tried phone sales. After activity analysis was performed, it was found that the revenue generated even by phone sales could not be justified. So the phone company went to direct mail solicitations. Even though total revenue was less than with sales people or phone sales, the net margin to the company after selling expenses was greater.

Another organization used ABC in their estimating department for yellow pages sales. They defined their activities as:

- Receive cost estimate from region
- Obtain additional information to complete estimate
- Develop supplemental data

- Produce cost estimate
- Perform variance analysis between estimate and actual cost
- Manage estimating department

Activity Map

Activities	Alternatives
Receive cost estimate	via mail via fax via telephone In person
Obtain additional information	Estimate from region Develop in house
Develop supplemental data	Estimate Contact printer Use historical datas Examine physically Use directory report
Produce cost estimate	Produce manually Use system program Mail Fax Telephone
Perform variance analysis	Don't perform Internal to department External to department

Cost drivers included desired turnaround time, number of estimates per proposal, complexity of enhancement, completeness of request, number of estimates, training of estimators, experience of estimators, and data available in database.

COLLEGE ACCOUNTS PAYABLE DEPARTMENT

A college looked at activity management in its accounts payable department and identified the following activities:

- Process mail
- Process invoices
- Maintain files
- Correspond with vendors
- Prepare documents for microfiching, copying, and auditors
- Reconcile backup documents and subledger to general ledger

- Administer production reports (balance to general ledger production statistics)
- Other (train, verify addresses, review control groups)

Activity Map

Activities		Alternatives	
Process mail		Process manually	Automate
Process invoices	Pay with credit	Process manually	Pay complete
	Pay partially		
Maintain files	Don't update	Batch process	Use real-time update
Correspond with vendors	Don't correspond	Telephone Write letters	Fax Meet
Prepare documents	Don't prepare	Prepare manually	Automate
Reconcile backup	Don't reconcile	Reconcile manually	Automate
Administer production reports	Don't prepare	Prepare manually	Automate

Cost drivers for processing mail include type of mail, types of purchases, number of purchases, time of month, skill of processor, and training of processor.

Activities	Total Cost $	Unit Measure	Units	Cost/ Unit $
Process mail	19,495	Mail pieces	50,000	.39
Process invoices	72,349	Invoices	35,365	2.05
Maintain files				
Correspond with vendors	34,658	Vendor contacts	4,100	8.45
Prepare backup	6,498	Documents	45,000	.15
Reconcile	6,065	Reconciliations	2,500	2.43
		Cost of processing invoices =		$13.47

The following activities were determined to be value-added: process mail and invoices, reconcile backup, administer production reports. File maintenance, correspond with vendors, and prepare documents were felt to be non-value-added.

HOSPITAL

Hospitals are great candidates for activity management, as they try to compete in an overcapacity marketplace. There is an excess of hospitals and hospital beds. As society clamors to control health care costs, noneffective hospitals will fall by the wayside. This will apply to both large and small hospitals.

Activity management is a perfect way to analyze a hospital's procedures. In creating a bill of activities, we can start at the beginning and walk all the way through until patient discharge and collection. The following is a partial list of activities for many patients:

Activities	Activity Measures
Schedule patient	Number of patients scheduled
Verify insurance	Number of verifications
Admit patient	Number of admissions
Prepare patient/room	Number of preparations
Review doctor's report	Number of reviews
Feed patient	Number of feedings
Order tests	Number of orders
Move to/from lab	Number of moves
Administer lab tests	Number of tests
Order pharmaceuticals	Number of orders
Complete reports	Number of reports
Check vital signs/assists	Number of vitals, assists
Prepare for operation	Number of preparations
Move to/from operatory	Number of moves
Operate	Number of operations of certain type
Collect charges	Number of collections
Discharge patient	Number of discharges
Bill insurance	Number of bills

From this partial list, the bill of activities is created in order to develop a bill for the patient. What's important about the bill of activities is that in preparing it cost drivers were identified. For example, poor doctor's writing may be a major cost driver in ordering lab tests and pharmaceuticals. Poor descriptions of hospital charges may cause multiple reviews by the insurance carrier before payment is made. The hospital can then determine which activities are value-added and which are not. For example, billing insurance would be value-added. Rebilling for insurance proceeds would be non-value-added. Presenting the correct food order by patient and/or doctor would be value-added. Presenting the wrong food and having to get the correct food would be non-value-added.

The bill of activities consists of a hospital charge for room and board. This is the cost of the room, TV, phone, and food. The patients pay the daily rate multiplied by this daily charge for each day of their stay. Then there should be charges for items like verifying insurance, admission, discharge, scheduling, and billing for insurance. These activities should be billed for only once, regardless of the length of stay. Rates for medical care, including testing, pharmaceuticals, nursing, and medical care such as operations, cardiac monitoring, physical therapy, and special nursing attention are all added.

In this way, a hospital could use rooms more effectively by tracing the costs to the correct activities. As it is now, long-term patients are subsidizing short-term patients. The reason for this is that built into the hospital per diem are one-time charges like admission. A patient who has a long stay pays for that charge over and over again. Meanwhile, a patient with a short stay is subsidized by the long-term patient for these one-time charges.

Also, if patients were charged for special services like assistance to the bathroom, hospitals and patients might work out an alternate method for getting this assistance completed.

Hospital Accounts Receivable Department

The following are activities in a hospital accounts receivable unit:

- Process mail
- Process lockbox
- Process Medicare/Medicaid
- Prepare deposits
- Cash checks
- Research inquiries
- Miscellaneous
- Administer (copy checks and handle inquiries)

Activity Map

Activities	Alternatives		
Process mail	Each clerk opens own mail	One clerk sorts; another clerk inputs	
Process lockbox	Receive bank report over modem, not tape	Receive bank receipts electronically	Patients mail to hospital
Process Medicare/Medicaid	Computerize outpatient part	Buy network version of Acculog to speed up input	
Prepare deposits	One person prepares both accounts	Prepare less frequently than daily	
Cash checks	Don't have cashier	Raise/lower check limits	Carry high/low amount to control volume of checks
Copy checks	Copy only checks, not cash	Buy optical scanner	Don't copy
Research inquiries	Research everything	Give others use of files to do own research	Limit kinds of items that will be researched

The following activity measures were considered for each activity:

Activities	% of Time	Activity Measures
Process mail	12	Number of batches or entries on report
Process lockbox	10	Number of batches or entries on report
Process Medicare/Medicaid	8	Number of RAs or entries on report
Prepare deposit	6	Number of deposits or number of checks
Cash checks	7	Number of checks cashed
Copy checks	6	Number of copies
Administer	11	Number of employees managed
Research inquiries	24	Number of items researched
Download data	5	Number of downloads
Miscellaneous	11	
	100%	

Finally, other natural expense categories were traced to various activities to determine in the bill of activities a cost per patient for the accounts receivable department for both Medicare/Medicaid patients and for those patients paying either through insurance or in cash.

AIRLINE

Airlines have a variety of activities that activity management would be well suited to. For example, consider the ground-handling department. These people have the following activities:

- Load baggage onto plane
- Unload baggage from plane
- Load cargo
- Unload cargo
- Locate mishandled bags on plane
- Direct plane to gate
- Direct plane from gate
- Fuel plane
- De-ice plane
- Communicate with pilot

Cost drivers for the activity unload baggage are: type of plane, type of un/loading equipment, amount of baggage, size of baggage, training of personnel, experience of personnel, baggage fallen off carts, desired turn-around times, weather conditions.

An activity measure could be cost per plane or per type of plane. It also could be cost per piece of luggage or cost per luggage cart. The choice of activity measure would be determined by what the airline was trying to accomplish. In some cases, the number of carts used might be more appropriate. On commuter planes, there are no luggage carts, just individual pieces of luggage. Either the airline could use two activity measures, carts and luggage, or just one measure, such as number of pieces of luggage.

With activities, the airline can track not only the cost per cart or per piece of luggage, but they can also track the time it takes to load a cart, and the quality with which it is loaded. Quality might be determined by number of bags falling off the conveyor or the number of bags loaded on the wrong plane.

RESTAURANT

The activities for a restaurant include:

- Set table
- Seat customers
- Take order
- Cook food
- Serve orders
- Take dessert order and serve
- Present bill and collect
- Clean table

The cost drivers for the activity set table are: whether a tablecloth is used, number of glasses and silverware, skill and training of setter, distance of glasses and silverware to table, neatness required, and time allowed.

Activities	Activity measures
Set table	Number of settings
Seat customers	Number of seatings
Take order	Number of tables or number of customers
Cook food	Number of customers
Serve order	Number of tables or number of customers
Take dessert order and serve	Number of tables
Present bill and collect	Number of bills
Clean table	Number of tables

What is interesting to point out in this example is that the activity measures for a number of activities are the number of tables being served and not the number of customers at the tables. The reason for this is that once food is being served, it really doesn't matter how many people are at the table; what really matters is that the waiter or waitress has to go to the table to serve the table. One could combine some of these activities. For example, it might make sense to have one activity called serve table. This activity might include take order, serve order, and present bill. Clean and set table could be combined into one activity. It all depends on the size of the restaurant and what the company is trying to accomplish.

TELECOMMUNICATIONS

A telecommunications company has the following activities that relate to their line personnel:

- Install new lines in home
- Install new phone lines
- Service callbacks/not working
- Repair lines in home
- Repair phone lines

Cost drivers for installing new phone lines are: soil condition (rock, gravel, mud, or sand); training and experience of installer; type of equipment; proximity to power lines; other types of lines underground; and size of transmission lines.

The following are activity measures:

Activities	Activity measures
Install new lines in home	Number of new lines in home
Install new phone lines	Number of poles or number of feet
Service callbacks/not working	Number of callbacks
Repair lines in home	Number of repairs in home
Repair phone lines	Number of repairs

Callbacks would be non–value-added. The other activities would be value-added. As the phone company works to lower cost and improve operations, it can focus on these activities.

RETAIL

The activities of a retail clerk might be:

- Hang new inventory
- Sell merchandise
- Handle complaints and returns
- Take markdowns
- Count inventory

The following are activity measures:

Activities	Activity measures
Hang new inventory	Number of racks or number of times inventory hung
Sell merchandise	Number of pieces sold
Handle complaints and returns	Number of complaints/returns
Take markdowns	Number of markdowns or number of pieces marked down
Count inventory	Number of inventories or number of pieces counted

Once the company understands the cost of these various activities, it can begin to determine who is the best person to perform these activities and whether these activities are worth doing.

U.S. AIR FORCE

Seaport Operations

A first pass at defining activities for Transcom's seaport operations yielded:

1. Receive cargo
2. Process cargo paperwork

3. Load database
4. Prepare/receive manifest
5. Check documentation
6. Verify items versus manifest
7. Prepare customs documentation
8. Prepare hazardous material documents
9. Order stevedore services
10. Determine equipment load requirements
11. Prepare load plan
12. Monitor loading of ship

After brainstorming, it was decided that the list might be reduced to the following five categories:

Receive cargo

Prepare documents (combine items 2, 4, 5, 6, 7, 8 above)

Maintain database

Prepare load plan (combine 10, 11 above)

Monitor loading of ship (combine items 9, 12 above)

They then defined the following inputs, output, and activity measures for their five activities:

Input	Output	Activity measure
Cargo delivery	Processed cargo	Number of receipts
Processed cargo paperwork	Manifest	Number of cargo manifest documents
Data elements manifest documents	Management information	Number of transactions
Manifest	Final load plan	Number of load plans
Load plan	Loaded ship	Number of loaded ships

Aircraft Configuration Management

The original brainstorming of activities came up with the following activities:

1. Maintain source control of engineering drawings
2. Maintain database of engineering changes
3. Maintain maintenance records
4. Maintain database maintenance procedures
5. Maintain database test/calibration equipment
6. Complete flight logs
7. Complete safety logs
8. Conduct configuration control board reviews
9. Establish configuration baseline

After some discussion, the group combined the above activities as follows:

1. Maintain source control of engineering drawings and establish configuration baseline
2. Maintain database of engineering changes and conduct configuration control board reviews
3. Maintain maintenance records
4. Maintain database maintenance procedures and maintain database test/calibration equipment
5. Complete logs (i.e., flight and safety)

They then defined the following inputs, output, and activity measures for their five activities.

Input	Output	Activity measure
Current drawings	Revised drawings	Number of drawings
Proposed changes	Accepted changes	Number of accepted changes
Current records	Revised records	Number of revisions
Current procedures	Revised procedure	Number of revised procedures
Completed flight	Completed log	Number of completed logs

Transfer Civilian Personnel

A first pass at defining activities for transferring civilian personnel yielded:

1. Prepare job descriptions
2. Develop selection criteria
3. Develop timeline
4. Train personnel
5. Pay personnel
6. Provide benefits
7. Promote employees
8. Move employees
9. Assess risks
10. Provide policy
11. Retire employee

After brainstorming, it was decided that the list might be reduced to the following five categories:

Select civilian personnel
Train personnel
Compensate personnel
Transfer personnel
Retire personnel

They then defined the following inputs, outputs, and activity measures for their five activities.

Input	Output	Activity measure
Personnel certificate	Selected personnel	Number of selected personnel
Selected personnel	Trained personnel	Number of trained personnel
Time card	Compensated personnel	Number of check statements
Selected personnel	Transferred personnel	Number of transferred personnel
Eligible personnel	Retired personnel	Number of retired personnel

Move Tanks

A first pass at defining activities for the business process move tanks yielded:

1. Identify requirements
2. Identify capability
3. Allocate capability
4. Schedule ship
5. Schedule train/truck
6. Determine resources to move
7. Report movement
8. Track movement
9. Bill customer
10. Contract support

After brainstorming, it was decided that the list might be reduced to the following five categories:

Identify requirement
Allocate transportation
Schedule transportation
Report movement
Bill customer and collect

They then defined the following inputs, outputs, and activity measures for their five activities.

Input	Output	Activity measure
Transportation request	Validated requirement	Number of validated requirements
Validated requirement	Mode allocation	Number of requests allocated
Mode allocation	Movement schedule	Number of schedules
Movement schedule	Position report	Number of reports
Position report	Paid bill	Number of paid bills

RESEARCH DIVISION OF MANUFACTURING COMPANY

A research division of a manufacturing company created the following activities and tasks:

Build/design equipment/instrumentation. Drawing, drafting, picturing, engineering, modeling or patterning equipment or instrumentation for the manufacture of a product.

Support/visit customers. Provide assistance to a company who has purchased product from the company in the past, or who the business believes might be a candidate for additional product purchases.

Document/communicate findings. Conveying the results of research to the appropriate members of the organization or of the scientific community.

Performing experiments and tests. Performing experiments and tests on materials, compounds or products.

Process engineering. Determining the correct engineering parameters to manufacture a product.

Design/plan/prepare for Experiments. Providing all necessary supplies for experimentation.

Handling materials. Acquiring supplies.

Investigate materials or ingredients. Researching and analyzing individual components.

Analyze/investigate data. Investigating the results of an experiment.

Perform housekeeping. Keeping work areas safe and clean.

Plan/monitor/control projects. Influencing the direction of a project.

Prepare materials/product. Making quantities of a finished good.

Develop a prototype. Modelling a mock-up of a potential product.

Develop methods. Designing an experiment to answer a particular question.

Provide professional training. Participation in meetings with staff, other employee groups or external customers and suppliers with the purpose of increasing technical knowledge.

Support qualify assurance. Determining how the quality of a product compares to the existing specification.

Perform routine analysis. Performing an experiment on a repetitive basis.

Solicit/gather information. Collecting data for the purpose of analysis in a research-related project.

Attend meetings. Participation in scheduled and unscheduled meetings with staff, other employee groups or external customers and suppliers.

Support regulatory. Adhering to the governmental requirements and regulations required by federal agencies.

Investigate competitive products. Researching and analyzing products sold by companies competing in the same market.

Troubleshooting. The process of fixing a process.

Administer department. Performing tasks related to the general planning and administration of the business.

U.S. POSTAL SERVICE

The U.S. Postal Service has the following distribution activities:

Distribute mail
Distribute mail to post office boxes

Distribute throwbacks

Take mail to carriers

Process nixie/markup mail

Process business reply mail

Prepare carrier route mail

Sign in/out accountables

Accept bulk mail

Prepare collection mail

Manage department

Train employees

The customer services support activities, input, output, and activity measures:

Activity	Input	Output	Output measures
Sell to major customers	Major customer	Sales call	Number of customers
Respond to customer concerns	Customer inquiry	Delighted customer	Number of inquiries
Maintain express mail program	Express mail customer	Express mail sale	Number of express mail pieces
Accept bulk mail	Bulk mail customer	Accepted mail	Number of bulk mail pieces
Distribute accountable mail	Requisition	Stamped shipment	Number of shipments
Administer rules to customers	Inquiring customer	Informed customer	Number of customers

FEDERAL GOVERNMENT AGENCY

An agency of federal government had a mission to design new cost accounting systems for the various branches of the federal government. It defined the following activities, and activity time and quality goals:

	Time		Quality	
Activity	From	To	From	To
Design solutions	2 weeks	2 days	20% missed customer requirements	0%
Develop solutions	6 weeks	2 weeks	10 test failures	0
Implement solutions	3 days	1 hour	230 reruns	100
Perform account management	1/2 day per week	2 days per week	customer satisfaction rating: 3	8
Introduce automated tools	50 days	200 days	Deployment: 20%	50%

MIS DEPARTMENT

The following are the activities, inputs, outputs, and output measures for a small MIS department:

Activity	Input	Output	Output measures
Handle complaints	Customer calls	Updated files	Number of complaints
Support applications	data files	Customer letters	Number of records
Run help desk	Internal calls	Satisfied customer	Number of inquiries
Develop imaging	Request	Plan	Number of requests met
Manage department	Employees	Managed department	Number of employees managed

The following are time and quality goals for the above activities:

	Time		Quality	
Activity	From	To	From	To
Handle complaints	5 minutes	3	20% call backs	16%
Support applications	2 minutes per record	1:45	8% errors	6%
Run help desk	2 minutes per inquiry	1:30	90% satisfaction	95%
Develop imaging	45 person days	40	80% first time acceptance	90%
Manage department	10% of time	10%	90% employee satisfaction	95%

ELECTRIC AND GAS UTILITY

An electric and gas utility has the following activities that relate to their installation personnel:

Install electricity to home

Install new electric lines for a community

Callbacks/not working

Repair electricity in home

Repair common electric lines

Cost drivers for installing electricity to home are: training and experience of installer; voltage to home; proximity to power lines; other types of lines underground; size of transmission lines.

The following are activity measures:

Activities	Activity measures
Install electricity to home	Number of home installations
Install new electric lines for community	Number of poles or number of feet
Call backs/not working	Number of callbacks
Repair electricity in home	Number of repairs in home
Repair common electric lines	Number of repairs to common electric lines

Call backs would be non-value-added. The other activities would be value-added. As the electric company works to lower cost and improve operations it can focus on these activities. It can benchmark with other electric utilities to determine how effective they are in terms of cost, time, and quality for these activities.

COMPUTER SOFTWARE LEASING COMPANY

A company wrote leasing software and handled leases for financial institutions. For the processing of leases, they defined the following activities. They also calculated their cost per unit of activity with and without excess capacity to determine how much additional cost was added to the activity because of excess capacity. These numbers have been adjusted to preserve confidentiality.

Activity	Cost/Unit With Excess Capacity $	Cost/Unit Without Excess Capacity $
Process lockbox payments	1.64	1.66
Management of customer lockbox operations	2.34	2.52
Update leases	1.84	1.98
Book new lease	26.38	28.90
Provide accounting management	284.10	304.40
File sales and use tax	83.48	88.74
File property taxes	100.22	107.60
Track titles	62.48	67.84
Collect delinquent accounts	6.92	7.46

This also gave the operating vice president some insight into her excess capacity. With this excess capacity information, she could decide whether to get rid of this excess capacity, save it for future growth, or lease it out.

This organization was already keeping detailed records on processing times for various tasks. So it could already tell how much time and effort were spent on various types of tasks. Therefore, it was very easy to calculate equivalent units for its various output measures. For example, lessees may call in: to simply update their address, to ask for a payoff amount, or to ask about an incorrect bill. Each of these subactivities required different amount of time and resources. Thus, equivalent units and costs could be calculated for each of these activities.

GLOSSARY

Abandonment analysis The process of determining whether it is more profitable to continue or discontinue a service or project.

Activity A combination of people, technology, supplies, methods, and environment that produces a given service. Activities describe what an enterprise does, that is, the way time is spent and the outputs of the process. *See* **Process**.

Activity accounting The collection of financial and operational performance information about significant activities of an enterprise.

Activity analysis The breakdown of an enterprise into manageable segments for detailed analysis regarding cost and performance.

Activity budget A quantitative expression of the expected activities/business processes of the organization reflecting management forecast of workload and financial and nonfinancial requirements to meet agreed strategic goals and planned changes to improve performance.

Activity budgeting The process of planning and controlling the expected activities/business processes of the organization to derive a cost-effective budget that meets forecasted workload and agreed strategic goals.

Activity dictionary A listing of generic activities according to the functions performed by a typical organization. It includes activity, activity description, business process, function, whether value-added, inputs, outputs, supplier, customer, output measures and cost drivers.

Activity management A formal management system that: supports excellence by compelling employees to understand their activities and how they contribute to achieving strategic objectives; changes traditional management practices to emulate best practices and establish process controls to ensure consistently good performance; and supports continuous improvement by providing new insights into the customers of activities/business processes and permitting the adoption of best practices that encourages employees to add greater value to the organization.

Activity measure A quantitative measurement unit selected as a surrogate of the level of activity. Activity measures are based on the output (e.g., a purchase order for the purchasing activity) of the activity considered to drive the activity cost in a linear way.

Activity unit The heading under which a group of related activities are grouped. Also known as a department, work center or cost center.

Actual cost Amounts determined on the basis of costs incurred (historical costs), as distinguished from predicted or forecasted costs.

Aggregation The process of combining activities into functions or combining tasks into activities.

Attributes Qualitative information about activities gathered during activity (i.e., primary *vs* secondary, required *vs* nonrequired, strategic, valued-added *vs* non-value-added).

Back flushing A costing system that first focuses on the throughput of an organization, and then works backward when allocating costs between cost of goods sold and inventory.

Bill of activities (BoA) A list of activities and activity volumes required to produce a service, project or business process. A bill of activities can be created to determine the cost of servicing different customers and different channels of distribution.

Bill of supplies (BOS) A list of direct supplies needed for the production of a given service.

Book value Original cost, less any accumulated depreciation.

Budget *See* **Activity budget** processes.

Budgeted activity/business process cost A cost that reflects the organization's opinion regarding future improvements to an activity/business processes.

Burden rate *See* **Overhead rate.**

Business process An orderly management of related activities operating under a set of procedures in order to accomplish specific objectives.

Business rule A rule that defines the goals, strategies, and regulations governing an organization.

Capacity The measured ability of an activity/business process to produce output.

Capital budgeting The making of long-term planning decisions for investments and their financing based on activities/business processes.

Cause A source event or factor that affects subsequent events or activities.

Changeover A partial setup in which not all procedures are required.

Chart of accounts A list of accounts maintained by a specific enterprise.

Contribution margin A margin equal to revenue (sales) minus all variable expenses.

Control of activities/business processes (1) Action that implements the planning decision regarding activities and business processes. (2) Performance evaluation that provides feedback of the results of activities/business processes.

Conversion costs Direct labor costs and overhead.

Cost Resources sacrificed or forgone to achieve a specific objective.

Cost accounting system The system in an organization that provides for the collection and assignment of costs to intermediate and final cost objects.

Cost accumulation Collection of cost data in an organized way via an accounting system.

Cost allocation The assignment and reassignment of a cost or group of costs to one or more cost objectives. Terms with assorted shades of meaning are cost relocation, cost assignment, cost apportionment, cost reapportionment, cost distribution, cost redistribution, cost tracing, and cost retracing.

Cost allocation base A systematic means of relating a given cost or cost pool to a cost objective.

Cost apportionment *See* **Cost allocation.**

Cost assignment *See* **Cost allocation.**

Cost behavior pattern Estimation of how activity/business process costs behave as activity/business process volume changes over a relevant range of activity/business process levels.

Cost center The smallest unit of an organization for which budgeted or actual costs are collected, and which has some common characteristics for measuring performance and assigning responsibility. A cost center can consist of one or more work centers, work cells, or workstations.

Cost driver A factor whose occurrence creates cost. The factor represents a prime (root) cause of the level of activity (e.g., the number of different types of services for service operation planning and control, vendor contracting). An activity or condition that has a direct influence on the operational performance and/or cost structure of other activities.

Cost elements Types of costs (e.g., labor, technology, travel occupancy supplies) associated with the service process.

Cost management The management and control of activities to determine an accurate service cost, improve business processes, eliminate waste, identify cost drivers, plan operations, and set enterprise strategies.

Cost pools A grouping of costs caused by the same activity measure for the purpose of identification with or allocation to cost centers, processes, or services.

Critical success factors Those factors deemed essential for the success of an organization.

Current cost The cost of purchasing a currently held asset if an identical asset were purchased today; also, the cost of purchasing the services provided by that asset if identical assets cannot currently be purchased.

Customer The recipient of a product or service, either external or internal to the organization.

Cycle time The amount of time between the point when supplies for a service enters an organization and the point when the service is delivered.

Decomposition The process of breaking down an activity into tasks.

Delphi method The identification of departmental costs and activities via interviews with department heads.

Direct activity An activity that can be traced to an output or service.

Direct cost A cost item that can be identified specifically with a single cost object in an economically feasible manner. A direct cost is applied to the cost objective based on the actual content of the resource consumed by the cost objective. For example, a service that requires five person hours costing $20 per hour is charged $100, whereas a service that requires two person hours is charged $40.

Direct labor The cost of labor that can be identified with a specific service.

Direct supplies Acquisition costs of all supplies that are identified as part of the finished services and may be traced to the finished services in an economically feasible manner.

Effectiveness The degree to which a predetermined objective or target is met.

Efficiency The degree to which inputs are used in relation to a given level of outputs.

Engineered cost Cost that results specifically from a clear-cut, measured relationship between inputs and outputs.

Environment Set of uncontrollable factors that affect the success of a process.

Event An occurrence.

Excellence The cost-effective integration of activities within all units of an organization to continually improve the delivery of products and services to satisfy the internal or/and external customer.

Factors of service operation All costs including labor, supplies, technology, utilities, travel, and so on.

Feedback In control systems, a comparison of the activity budget with actual activity results.

Financial accounting External reporting emphasizing the historical, custodial, and stewardship aspects of accounting. Heavily constrained by generally accepted accounting principles.

Fixed assets Noncurrent, nonmonetary, tangible assets used in normal operations of an organization.

Fixed cost (1) Operating costs that do not vary with changes in the level of activity over a relevant range of such activity. (2) Those costs that will be unaffected by variations in activity level in a given period.

Function A group of activities having a common objective within an organization.

Full cost Cost of all activities/business processes required to produce a service plus an allocation of sales and administration cost. Also called fully distributed cost, fully allocated cost.

Gross margin Excess of sales over the cost of the goods sold. Also called gross profit.

Homogeneous cost Cost in which each activity included has the same or a similar cause-and-effect relationship to a cost objective.

Indirect activities Activities that are not directly attributable to a service (e.g., human resources).

Indirect cost (1) Costs common to a multiple set of cost objectives. Such costs are usually allocated by systematic and consistent techniques to services and business processes. (2) Costs that are not directly assignable/traceable to a service or business process. (3) Expenses that do not have a close causal relation with the service being provided. Management is an example of an indirect cost.

Indirect labor cost All service wages other than for direct labor.

Indirect service costs All costs other than direct supplies and direct labor that are associated with the service process. Also called service burden, service overhead, administrative expenses, and general overhead.

Input Physical documents or time-based schedules that trigger an activity.

Investment management Part of a service's process planning and development activity; it directly affects the selection and acquisition of the technology used to provide the service.

JIT *See* **Just in time.**

Just in time (JIT) System whereby each component on a service line is produced immediately as needed by the next step in the service line. Abbreviated as JIT service operation. A logistics approach designed to result in minimum inventory and waste during the service operation process.

JIT costing Hybrid costing used in conjunction with just-in-time service operation systems.

Job order Basic document used by job order costing to apply service costs. Also called job cost record and job cost sheet.

Job order costing System used by organizations whose services are readily identified by individual units or batches, each of which receives varying inputs of direct supplies, direct labor, and service overhead.

Joint cost Cost of a single process that yields two or more services simultaneously.

Joint services Two or more services that (1) have relatively significant sales values and (2) are not separately identifiable as individual services until their split-off point.

Lead time The span of time between the request for delivery of service and the actual delivery of that service.

Life-cycle costing Accumulation of costs for activities that occur over the entire life cycle of a service, from inception to abandonment by the service producer and the consumer.

Machine hours The measurement of time used by a machine (e.g., a computer, scanner) to monitor specified levels of output.

Make/buy decision The act of deciding whether to produce a service in-house or buy it from an outside vendor.

Management accounting Identification, measurement, accumulation, analysis, preparation, interpretation, and communication of information that assists executives in fulfilling organizational objectives. Also called internal accounting.

Management information system (MIS) An organizer's method of providing past, present, and prospective information relating to internal operations and external intelligence. It supports the planning, controlling, and operational functions of an organization by providing information in the proper time frame to assist decision makers. Also known as Information Technology (IT)

Market research The collection and interpretation of information about markets, market trends, and customer preferences.

MIS *See* **Management information systems**.

Natural expense category The basic classifications of cost that are universal and organization independent (e.g., wages, supplies, travel, occupancy).

Non-value-added cost A cost or activity other than the minimum amount of equipment, supplies, space, and workers' time that is absolutely essential to add value to the enterprise.

Operation The smallest unit of work used for planning or control purposes.

Operations Service activities in which work is performed to produce the service.

Organization structure The arrangement of lines of responsibility within the organization.

Output The result of an activity. It is what users receive or what people produce.

Overhead cost Cost other than direct cost.

Overhead rate The percentage rate at which overhead is applied to services.

Overtime premium Cost of the wages paid to all service workers (for both direct labor and indirect labor) in excess of their straight time wage rates. Overtime premium is usually considered a part of overhead.

Performance driver The prime factor influencing the performance of an activity (e.g., the level of service may determine staffing requirements).

Period costs Costs always expensed in the same period to which they are incurred.

Planned cost A cost derived from the strategic and operational planning systems.

Planning Delineation of goals, predictions of potential results of various ways of achieving goals, and a decision of how to attain the desired results.

Prime costs Direct supplies costs plus direct labor costs.

Process A combination of people, technology, raw materials, methods, and environment that produces a given service. An activity.

Process costing System of applying costs to like services that are mass-produced in continuous fashion through a series of service steps called business processes.

Product cost *See* **Service cost**.

Product development *See* **Service development.**

Production lead time *See* **Service lead time.**

Production planning and control system A system that ensures a balance between resources and activities.

Profit center Responsibility center that is accountable for costs and revenues.

Profit velocity The ratio of service profit to service lead time.

Project Complex job that often takes months or years to complete and requires the work of many different departments, divisions, or subcontractors.

Project management Scheduling and organizationing activities/business processes to control service operations.

Quality Conformance of a service to specifications.

Quality control activities Checking, physical inspection, and testing of the service.

Resources Factors of service operation such as labor, technology, and supplies.

Responsibility accounting System that measures the plans and actions of each responsibility center.

Service An output resulting from a collection of activities/business processes.

Service cost Traditionally costs, including costs for supplies, direct labor, and technology, that are directly or indirectly involved in the production of services for sale to customers or the production of services for the citizens of a governmental entity. Indirect costs include such items as equipment maintenance, office utilities, and wages for facilitating services in the office. Indirect costs are customarily assigned to services by an appropriate allocation technique. An activity service cost is the cost of all activities required to produce a service.

Service development All activities required to define, design, develop, test, release, and maintain the complete description of the services to be produced.

Service lead time Time from the first stage of service to the stage when the finished service comes off the service line or is delivered to the customer or citizen.

Service overhead All costs other than direct supplies costs and direct labor costs that are associated with the service process. Also called service burden, indirect service costs, service expenses, and service overhead.

Service operation Transformation of supplies into a service through the use of labor and technology.

Service/support center A work center whose primary mission is to provide specialized support to other departments.

Setup The process of preparing equipment or a work center the first time for producing a service.

Standard cost Traditionally, the process of calculating the anticipated cost of a specific service at a given level of volume and under an assumed set of circumstances.

Strategic planning A planning process that summarizes and articulates the basic operational tasks, objectives, goals, and strategies for the organization.

Sunk costs Costs that have been incurred, but not consumed, for generating future revenue.

Supplies management The function that regulates the movement of supplies and finished services through the office or facility.

Target cost A market-based cost that is calculated using a sales price necessary to capture a predetermined market share. Target cost = sales price (for the target market share) − desired profit.

Task How the organization performs an activity. The level at which activities are improved.

Technology cost The purchase price, start-up cost, interest, current-market value adjustment, and risk premium of technology acquisition.

Throughput The total time of operations through a facility (office, equipment, work center, department).

Time charging A reporting system that tracks labor by task and flags shortfalls due to absences.

Total quality management A management strategy in which all business functions work together to build quality into the services and prevent quality defects.

TQM *See* **Total quality management**.

Tracing The process of establishing a cause-and-effect relationship.

Transaction Physical (including electronic) documents associated with activities that affect information.

Transfer price Price charged by one segment (subunit, department, division, government entity) of an organization for a service supplied to another segment of the same organization.

Value-added cost The incremental cost of an activity to complete a required task at the lowest overall cost.

Variable cost (1) A cost that increases as the volume of an activity increases and decreases as the volume of an activity decreases. (2) Those costs that are affected by the level of activity in a period.

Waste The net total process output minus good process output.

Whole life cost The cost to the customer from service purchase to abandonment.

WIP *See* **Work in progress**.

Work center A specific area of the office or organization consisting of one or more people or pieces of equipment that perform essentially the same activities or can be treated in the same way. A work center may consist of one or more work cells or work stations.

Work in progress (WIP) The investment in supplies or labor in the process of producing a service.

Work measurement Careful analysis of a task, its size, the method used in performance, and its efficiency. The objective of work measurement is to determine the workload in an operation and the number of workers needed to perform that work efficiently.

INDEX